SEARCH
for a NATION

Canada's Crises in French - English Relations from 1759

3rd edition

Published in Canada by Fitzhenry & Whiteside,
195 Allstate Parkway, Markham, Ontario L3R 4T8

Published in the United States by Fitzhenry & Whiteside,
311 Washington Street, Brighton, Massachusetts 02135

www.fitzhenry.ca   mail to:godwit@fitzhenry.ca

10 9 8 7 6 5 4 3 2 1

Library and Archives Canada Cataloguing in Publication

Morchain, Janet Kerr, 1936-2006
Search for a nation : Canada's crises in French-English relations from 1759 / Janet
Kerr Morchain ; general editors, Mason Wade, John Trent. -- 3rd ed.

Includes bibliographical references and index.
ISBN 978-1-55041-594-0

1. Canada--English-French relations--History. I. Wade, Mason, 1913-1986
II. Trent, John E. III. Title.

FC144.M67 2010   971   C2010-905906-9

Fitzhenry & Whiteside acknowledges with thanks the Canada Council for the Arts,
and the Ontario Arts Council for their support of our publishing program.
We acknowledge the financial support of the Government of Canada through the
Canada Book Fund (CBF) for our publishing activities.

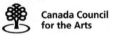 

Canada Council   Conseil des Arts
for the Arts   du Canada

ONTARIO ARTS COUNCIL
CONSEIL DES ARTS DE L'ONTARIO

Design by Tanya Montini
Cover image by ImageegamI, Istockphoto
Printed in Canada

SEARCH
for a NATION

Canada's Crises in French - English Relations from 1759

3rd edition

Janet Kerr Morchain, M.A., Ph.D.

GENERAL EDITORS
Mason Wade, M.A., Ph.D.
John Trent, M.A., Ph.D.

Fitzhenry & Whiteside

COPYRIGHT ACKNOWLEDGEMENTS

Grateful acknowledgement is made to the following for permission to include copyright material in this book.

Pierre Asselin: excerpt from *L'Oeuvre de l'abbé Groulx* by Olivar Asselin.

Barnes and Noble Incorporated: excerpt from *Charlevoix's Journal of a Voyage to North America* by L.P. Kellogg.

Jean-Jacques Bertrand: excerpts from a speech in the Quebec Legislature, 8 May 1963.

Canadian Historical Association: excerpts from *Guy Carleton, Lord Dorchester 1724–1808*, Booklet Number 5 by A.L. Burt.

Centre de Psychologie et de Pédagogie: excerpt from *Histoire de la Province de Québec* by R. Rumilly.

Marcel Chaput: excerpt from *Pourquoi Je Suis Séparatiste* by Marcel Chaput.

Clarke, Irwin & Company Limited: excerpts from *Arthur Meighen:* Vol. I, *The Door of Opportunity,* and Vol. II, *And Fortune Fled* by W.R. Graham.

Columbia University Press: excerpt from *The Crisis of Quebec 1914–1918* by E.H. Armstrong.

Le Devoir: excerpt from *Why the Navy Act Should Be Repealed* by Henri Bourassa; an editorial by André Laurendeau, 4 July 1958; an interview with René Lévesque by Jean-Marc Léger, 5 July 1963.

Les Editions de l'Homme: excerpts from *Les Insolences du Frère Untel* by Pierre-Jérôme.

Les Editions du Jour: excerpts from *La crise de la conscription 1942* by André Laurendeau; excerpt from *La Véritable Histoire du F.L.Q.* by Claude Savoie.

Les Editions Leméac Inc.: song by Georges Dor entitled "Je Suis Québéquoi"

Gouvernement du Québec: excerpt from *Quebec-Canada: A New Deal.*

Harvest House Limited Publishers: excerpts from *The True Face of Duplessis* by Pierre Laporte; excerpts from *For Pity's Sake* by Jean-Paul Desbiens.

Léger, Jean-Marc: excerpt from article entitled "Sovereignty, the Condition of Salvation" appearing in *Le Devoir,* October 1967.

Librairie Beauchemin Limitée: excerpt from Great Britain and Canada by Henri Bourassa; excerpt from *Les gerbes canadiennes* by L.O. David.

Longmans Canada Limited: excerpts from *The Incredible Canadian* by Bruce Hutchison; excerpts from *The Birth of Western Canada* by George F.G. Stanley.

McClelland & Stewart Limited: excerpts from *The Dangerous Delusion* by Donald H. Fullerton; poems by Earle Birney in *Selected Poems 1940–1966* and *Near False Creek Mouth;* excerpt from *White Niggers of America* by Pierre Vallières; excerpt from The *French Canadian Outlook* by Mason Wade; excerpt from William Weintraub's *The Underdogs.*

The Macmillan Company of Canada: excerpts reprinted from John A. Macdonald: *The Young Politician* and *John A. Macdonald: The Old Chieftain* by Donald Creighton, by permission of the Author and The Macmillan Company of Canada Limited; excerpts reprinted from *Revolt in the West,* Great Stories of Canada Series by Edward McCourt, by permission of the Author and The Macmillan Company of Canada Limited; excerpts reprinted from *The French Canadians 1760–1945* by Mason Wade, by permission of the Author and The Macmillan Company of Canada Limited.

Mrs. A.R. Menzies: excerpts from *Life and Letters of Sir Wilfrid Laurier* by O.D. Skelton.

John Murray (Publishers) Limited: excerpt from *Sir Wilfrid Laurier and the Liberal Party* by J.S. Willison.
Musson Book Co. (A Division of General Publishing Co.): excerpt from *Canada without Quebec* by John D. Harbron.

Les Nouvelles Editions de l'Arc: the song "Mon Pays" by Gilles Vigneault.

Oxford University Press: excerpts from *The Quebec Act: A Study in Statesmanship* by

Reginald Coupland; excerpt from *Broken Promises: A History of Conscription in Canada* by J.L. Granatstein and J.M. Hitsman.

La Presse: excerpt from 17 November 1965 issue; excerpt from 18 May 1963 issue.

Les Presses de L'Université Laval: excerpt from *Le Canada, expérience ratée ou réussie? (The Canadian Experiment: Success or Failure?),* Congress on Canadian Affairs; excerpt from *Papineau: textes choisis et présentés* by Fernand Ouellet.

Library and Archives Canada: excerpts from the Denison Papers, Volumes 5 and 35.

The Ryerson Press: excerpt from *A History of Canada by Charles G.D. Roberts;* excerpts from *Quebec: The Not-So-Quiet Revolution* by Thomas Sloan.

Pierre Elliott Trudeau: excerpt from *Cité Libre* by Pierre Elliott Trudeau.

The University of Toronto Press: excerpts from *Sir Guy Carleton* by A.G. Bradley; excerpts from *Movements of Political Protest in Canada 1640–1840* by S.D. Clark; excerpt from *The Politics of John W. Dafoe and the Free Press* by Ramsay Cook; excerpt from "Survival or Disintegration" by Ronald L. Watts in *Must Canada Fail?* edited by Richard Simeon; excerpt from "The Colonial Policy of the Whig Ministers, 1803–1837," *The Canadian Historical Review* by Helen Taft Manning, by permission of the author; excerpt from *The Progressive Party in Canada* by W.L. Morton; excerpts from *The Union Nationale* by Herbert Quinn; excerpts from "Conscription 1917: A Brief for the Defence," *The Canadian Historical Review* by A.M. Willms, by permission of the author.

Wherever possible, the source of quoted material has been traced and acknowledgement given. Apology is made for any inadvertent errors or omissions.

COPYRIGHT ACKNOWLEDGEMENTS
CHAPTERS 21-22

The Publishers gratefully acknowledge permission to include the following material.

Uni.ca: "The Backstabbing That Never Was" by Roland Rainville

Michael Hill: "Is Quebec A Nation?" from Quebec: A Nation, the Southern Patriot

Justin Trudeau: excerpt from "J'accuse" by Pierre Elliot Trudeau

John Trent: "Eleven Good Reasons Why Quebecers Should Want To Remain In Canada"

Intellectuals for the Sovereignty of Quebec (IPSO): excerpts from "Quebec Sovereignty: A Legitimate Goal"

ADDITIONAL ACKNOWLEDGEMENTS

The reference librarians at Library and Archives Canada were of great help in the research of the edited version, especially retired librarian Norma Gould, Don Carter, Gilles Leclerc, Anne Pichora, and consultation and reference officer Lynn Lafontaine. Librarians at the Ottawa Public Library, the Cornwall Public Library, and the Archives of Ontario also provided helpful information. In addition, Valerie Glenn, librarian at the University of Alabama Library assisted in finding a difficult source, which the Birmingham Public Library in Alabama promptly forwarded.

Foreword to the First and Second Editions

Janet Morchain has performed a very useful service for Canada by summarizing the major episodes in which English and French Canadians took different and sometimes conflicting views during Canada's evolution into nationhood. And she has put both kinds of Canadians in debt to her by including as an integral part of this book a collection of sources and documents illustrating both points of view, to which references are supplied in her narrative. For it has been too long the tradition of both English- and French-Canadian education to concentrate on one part of the Canadian tradition and ignore or even misrepresent the other. It is absurd to bring up people in watertight cultural compartments, convinced of the righteousness and inevitable superiority of their own tradition, and then expect them to achieve a harmonious *modus vivendi* with others equally devoted to another tradition. Happily, in the years since 1945, there has been much better communication between what Hugh MacLennan justly described as the "Two Solitudes" of prewar Canada—and Canadians have become much more conscious of what they have in common and less given to dwelling on what divides them. Dr. Morchain's book should do much to further the process of English-French accommodation by which Canada has become a nation and which must be continued if Canada is to remain one, after a century of common effort by men of good will who were willing to make sacrifices for the common good.

Mason Wade
University of Western Ontario
London, Ontario

Foreword to the Third Edition

It is both a pleasure and an honour to be invited to prepare a foreword for this book. A pleasure because it is wonderful to be part of Janet Morchain's still innovative and highly useful third edition of *Search for a Nation*. An honour to be asked to follow in the footsteps of Mason Wade, the historian whose rigorous scholarship made the greatest contribution to the understanding of the French-Canadian people and to improving French-English relations in Canada.

One of the difficulties in interethnic relations is that nationalists on one side or the other seem to be able to get to the podium first and speak more loudly. They normally proclaim just their side of the story, thus tending to exacerbate already tendentious relations. Those with a more reasoned voice, who try to look at both sides of the question, tend to be ignored. Glamour and partisanship are not in their favour. But if we are looking for ways to build bridges in multicultural societies, it is essential to have ready access to, and to be able to compare and analyze, divergent points of view. Fitzhenry & Whiteside are to be congratulated for their foresight and persistence in understanding that Morchain's volume of history, documentation, and opinion is an immense aid to students of all ages and an essential part of any Canadian scholar's bookshelf.

French-English relations are the substratum, the bedrock, of Canadian cultural and political life. It can be argued that this relationship, with its highs and its lows, has been the springboard to bilingualism, minority rights, multiculturalism, and appreciation of diversity that characterize twenty-first-century Canadian culture. It can also be maintained that the incapacity of Canadians to deal with Quebec's need for greater constitutional protection—as demonstrated in Morchain's two new chapters (Chapters 10 and 11)—has made it likely that accommodation of the Quebec reality still needs to be made within the Canadian polity. Furthermore, the author's judicious selection of basic texts will help students of Canada to have at their fingertips a knowledge of the facts and motivations that underlie Canada's past and that will help us prepare for its future. The handicaps under which Janet Morchain and her friend Michael Wall laboured to bring this third edition to fruition makes the achievement even more impressive. As this edition has been published posthumously, it also stands as a memorial to the great contribution Dr. Morchain has made to the study of Canadian history and, in particular, French-English relations.

John E. Trent
Chelsea, Quebec

PART I

SEARCH FOR A NATION

PART II

SOURCES AND DOCUMENTS

PART I

SEARCH FOR A NATION

1 ⚡ THE PROBLEM OF THE NATION

For Canada, unity has been the most difficult of problems. There is a French version and an English one. We search for the elusive common ground between the two, a single national identity. Some outsiders have noted our internal dissension, the tension at the heart of things. "I found," Lord Durham reported, "two nations warring in the bosom of a single state." "*Vive le Québec libre!*" Charles de Gaulle exclaimed at our Centennial celebrations. We feel our self-doubts; often, perhaps too often, we look inward. History records our periodic crises, sometimes resolved, sometimes simply passing—but ever recurring. In his retirement speech in June 1984, Prime Minister Pierre Elliott Trudeau described Canada as "the country that refuses to die." At times, we question our own existence, with two peoples pulling separate ways. Could this nation be a mistake? Our ancestors did not think so, but perhaps times have changed to the point where their vision is no longer valid.

We came together in the mid-nineteenth century, a nation-building age. Germany, Italy, the United States, and Australia, among others, were being formed. There was a worldwide drive for national unification. But today, in the early twenty-first century, there are separatist movements everywhere. It is an age of independent states, dying empires, and fragmentation, even in long-established states like our historic motherlands. In Britain, there are proponents of devolution for Wales and Scotland; in France, there are the Basque, Breton, and Corsican separatists. Can we stand against the current of the times?

We have faced at least three challenges, the combination of which makes us unique. The first has been the challenge of living in a northern environment, not in a primitive condition but in an advanced industrial civilization. The second has been to maintain our identity beside the huge American nation that could easily erase the border economically and culturally. The third is the one that concerns us here—the duality at the base of our culture, French and English.[1] We are one of the few nations in history that has endured so long with two cultures, without civil war and without assimilation of one by the other.

Other nations have suffered from foreign invasion, massive famines, and the agony of class revolutions. Compared to them, we have led a charmed existence. But Canada cannot be taken for granted. Our nation has been from the beginning an experiment that might not work. Can French and English Canadians live together and act effectively as a single state? Only when our two peoples cooperate as free and voluntary partners can we function successfully as a nation. Unilateral action has been tried, but it has never worked well. There have been no quick and easy solutions along the road of partnership, much less final ones. The price of nationhood has come in the form of recurring crises.

Originally, there was concern that neither would accept the other. Canada had two beginnings: one French and the other English. The French considered Canada theirs alone. Their fur traders, their missionaries, and their explorers (not the English to the south) were the ones who ran the risks of cold and hunger in the northern land. They were here first. Then the English arrived, first as soldiers on the Plains of Abraham and later as Loyalist refugees from the Thirteen Colonies. They won Canada by right of conquest and through immigration by force of numbers. They thought Canada was theirs alone. They even tried to expel the French from Acadia. But the French came back and proceeded to counter English immigration through *la revanche du berceau*. Finally, each admitted, albeit reluctantly, that the other was here to stay.

In *Search for a Nation,* we will look at the great crises in Canada's history, ten to date: the Conquest (1759–1774), the Rebellions (1837–1849), Confederation (1860–1867), the Riel Rebellions (1869–1885), Laurier and the Imperialist Crisis (1896–1914), the Conscription Crisis (1917 and 1942–1944), the Quiet Revolution (1960s), the Crisis of Separatism (1970–1980), the Constitution Crisis, 1982-1992, and the 1995 Referendum Crisis. Each crisis brought home the simple truth that if the two peoples did not work together, there would be no country left. More than once, the question was raised: Would it not be easier to sever the ties and go our separate ways?

Before studying the crises, we need to define our terms. What is French Canada? What do we mean by English Canada?

Historically, Quebec has been the pillar of the French fact in North America. Its geographic area is 1,356,797 km², which represents 14.7 percent of our total land mass. By 2001, its population was 7,237,479, representing 24 percent of the Canadian total of 30,007,094—down from 26 percent in 1981. Quebec is home to almost 90 percent of French-speaking Canadians, and within the province, the·proportion of those who listed French as their mother tongue was holding steady at around 81 percent. A noticeably declining number listed English, a drop from 12.7 percent in 1981 to 8 percent in 2001. However, there was a dramatic increase in the number who spoke nonofficial languages as their mother tongue: 709,420, or 10 percent, in 2001. In 1991, this third group was at 7.5 percent of Quebec's total. According to the Canadian census of 2006, 575,555 (7.7 percent) of the population in Quebec declared English as their mother tongue, 744,430 (10 percent) used mostly English as their home language, and 918,955 (12.9 percent) comprised the Official Language Minority, speaking English as their first official language.

These statistics, which related solely to Quebec, fall short of describing French Canada. They do not include the Maritime Acadians and the French minorities in the other provinces, collectively known as *les francophones hors Québec*. And they also fail to reflect the presence of the English minority in Quebec, once a million strong but cut in half by 2001 to 557,040. The English minority in Quebec was weakened mainly because of migration patterns and fear of the nationalist movement leading to separation. It was losing more members than it could replace. This has always been the case, but the rate of loss was increasing, largely because of fear of separation.

The French-Canadian minorities outside Quebec are threatened by assimilation; even in New Brunswick, where they are protected by official language status, the assimilation rate is high. *Non-Québécois* francophones generally identify with their own provinces, calling themselves Franco-Ontarians or Franco-Manitobans, for example. The difficulty of defining French Canada might be resolved by considering those who list French as their mother tongue. Ontario has the largest number outside Quebec: some 485,630 people. But many have ceased to speak their mother tongue.

Another way of defining French Canada is to look at the attitudes and beliefs shared by many francophones. French Canadians believe in varying degrees (some are nationalists; some are not) that they possess the attributes of a nation—a common language, religion, code of law, history, folk institutions, and literature—and the will to make sacrifices to preserve and promote them. Mason Wade described this collective psychology:

> The French Canadians are the *Sinn Feiners* of North America, for their strong group consciousness and cohesiveness arise from a basic loneliness and insecurity. It is the sense of "ourselves alone" that motivates efforts at enhancement by stressing French Canada's peculiar ties with France and Rome. The attitudes of minority groups can often be explained only in psychological terms, and French Canada is no exception to this rule. Sir Wilfrid Laurier ... once formulated this fact in the observation that "Quebec does not have opinions, but only sentiments."[2]

The more extreme nationalists were traditionally hostile to what they conceived to be Anglo-Saxon materialism, militarism, imperialism, Protestantism, individualism, and egalitarian democracy. They stressed the role of the Roman Catholic Church in preserving the French nationality by extending its parishes as settlement expanded beyond the St. Lawrence. They also emphasized the distinctive customs of Quebec, such as the celebration of St-Jean-Baptiste Day. *"Restez d'abord nous-mêmes,"* the Abbé Groulx, a nationalist historian and teacher, told his students in the classical college. He believed that a new state, *La Laurentie,* could be established in eastern Canada:

> Reality is the fact that we are two million French Canadians in the Dominion of Canada. We have an impregnable foothold in the province of Quebec; we occupy a territory with geographical unity; we have all the wealth of the soil, all the channels of communication, all the outlets to the sea, all the resources which assure the strength and independence of a nation. We can, if we wish, if we develop all the powers of our race and our soil, become strong enough to lend vigorous assistance to our dispersed brethren … God will not let perish that which he has conserved by so many miracles.[3]

Four times nationalist parties have come to power in the history of Quebec: the Parti Patriote in the 1830s, the Parti National in the 1880s, the Union Nationale in the 1930s, and the Parti Québécois in the 1970s. But until the last of these, there was no coherent policy to change Quebec's situation radically. Then René Lévesque, who had claimed, "We are a true nation, but a nation unattended by sovereignty," became the premier of Quebec.[4] He promised a referendum (two, if need be) to put the independence issue to the people, thereby making the problem of the nationalists in Quebec a problem for the whole country.

This issue of sovereignty disturbed English Canada. It also disturbed many French Canadians who cherished the belief in their nationality but were reluctant to sanction it politically. They identified with Quebec and with Canada. The one was close at hand and familiar, arousing emotional loyalty; the other was farther away, less well known, to a degree foreign, but still a matter of habit and commanding rational allegiance. André Laurendeau, editor of *Le Devoir* and co-chairman of the Royal Commission on Bilingualism and Biculturalism (1963–69), described the matter succinctly: "In Quebec we do what we like; in Ottawa we do what we can."

If French Canada can be defined as a nation within a larger state, what about the other part? What is English Canada? In geographic terms, it is the other nine provinces, encompassing 85.3 percent of the total land area. Subtracting the area of Quebec from the 9,221,016 km² of Canada leaves English Canada with 7,864,219 km²—less a small portion for the "bilingual belt" (this extends in an arc around Quebec through Labrador, northern New Brunswick, and eastern and northern Ontario).

English Canada can also refer to a population group, all of whom are not French Canadian. Quebec has 24 percent of the English-Canadian population, and the rest of the country has 76 percent. In 2001, 2,672,085 people in Ontario listed themselves as speaking nonofficial languages as compared to only 709,429 in Quebec. This is known as the "Third Force," or the "allophones," a term originally applied to the Europeans who came to Canada after the Second World War but which now includes the more recent immigrants from Asia, Africa, Latin America, and the Caribbean. The "English" side of Canada's culture maintains its numbers largely through such immigration and the assimilation of many immigrants. This accounts for English Canada's more heterogeneous character; indeed, it is more properly referred to as multicultural, especially in its large cities, such as Toronto. The French side traditionally maintained its numbers through a higher birth rate. Quebec's more homogeneous character stems from the fact that fewer immigrants have settled there. But this, too, is changing, as the birth rate has dropped and immigration has increased, including immigration from non-French-speaking countries.

English Canada might be defined by the use of the English language, but even this is not entirely satisfactory. The definition obscures the fact that many immigrants adopt English only for business purposes and continue to use their native language at home. Of special interest is the increase in those listing themselves as bilingual in English and French. In 1971 this group numbered about 2.9 million, or 13.5 percent; by 2001, the figure had increased to 5,231,500, or 17.7 percent. Between 1996 and 2001, the increase was 8.1 percent. Nationally, 43.4 percent of francophones listed themselves as bilingual, compared to 37.8 percent in 1996 and 35.4 percent in 1991. Outside Quebec, the rate was almost static: 10.3 percent in 2001 from 10.2 percent in 1996.

Quebec had the highest rate of bilingualism. Among anglophones in 2001, it was 66.1 percent, and among francophones, it was 36.6 percent. It was increasing in every age group. Among allophones in Quebec, who had to learn two second languages, bilingualism was high and climbing. Between 1996 and 2001, it rose from 46.7 percent to 50.4 percent. In 2001, 73.1 percent of allophones spoke conversational French, and 69.1 percent could speak English.

The least bilingual of the linguistic groups in Canada were the anglophones outside Quebec. Most learned French at school, and the most bilingual age group was 15–19. In 2001, 14.7 percent aged 15 to 19 spoke French—twice the proportion for the anglophone population as a whole, which was 7.1 percent. Unlike the francophones and allophones, the rate was dropping slightly between 1996 and 2001, especially in the provinces west of Quebec. Young anglophones also tended to lose their French; fewer spoke French in 2001 than in 1996, and the decline was even greater dating from 1991.[5] Lack of practice and lack of necessity probably accounted for this situation. Francophones and allophones felt the need to learn second and third languages, whereas anglophones, being in the majority, felt comparatively little pressure to do so.

Is Canada better described as multicultural or as bicultural? The existence of varied ethnic groups within English Canada brings us to the truly difficult question of identifying an English-Canadian consciousness. It is amorphous and contradictory, full of diverse elements. "English Canada," wrote André Laurendeau, "manifests, through its newspapers, curiosity and uneasiness about Quebec opinions; but it expresses scarcely any attitude of its own. It maintains towards us a great silence."[6]

In the nineteenth century and earlier, English Canada was much more homogeneous than it is now. It was strongly Anglo-Saxon in origin, with a common historical experience: the perilous journey across the ocean or north from the rebel colonies and then the struggle on the agricultural frontier, now only a memory reconstructed in tourist spots like Upper Canada Village on the St. Lawrence River.

English Canada had its distinctive associations, such as the Imperial Federation League, the Sons of England, the Orange Order, and the Imperial Order of the Daughters of the Empire. It celebrated festivals such as July 12, the anniversary of the Battle of the Boyne; Victoria Day; and the anniversary of the Battle of Queenston Heights, October 13, 1812, in Upper Canada. The Loyalist Centennial held in Niagara-on-the-Lake in 1884 looked to the past of the English-Canadian nation and reviewed its glorious victories over the French and the Americans. This celebration was very different in tone from the Bicentennial in 1984, which stressed the multicultural aspects of Ontario's heritage.

English Canadians shared a strong sense of allegiance to Britain and the monarchy. The Tories of Ontario, it was said, were more loyal than the Queen. This sentiment was embodied by Alexander Muir in his song "The Old Union Jack":

Up with the standard, our brave fathers bore,
In the defence of their loved Canadian shore;
On hard-fought fields, they proved their valour true,
And victory crowned them Red, White, and Blue.
The flag, Wolfe planted on Abraham's Plain,
Waved on Queenston Heights and on Lundy's Lane,
Round it, they rallied—and stood firm on the rocks,
And conquered, led on by Drummond and Brock.[7]

There had been no break with the motherland such as the one French Canada experienced in 1789.

English-Canadian nationalists believed in a unilingual Canada. As they became the majority through great waves of immigration from the British Isles, they sought to make English compulsory in the schools and the sole official language. The drive to suppress the use of French spanned seventy years. Its landmarks were catalogued by the Abbé Lionel Groulx:

1864 — Nova Scotia: French-speaking Catholic Acadians are forbidden to have French schools.

1871 — New Brunswick: Catholic schools are closed and the teaching of French (and in French) is forbidden in public schools.

1877 — Prince Edward Island: Catholic and French schools become outlawed.

1890 — Manitoba: Separate (Catholic) schools are outlawed and the teaching of French (and in French) is forbidden at the secondary level.

1892 — Northwest Territories including what is now Alberta and Saskatchewan: Teaching in French is outlawed in public schools and Catholic schools are prohibited.

1905 — Alberta and Saskatchewan: The regulations of 1892 (Northwest Territories) are confirmed.

1912 — Keewatin: Denominational (Catholic) schools are suppressed and the teaching of French is forbidden.

1912 — Ontario: By regulation (regulation No. 17) French is outlawed in Ontario schools.

1916 — Manitoba: The teaching of French is prohibited at all levels.

1930 — Saskatchewan: The teaching of French is prohibited even outside school hours.[8]

English-Canadian nationalists supported Britain in the two world wars. For them, Canadian patriotism was bound up with British imperialism. Even well after the last war, in 1964, echoes of these sentiments could be heard in the flag debates among supporters of the Red Ensign. When Canada rejected that flag, it was adopted by Ontario and Newfoundland. But the old sense of the rightness of British ways and their relevance to Canada was gone. English Canada was standing psychologically without its motherland as French Canada had long done.

Meanwhile, English Canada had also become home to many newcomers. The majority of these new Canadians tended to bypass the Maritimes and Quebec, as those areas had retained more of their original cultural duality. Immigrants usually favoured Ontario and the West, making these provinces more multicultural and lessening Canada's historical duality. In 1979, the Task Force on National Unity noted:

> Because many English-speaking Canadians think of their country as a cultural and geographic mosaic, they tend to regard French-speaking Canadians as members of one of the many minority groups that make up the Canadian mosaic. They do not spontaneously think of their country in a dualistic way.[9]

Governor General Edward Schreyer's inaugural address of February 1979 was the first to be given in five languages (English, French, Ukrainian, German, and Polish). Adrienne Clarkson became Canada's first Governor General of Asian extraction. She was succeeded by Michaëlle Jean, a black woman of Haitian origin. As Clarkson rose in the English-language media, so Jean became a star in Quebec and later in English Canada. Both stressed the ideals of freedom and opportunity in their new homeland. Canada was moving in the direction of multiculturalism, if not multilingualism. In Quebec, the allophones could be counted on to vote 90 percent federalist, along with the anglophones, to maintain Canada's unity. But it would be decades before their full influence, proportionate to their growing numbers, would be felt in our political and economic hierarchies.

These newcomers may eventually moderate our classic duels, but it will take time before they achieve power in proportion to their numbers. And when they do, they may not choose to act as an independent third group. John H. Porter, economic historian, found that despite steady immigration from non-British and non-French countries since 1900, those who held power in Canada were overwhelmingly English and French. Eighty-five percent of the members of Parliament came from the two charter, or founding, peoples.[10] In the economic establishment, the new Canadians were even less represented; they were spectators, rather than participants.[11]

We shall examine ten crises in the relationship between Canada's two founding peoples. In doing so, we should ask ourselves these questions: What caused the crisis in each case? Could it have been averted? Was it resolved or did it just go away with time? Of the alternative actions, was the best one taken? Why did another crisis occur within a few years? Is crisis between French and English a chronically recurring state in Canada? Why has Canada not yet found an answer to this issue of discord or accord at its core?

Both French- and English-Canadian writers have expressed their views in a variety of literary sources. For samples of prose and poetry that seek to explain the nature of Canada, see Chapter 12, Controversy over the Problem of the Nation.

NOTES

1   Originally, the French called themselves *"Canadiens"* and the newcomers *"Anglais."* In the nineteenth century, they began to use the term *"Canadiens français"* to distinguish themselves from English-speaking Canadians. For the most part, in the early historical section of this book, we will use the traditional expressions, "French Canadians" and "English Canadians." In the latter chapters, however, we shall employ the words coined by the Royal Commission on Bilingualism and Biculturalism (1963–69)—"anglophone" and "francophone"—and the term "Québécois," or "Quebecker," favoured by the Parti Québécois.

2   Mason Wade, The French Canadians 1760–1945 (Toronto, 1955), vii.

3   Oliver Asselin, L'Oeuvre de l'Abbé Groulx (Montreal, 1923), 90.

4   Le Devoir, 5 July 1963.

5   "Bilingualism Losing Some Ground among Young Anglophones outside Quebec," in Profile of Languages in Canada: English-French Bilingualism (Ottawa, Statistics Canada).

6   André Laurendeau, qtd. in "The Silence of English Canada," in The Essential Laurendeau, ed. Ramsay Cook and Michael Behiels, trans. Joanne l'Heureux and Richard Howard, Issues in Canadian History, gen. ed. J.L. Granatstein (Vancouver, 1976), 253–54.

7   Archives of Ontario: Denison Papers, vol. 5, personal copy sent to G.T. Denison.

8   André Bernard, What Does Quebec Want? (Toronto, 1978), 27. The list was originally taken from Abbé Lionel Groulx, L'Enseignement français au Canada (Montreal, 1935).

9   The Task Force on Canadian Unity, A Future Together: Observations and Recommendations (Ottawa, 1979), 26.

10   John Porter, The Vertical Mosaic (Toronto, 1965), 386–89.

11   Peter C. Newman, The Canadian Establishment, vol. 1 (Toronto, 1975), 84–88.

2 ❧ THE CRISIS OF THE CONQUEST, 1759–1774

The British Conquest was the first great crisis in Canadian history. The Conquest reminds us forcibly that long before English Canada existed, there was French Canada. The motto of the province of Quebec is *Je me souviens*. By this, French Canadians mean that they remember their past before the Conquest, that golden age when Canada was entirely French. *Notre maître, le passé*, was the imperative the Abbé Groulx taught his students.

The tendency of the nationalist historian is to over-glamorize the past, but there is no doubt that French Canada had its romantic age. The ideal sense of romance was captured by William Kirby when he wrote *The Golden Dog*, a novel of aristocratic life in old Quebec. The more prosaic but still fascinating reality was recorded by travellers. One, the Baron de Lahontan, described the peasants of New France in 1683:

> The Canadians are well built, sturdy, tall, strong, vigorous, enterprising, brave, and indefatigable. They lack only the knowledge of literature. They are presumptuous and full of themselves, putting themselves ahead of all the nations of the earth; and unfortunately they do not have the respect that they might for their relatives (the French). The blood of Canada is very good; the women are generally pretty; brunettes are rare, the wise are common, and the lazy are found in great enough number; they love luxury dearly, and it falls to the one who best traps a husband.[1]

Another traveller, Père Charlevoix, a Jesuit who visited New France in the early eighteenth century, made this comparison between the French Canadians and the English settlers in the Thirteen Colonies. It might be seen as the first commentary on French-English relations in North America:

> The English colonist amasses means and makes no superfluous expense; the French enjoys what he has and often parades what he has not. The former works for his heirs; the latter leaves his in the need in which he is himself, to get along as best they can. The British Americans dislike war, because they have so much to lose; they do not humour the Savages, because they see no need to do so. The French youth, on the contrary, loathe peace and get along well with the natives, whose esteem they easily win in war and whose friendship they always earn.[2]

It has been this marked difference in values, noted so early, that lies at the root of each French-English crisis in Canada.

What was French society like before the Conquest? The most glamorous of the French were the *coureurs de bois*. They are today the great heroes of French-Canadian folklore. Every schoolboy in Quebec knows of Adam Dollard and his stand against the Iroquois at the Long Sault. He knows, too, that it was the *coureurs de bois* who carried the *fleur-de-lys* for the King of France and laid claim to vast tracts of land up the St. Lawrence, beyond the Great Lakes, south on the Mississippi, north to Hudson Bay, and west on the Saskatchewan. Their numbers were never large (for example, just five hundred in 1679), but their energy and their dreams for a continental fur empire based on the St. Lawrence were boundless. Today economists argue that they over-reached themselves, that the fur trade was a drain on the resources of New France, rather than a profitable endeavour, and that it would have been more sensible to have concentrated on agriculture along the St. Lawrence. Undoubtedly, the fur traders would have gained economically had they chosen to join the Thirteen Colonies. But they did not. They were the first Canadians.

The *habitants* and their *seigneurs* lived more prosaically, but they ensured through their patient toil the permanent existence of Canada as a nation. They were not numerous compared to the English colonists to the south—only about 70,000 instead of a million and a half. But they were strong in patience and in the self-reliance required of those who inhabit a northern land. Their farms were laid out in long, narrow strips, which can be seen today on the hills near Quebec City, running back from the St. Lawrence. Each *habitant* had his river frontage; his piece of flat, fertile meadow; and his woodland on the hill, according to the democratic custom of the frontier. The homes were set close together in little clusters along the river, the original highway winter and summer, and they were joined by an inland road to the church. The *habitants* were always an agricultural people, not much tempted by the incentives and subsidies offered by Jean Talon, the famous intendant sent out by Louis XIV, in a burst of unusual energy and efficiency, to encourage shipbuilding, lumbering, milling, iron mining, and domestic industry. Compared to the bustling traders and manufacturers to the south, the *habitants* seemed backward people.

Critical observers at the time ascribed this relative inactivity to the influence of the *curés*. The Baron de Lahontan wrote:

> One cannot have any pleasure, either at cards or in visiting the ladies, without the *curé* being told of it, and without his denouncing it from the pulpit. His indiscreet zeal goes so far as to name persons; and if he goes so far as to refuse Communion to noble ladies for wearing coloured ribbons, for the rest you can judge for yourself ... I vow they are ridiculous in their actions: they excommunicate maskers, and even run to places where they are to be found, in order to unmask them and cover them with

opprobrium … They persecute people who do not go to Communion monthly … They forbid and burn all books which are not concerned with devotion.[3]

If the influence of these zealous and puritanical clergymen was strong, it was also well deserved. The French clergy—parish priests and nuns, bishops like the great Laval and Jesuit missionaries like the martyred Brébeuf—were truly builders of Canada, her first spiritual mentors. Without their learning and their zeal, one could very well ask if early Canada would have had any cultural life or social discipline; without them, early Quebec would have been a rough, unlettered, crude society. They carried civilization to the wilderness. And they remained after the Conquest in Canada, along with the *habitants* and the *coureurs de bois*, when the French officials and many of the *seigneurs* went home to France.

This, then, was the society of New France. But for all the glamour of its *coureurs de bois*, for all the pluck of its *habitants*, and for all the power of its *curés*, it could not compete with the society to the south. It was numerically, economically, and militarily inferior. It could not defend itself without outside naval support. Unfortunately, the French in France, unlike the British, were a continental people who looked inward to Europe. Colonies to them were dipensable luxuries, mere extras that cost little, rather than necessities, the lifeblood of raw materials and of trade, as they were to the British. Louis XIV's finance minister, Jean Colbert, thought colonies were good only insofar as they were good for France.

The basic inequality between the two societies in the New World spelled disaster for New France on the Plains of Abraham in September 1759. There, all the courage of the French forces and all the brilliance of Montcalm were of no avail in the face of the greater resources and efficiency of the British. Even then, the defeat on the autumn fields outside Quebec might not have been final. If, when the ice left the Gulf of St. Lawrence the following spring, a French fleet bearing reinforcements had sailed up the river, all might not have been lost. But it was the British fleet that appeared, and that sealed the fate of Canada.

Francis Parkman, a nineteenth-century New Englander of proud, old colonial stock and the foremost historian of the French and Indian Wars, saw the issue as a clash between an agricultural, feudal, Roman Catholic society and an industrial, democratic, Protestant one. In his view, the events of 1759 and 1760 signalled a conquest—of the French by the English. French nationalist historians disagreed. The Abbé Groulx argued that the French people had not been conquered, nor had the British army been victorious. The French in Canada had not really been defeated on the Plains of Abraham in 1759. After all, a second French army under Lévis had remained undefeated in the colony, and it was victorious at the battle of Ste. Foy in 1760. But the French Canadians were abandoned by the government at Versailles, which was steeped in graft and corruption, and left to their fate. They made an honourable peace with the English in the fall of 1760—they did not surrender.

Both English and French historians agree, however, that a change of government occurred. The colony previously governed by France became part of the British Empire. The British administrators, operating in those easy days before the rude awakening of the American Revolution, considered the problem of this foreign colony. How could these aliens possibly be fitted into an empire of British settlers? Should they be allowed to remain alien, French, and Roman Catholic? Or should they become British and Protestant, to match the rest of the empire? By 1763, the British government had decided that Quebec should become a British colony like the others. The Ohio country was chopped off from the St. Lawrence region; British courts were established; lands were set aside for the support of the Protestant clergy and schools; the English language was made official; provision was made to encourage immigration of British settlers from the crowded south; and a democratic assembly was granted—that is, as democratic an assembly as then existed in the Thirteen Colonies. How simple it all seemed in London!

What looked so neat and logical on paper in the Proclamation of 1763—the policy of assimilation as it has since been called—proved totally unrealistic and impractical. There were at this time thirty French Canadians to each English settler in Quebec. To turn a French colony into a British one was easier said than done. It was not many years before the British governors of Quebec, those who were actually on the spot, saw this. Governors James Murray and Guy Carleton wrote home that it would be difficult to introduce a democratic assembly here, where there had never been one. They pointed out that there might be resistance from the Roman Catholic *habitants* if they were asked to support a Protestant clergy. And it might be confusing to introduce English common law into a society reared on the French civil code. Further, Carleton questioned whether it was really desirable to recast this peaceful colony, ruled by its seigneurs and curés, in the image of the rebellious south?

Finally, the British were persuaded to abandon assimilation. At the last moment, they yielded to the advice of the men on the spot and decided to fortify the old citadel of Quebec, the only visible bulwark against the growing forces of the American Revolution. They decided to recognize *le fait français* and hoped that their generosity would be repaid in loyalty. French Canada was granted its Magna Carta in the *Quebec Act* of 1774. The Ohio hinterland was restored to the St. Lawrence for the fur trade; the French were guaranteed their ancient civil law; the Roman Catholic Church was assured its freedom and its legal right to tithes; and an assembly was granted but postponed as "inexpedient." The act was meant to mark the beginning of a new age of accommodation between French Canada and the British government.

The Thirteen Colonies were outraged. To the north, a French, authoritarian, and Roman Catholic society would be made permanent. In 1774, bidding against the British government for the loyalty of the *habitants,* the Continental Congress made a counterproposal. In the "Address to the Inhabitants of the Province of Quebec," the rebelling colonists invited the *habitants* to join them:

Seize the opportunity presented to you by Providence itself. You have been conquered into liberty, if you act as you ought. This work is not of man. You are a small people compared to those who with open arms invite you into fellowship. A moment's reflection should convince you which will be most for your interest and happiness, to have all the rest of North America your unalterable friends, or your inveterate enemies. The injuries of Boston have roused and associated every colony, from Nova Scotia to Georgia. Your province is the only link that is wanting to complete the bright strong chain of union.[4]

The offer was a democratic assembly and freedom from the British government, from feudal dues, and probably from the tithe. The terms were associated with the *Bostonnais*, their old enemies in the French and Indian Wars, and probable assimilation into the Protestant, Anglo-Saxon society of the south. Material advantage was the trump card the Continental Congress offered; the price was the Roman Catholic religion and French culture.

It was a hard choice—between dollars and distinctiveness. The *habitants* hesitated. They asked their curés for advice and invariably received the reply, "The Yankees are godless." They observed that the American invaders, while promising prosperity in the future, often failed to pay hard cash for the supplies to which they helped themselves. At best, the *habitants* offered an uncertain welcome to the Americans. It would have taken a highly organized and efficient force to have captured the old citadel of Quebec, and the Americans under Montgomery were anything but organized and efficient in 1776. They failed to capture the city, and they found the winter cold unbearable. When spring brought British reinforcements up the St. Lawrence, they returned home, leaving the British still the masters of Quebec. The *habitants* noted this, and then they listened carefully to the terms of the *Quebec Act* as explained by the *curés* and the *seigneurs*. There were the promises of support for culture and religion and of resistance to encroachments from the south. In the end, it paid the British government to grant the *Quebec Act*: the "Fourteenth Colony" did not rise in revolution.

The *habitants*, then, were not to become future American citizens. With the advent of peace after the Revolution, a large measure of contentment came to Canada. The Crisis of the Conquest seemed to have been solved by the *Quebec Act,* and the French settled down to live under its guarantees. Those who could not swallow British rule returned to France; the rest were content for the moment. The British government was too far away to really interfere, but the fleet was there to protect. The French were a large majority in the northern land, and the English only a handful—a group of merchants who had moved north from Albany and bought up the fur-trading companies. There was no hint of a second crisis. The generation after the Conquest enjoyed its quiet decades and smiled at its conquerors. According to the Abbé Groulx, this was the generation that slept.

The terms of Quebec's surrender, excerpts from the Quebec Act, and opinions revealing the storm of controversy over the Conquest can be found in Chapter 13, Reflections on the Conquest.

NOTES

1   R.G. Thwaites, ed., *New Voyages to North America by the Baron de Lahontan,* vol. 1 (Chicago, 1905), 391.

2   L.P. Kellogg, ed., *Charlevoix's Journal of a Voyage to North America,* vol. 1 (Chicago, 1923), 117–18.

3   Thwaites, *New Voyages to North America,* vol. 1, 89–90.

4   Address of the General Congress to the Inhabitants of Quebec, 26 October 1774.

3 ❧ THE CRISIS OF THE REBELLIONS, 1837–1849

Two events disturbed the lull after the Conquest: the French Revolution and the arrival of the Loyalists.

The Loyalists moved north to the Maritimes, Upper Canada, and Quebec, and once settled, complained that they could not live in a French environment. So it became necessary, as early as 1791, to grant them their own assemblies, English common law, the use of the English language, and land reserves for the support of the Protestant clergy.

In France, the greatest of all revolutions changed the face of the old land from which the French Canadians had come. The *tricolore* replaced the *fleur-de-lys* of the Bourbons; the feudal nobility lost their privileges; the Roman Catholic Church was disestablished; and the Paris mob ran through the streets. The proponents of *liberté, égalité, fraternité* dismantled the ordered hierarchy of the *ancien régime*. French Canadians looked on in horror as the godless Robespierre and the upstart Napoleon seized power. It was the first but by no means the last time that the Old World proved more radical than the New. Quebec became the guardian of Old France and received on its shores some fifty *émigré* royalist clergy.

As the nineteenth century began, French Canada was one of five provinces in British North America. Its citizens were a minority. It was cut off from the old wellsprings of its culture. The French Canadians were cast adrift in an Anglo-Saxon sea. The second crisis of French-English relations—the Rebellions—was long in coming from the days of the Conquest but bitter when it broke. In 1837, violence erupted for the first time in eighty years. Again, the French fought the English in the land of the *Quebec Act*—in the streets of Montreal and in the small villages along the Richelieu and the Ottawa rivers. Doubts were raised about the future of the northern land. Could the nation—born through the Conquest and reborn through the Loyalist migration—endure the agony of strife between its two peoples?

The 1837 Rebellion in Lower Canada was in large part an economic conflict. Since the Conquest, as before it, the French had been an agricultural people. They farmed in the traditional way of their feudal past—mixed farming for subsistence. Very few people in Quebec produced specialty crops for the export market. They lived by themselves, feeding themselves, independent of and isolated from the world of trade, which was British. The French upper classes sent their sons into the professions—the law, the Church, and medicine—and here, too, they lived apart from the world of trade. By contrast, the English newcomers were capitalists and merchants, land speculators, and canal builders. They demanded that the *habitants* pay taxes to deepen the St. Lawrence, and the *habitants* refused. An agrarian society clashed with a commercial one; the country opposed the town. And because business yielded greater returns than agriculture and the professions, it was a struggle between the haves and have-nots, a struggle as old as human history.

To the economic cleavage was added a social one. The French became the lower classes, a status galling to the descendants of *seigneurs,* and the English became the upper. Governor James Craig, whose rule in Quebec is referred to by French Canadians as "the reign of terror," noted the social tension:

> ... the line of distinction between us is completely drawn. Friendship (and) Cordiality are not to be found—even common intercourse scarcely exists—the lower class of people, to strengthen a term of contempt, add Anglois—and the better sort, with whom there formerly did exist some interchange of the common civilities of Society, have of late entirely withdrawn themselves—the alleged reason is that their circumstances have gradually declined in proportion as ours have increased in affluence.[1]

The religious difference compounded the economic and social conflict. The English newcomers were largely Protestant, while the French remained strongly Roman Catholic. Although they were only a small minority in Quebec, the Church of England clergy under the leadership of Bishop Mountain campaigned for the disestablishment of Roman Catholicism and for the privileges of official status for themselves. As early as 1804, Herman Ryland, an Anglican layman and close friend of the Bishop, complained to London about the privileged position of the Roman Catholic clergy:

> I call them "Popish" to distinguish them from the Clergy of the Established Church, and to express my contempt and detestation of a religion which sinks and debases the human mind, and which is a curse to every country where it prevails. This being my opinion, I have long since laid it down as a principle, which, in my judgement, no Governor of this Province ought to lose sight of for a moment ... by every possible means which prudence can suggest gradually to undermine the authority and influence of the Roman Catholic priests ... We have been mad enough to allow a company of French rascals to deprive us for the moment of the means to accomplish this.[2]

The British government never did yield to these importunities, but the Catholic faithful in Quebec lived in a state of anxiety that it might.

Where there are deep schisms in society, politics is fraught with turmoil and confusion. By the 1830s, a power struggle deadlocked the province. Intercourse between the Council, to which the governors appointed the English (along with some tame French officials), and the Assembly, where the populace returned a French majority of its own choosing, became less and less frequent, and the wheels of state ground slowly to a halt. The Council in popular parlance became known as the "Château Clique." These were the Governor's pampered pets, the wealthy traders like the Richardsons and the McGills of Montreal, the commercial élite, the oppressors of the people. In the eyes of the Council, the Assembly was an ignorant rabble led by loud-mouthed troublemakers, who delighted in blocking all schemes to improve the roads and canals, who talked and talked while the province slipped deeper and deeper into debt and lagged further behind its southern rivals.

Lord Durham, British North America's first Governor General, was sent out to find a solution to the colony's ills and wrote a report about the situation in 1839. He believed that the trouble went beyond the council chamber and the assembly hall. It was not political principles that were at stake, nor social distinctions, nor economic jealousies. "I expected to find a contest between a government and a people, " he wrote after months of observation and much reading of reports. "I found two nations warring in the bosom of a single state: I found a struggle, not of principles, but of races." Did a total split exist in the rebellion in Lower Canada? Were the French really united against the English? Let us examine the career of the leader of the rebellion, Louis-Joseph Papineau. He was a tall, aristocratic *seigneur* of the old school, who had inherited from his father the *seigneury* of La Petite Nation on the Ottawa River. He possessed a brilliant mind filled with liberal ideas and a gallant heart overflowing with love for his people. There was about Papineau an air of *noblesse oblige* in its finest and purest form. Like those of most prominent men in history, his actions have been controversial. Was he a hero or a scoundrel? *Un ange ou une bête?*

English-Canadian historians considered him a dangerous traitor. D.B. Read, for instance, writing in 1896, said that Papineau was "only a petty leader in a really petty cause, leading his confiding countrymen to certain destruction."[3] On the other hand, the Abbé Groulx revered Papineau as a great national hero. How difficult it is even for professional historians to be objective about events that arouse deep emotions! Gérard Filteau in his *Histoire des Patriotes* observed that in historiography "Les Patriotes se sent ainsi vus condamner sans retour ou glorifier sans mesure."[4] (The Patriots thus see themselves as condemned without reprieve or glorified without limit.)

In his youth, Papineau had great faith in British institutions. To him, British rule had liberated, rather than enslaved, the French Canadians. In 1820, on the death of George III, Papineau eulogized him:

> ... Suffice it then at a glance to compare our present happy situation with that of our fathers on the eve of the day when George III became their legitimate monarch ... Under the French government ... the interests of this colony had been more frequently neglected and maladministered than

those of any other part of its dependencies … with a trade administered by monopoly companies … personal liberty daily violated … Such was the situation of our fathers; behold the change! George III, a sovereign revered for his moral character, attention to his kingly duties, and love of his subjects, succeeds to Louis XV … From that day the reign of the law succeeds to that of violence … Soon after are granted to us the principles of its free constitution … Now religious toleration … All these advantages have become our birthright … Let us only act as becomes British subjects.[5]

Papineau believed that the power of the democratic Assembly in Quebec and the guarantees of the *Quebec Act* were all that were needed to ensure the place of French Canada within the British Empire. He served as Speaker of the Assembly and studied the British Constitution with care. In the 1820s, with the united French nation at his back and staunch allies like John Neilson, the liberal-minded Scottish editor of the *Quebec Gazette,* he secured steady advances for the powers of the Assembly through the constitutional means of petitioning and pressuring the British government. He believed in British parliamentary democracy—not for its own sake but for the sake of what it could bring French Canada. His goal was self-government for Quebec under the British Crown. He was proud to be part of the empire of freedom.

In his middle age, Papineau lost this early faith. He became disillusioned and impatient with the snail's pace at which the British moved in constitutional reform. The Governor, surrounded by the "Château Clique," seemed to block the Assembly at every turn. And Papineau wearied of sending appeals to London that went unanswered for months. Parliament, as it existed in French Canada in the 1830s in the form of an Assembly, could be dismissed by the Governor at will; so Papineau came to view it as a poor vehicle from which to launch the French-Canadian ship of state. Slow and woefully inadequate, it yielded too little too late. Papineau turned from the British example and looked with increasing longing at the American one. He grasped at the idea of an elected executive as a way of getting things done fast. He grew to admire the American insistence on independence and on fundamental individual rights. A democratic republic for the French nation, a sovereign state in North America, *une nation canadienne!* Such was the stuff of his ambitions by 1837.

How was this vision to be realized? Through an American-style revolution, fought by the *habitants* with American aid. The irony was that as Papineau became more radical and increased his demands for the French-Canadian nation, he began to lose his support among those very people. The moderate French Canadians, those who eschewed violence and preferred to compromise with the British (for, after all, le *fait britannique* was not to be ignored), left the Patriots. The moderates were denounced as *chouayens,* or *vendus,* but they were joined by many of Papineau's English allies, including Neilson. The Patriot movement became less French, more Irish, and more radical. Few French Canadians had ever expressed the depth of hatred for the British government poured out by O'Callaghan's *Vindicator* in Montreal: "Henceforth, there must be no peace in the province! No quarter for the plunderers. Agitate! AGITATE!! AGITATE!!! Destroy the revenue; denounce the oppressors. Everything is lawful when the fundamental liberties are in danger. The guards die—they never surrender."[6] Originally a parliamentary party, the Patriots now left the Assembly and took to the streets and the fields. They held large rallies, where speaker after speaker whipped up the emotions of the crowds. To the alarm of the moderate French Canadians, the horror of the bishops, and the terror of the English minority living in Quebec, Patriots began calling for civil disobedience, trade boycotts on British goods, American aid in arms, and direct resistance. Wolfred Nelson, later a Patriot military commander who took refuge in the United States, shouted, "Let us have no petty expedients, the time has come to melt our spoons into bullets!"

At Saint-Charles, the independence resolutions had a familiar ring, "That, in accordance with the example of the wise men and heroes of 1776, we hold as self-evident and repeat the following truths: That all men are created equal; that they are endowed by their creator with certain inalienable rights ...." The young Patriots of Montreal took the name *Fils de la Liberté,* and they roamed the streets looking for a fight with armed bands of young Tories. In his old age, Papineau had cause for bitterness. Once the hero of the French nation, and enjoying its solid support for constitutional reform, he saw in the violence of 1837–1840 not a revolution won but a movement that faded away. The French-Canadian moderates, the French-Canadian clergy, many of the *habitants,* and the English sympathizers all deserted Papineau. The Patriot movement became dominated by the Irish, lawless elements among the French, and American sympathizers. In the end, it was put down ruthlessly by British troops, English-Canadian volunteers from Quebec and Glengarry County in Ontario, and the French *chouayens.*

The revolution might have succeeded even then, if American aid had appeared. But President Van Buren, the "Red Fox," refused to commit the American government officially and observed a studious neutrality. Granted, some arms and supplies did cross the border. They were sent by the mysterious Hunters' Lodges, a clandestine organization of American sympathizers, whose local cells from Maine to Wisconsin tried to aid the rebels. It was a great game to "go hunting in the north woods," and many were the mysterious signs and symbols traced in the snow over the border. But the Hunters were really just playing at revolution for lack of something better to do, and when it became evident that the Canadians were not rising *en masse* to hail their deliverers, they gave up easily.

The United States did, however, offer asylum to Papineau. He fled south, and a generation of French Canadians turned their backs on him. In later years, the French moderates such as LaFontaine and Cartier cursed him. *"C'est la faute à Papineau,"* they said when things went wrong.

Was this "racial war" in Quebec as Lord Durham had said? It is a fact that early in the conflict, a majority of the French Canadians were united behind Papineau against the English. It is also a fact that toward the end, the French were sorely divided, as were the English—the former as to whether the rebellion should take place, the latter as to whether it should be crushed by force. The French *chouayens* and the English sympathizers prevented a thorough racial cleavage. The day was shortly to come when they, and not the extremists, would hold the fate of Canada in their hands. When the gun smoke cleared from Saint-Eustache, Saint-Denis, and Saint-Charles, the moderates on both sides came forward and tried to catch the ear of Lord Durham. In 1839, he presented to the British government his report, the Grand Answer to the Rebellions, which every school child in Canada knows. But which version have Canadians learned in school: the English one or the French? Opinion on the report serves powerfully to remind us that there are two Canadas. English-Canadian school children learn that the report was a charter of liberties, a Magna Carta for the land; French-Canadian school children learn that it was a charter of oppression, every page a denial of freedom.

Lord Durham recommended that responsible government be given to the Canadas. We take self-government through the Cabinet system for granted today, but in 1839, this was a daring and courageous innovation. He also advised the assimilation of the French Canadians. As the final solution to domestic conflict, Durham demanded the union of the two Canadas. Into this union, he urged the rapid and assisted immigration of the British poor—to relieve the motherland and to swamp the French. Such a union could be granted responsible government quite safely, because the English would soon form the majority there. In French Canada, it was little wonder that the report was hailed with something less than enthusiasm and its author mistrusted. It was considered a fine blueprint for the slow death of French Canada. A far cry from the Patriot's dream of *une nation canadienne!*

The only future Lord Durham saw for Canada was an English-Canadian one. Both he and his assistant Stuart Derbishire held a low opinion of French Canadians. After a few days' travel about the province, Derbishire wrote:

> The *habitants* are a sluggish race, fond of indolent pleasures, lighthearted and gay. They resemble the French [in Europe] in many of their qualities, and have all the national conceit of that people … I believe that from the highest to the lowest they live in a perpetual atmosphere of self-adulation. They are, I believe, an innocent and virtuous race, [and] have retained a character of primitive simplicity … The ambition of bettering their condition seems never to have visited their minds: locomotive faculties they seem to have none

... There seems to be no decorative taste in the people, no active spirit of improvement, no ambition beyond the mere supply of the wants of nature.[7]

A pleasant people, charming as peasants are, but lazy, dull, and backward. Hardly the stuff out of which to build an empire. Lord Durham felt much the same way about them:

> ... They cling to ancient prejudices, ancient customs and ancient laws, not from any strong sense of their beneficial effects, but with the unreasoning tenacity of an uneducated and unprogressive people ... The Conquest has changed them but little ... The continued negligence of the British government left the mass of the people without any of the institutions which would have elevated them in freedom and civilization ... They remain an old and stationary society in a new and progressive world.[8]

And in the aftermath of the rebellion, he read the mood of the French thus: "They brood in sullen silence over the memory of their fallen countrymen, of their burnt villages, of their ruined property, of their extinguished ascendancy, and of their humbled nationality. To the Government and the English they ascribe these wrongs, and nourish against them both an indiscriminating and eternal animosity."[9] Lord Durham felt that the old policy of assimilation of 1763 should never have been abandoned. But in 1839 it was not too late to take it up again because:

> ... It will be acknowledged by everyone who has observed the progress of Anglo-Saxon colonization in America, that sooner or later the English race was sure to predominate even numerically in Lower Canada, as they predominate already, by their superior knowledge, energy, enterprise, and wealth.[10]

However, it became evident within a few years that this recommendation was futile. Under responsible government, the first great ministry in Canada was not based on a solid English majority headed by one English Prime Minister as Durham had advised, but on a French-English partnership under Robert Baldwin and Louis-Hippolyte LaFontaine.

Henceforth in Canada, it was to be almost impossible to have a successful government without the cooperation and participation of the French. The best governments of Canada have always been, like its first, partnerships. Between the French extreme of Papineau's independent state and the English extreme of Durham's assimilative state, a compromise was attempted in the 1840s—a partnership within a single state. Whether it would work out or not was a question for the future. In 1848, all that was known was that a dual ministry existed, and in 1849, the British Governor had accepted his first piece of controversial legislation, the Rebellion Losses Bill.

The first ministry was a personal triumph for Baldwin, the author of the idea of responsible government in Canada and its patient advocate through discouraging years. It was also a personal triumph for LaFontaine, who made it possible in the realm of practical politics. Without the adhesion of the French, no ministry could have commanded a majority of the Assembly and been a truly responsible ministry. LaFontaine and the French moderates participated despite the terms of representation, which worked to their disadvantage. In 1840, Lower Canada had 600,000 inhabitants and Upper Canada had only 400,000, and yet each was awarded equal representation in the joint Assembly.

The French entered the Union, therefore, with sober optimism. But despite their cooperation, the judgement of Lord Durham would, in time, begin to haunt them. Without assimilation, they were doomed to an inferior status:

> ... It would appear that the great mass of the French Canadians are doomed, in some measure, to occupy an inferior position, and be dependent upon the English for employment. The evils of poverty and dependence would merely be aggravated in a ten-fold degree, by a spirit of jealous and resentful nationality, which would separate the working classes of the community from the possessors of wealth and employers of labour.[11]

The dual ministry was, nevertheless, a guarantee that there would be a future. It was a symbol of the cooperative potential of the nation and of its capacity to endure.

The Rebellions and the Report gave contemporaries and later scholars much food for thought, as can be seen from the documents contained in Chapter 14, Both Sides of the Rebellions.

NOTES

1   Craig to Liverpool, 1 May 1810.

2   Robert Christie, *A History of the Late Province of Lower Canada*, vol. 6 (Quebec, 1848), 72–73; Ryland, 23 December 1804.

3   D.B. Read, *The Canadian Rebellions of 1837* (Toronto, 1896), 27.

4   Gérard Filteau, *Histoire des Patriotes*, vol. 1 (Montreal, 1938), 7.

5   A.D. De Celles, *Papineau*, vol. 5 of Makers of Canada Series (Toronto, 1926), 35–37.

6   *Vindicator* (Montreal) April 21, 1837 Number 48.

7   Qtd. in *Canadian Historical Review 18* (1937): 57.

8   *Lord Durham's Report on the Affairs of British North America*, vol. 2, *Text of the Report*, ed. C.P. Lucas (Oxford, 1912), 30.

9   Ibid.

10 Ibid.

11 Ibid.

4 ❦ THE CONFEDERATION CRISIS, 1860–1867

After the rebellions and the report, French and English Canadians settled down to live together in the Union. The alliance of Robert Baldwin and Louis-Hippolyte LaFontaine in the Reform Party and the counteralliance of Tories under William Henry Draper and the young John A. Macdonald with French Conservatives were living proof of Canada's will to make the partnership work. The Union prospered. The St. Lawrence route was improved by a series of canals. The government gave aid to the railways, whose lines spread like spiders' webs across the united provinces. Wheat from Upper Canada, now Canada West, and from the American Midwest poured down the golden funnel of the river and across the Atlantic to waiting buyers in Britain.

Immigrants came up the river to Canada West, and there they pushed back the agricultural frontier, back from the lakeshore settlements of the Loyalists into the interior. There they founded towns and villages and laid out prosperous farms north of Toronto and to the west in the Huron Tract. In Canada East (Quebec), the *habitants* multiplied rapidly and began their expansion north of the river, west into the Ottawa Valley, east of Quebec City and south to the Eastern Townships and northern New England. Busy pursuing the hard cash to be made on the new farms, English and French Canadians were too preoccupied to reopen old wounds. Nevertheless, changes occurred throughout the quiet years, bringing crisis once more to the nation. Though both Canadas were growing, Canada West (Ontario) was growing faster. These were the years of the potato famines in Ireland, hard adjustments in the industrialization of England, grinding poverty in Scotland, and hence the "Great Migration" to the New World. By 1861, the census told the story: there were 300,000 more souls in Canada West than in Canada East. And unlike the French and English Canadians already living in the Canadas, the new British immigrants would not tolerate underrepresentation!

The cry went up for "rep by pop" ("representation by population"). The Clear Grit Party, strong among the independent Scots, organized in Canada West to pressure the government of the day for changes. The ugly question was raised: Must we live under "French and Roman Catholic domination"? The French were forced into a defensive position. The accord of 1840 was threatened. In 1860, twenty years later, the new majority were demanding their rights against the minority. Who would win? Or who could win?

In the face of these fundamental questions involving the life of the Union, government ground slowly to a halt. It became increasingly difficult to form a Cabinet supported by the double majority (a majority of English and a majority of French) demanded for the success of the Union. The Tories, under John A. Macdonald and his French lieutenant, George Etienne Cartier, were becoming a party of the French, woefully weak in English Canada. The Reformers, or Grits, as they were called before the name "Liberal" was officially adopted, were led by George Brown of the Toronto *Globe*, and they were becoming a party of the English, woefully weak in French Canada. On every issue, the two sides moved further apart. Reactions to the Separate Schools Bill provided a classic example of the chasm between the two parties. The bill was cherished by the Roman Catholics of Canada East but was anathema to the Protestants of Canada West. Donald Creighton, historian of the Confederation period and biographer of Macdonald, wrote of the dilemma of the Reform government:

> ... The whole history of the Scott (Separate Schools) bill was, in itself, a faltering, unhappy confession of weakness. The ministry as a whole, fearful of losing its strong support in Canada West, had not dared to introduce the bill as a government measure; but the ministers individually, worried by the prospect of arraying the whole of Canada East against them, had decided that they must give it their support ... The Scott Separate School Bill passed, but in a fashion characteristic of such measures. A majority of the whole House voted in its favour; a majority of the members from Canada West voted against it. It was, in other words, a sectional, a "single" majority. Yet Double Majority was professedly the fundamental guiding principle of the government. What would it do? What explanation could it possibly give? It did nothing. It said nothing. It gave no explanations, yet it continued in office.[1]

A growing sense of futility descended on the debates in the Union Parliament. Unable to work together, French and English sought freedom from each other. There had to be a way out or Canada would break up.

The answer was found in Confederation, which shattered the old Union and built a new nation. Confederation was many things. It was constitution making *par excellence;* it was the framework for a transcontinental economy; it was the British answer to American encroachments on the Prairies and in British Columbia; it was the product of Canadian fears of the recently (post–Civil War) unemployed army of the American North. But above all, it was the catalyst for another crisis.

Confederation meant a union of all the territories in British North America. It was not a new idea. The first Loyalists had dreamed of a united northland. Jonathan Sewell and William Smith, for instance, had been its fervent advocates in the 1780s. Such a state would be the brightest jewel in the Empire they had fought to preserve, and it would be the envy of the traitorous Yankees. Smith was confident that the French could be absorbed in such a union, citing the example of the Thirteen Colonies, where he had observed the successful integration of peoples "addicted to foreign laws and usages and understanding none but a foreign language."[2] The same could be done in Canada. In 1840, Lord Durham took up the old Loyalist idea with enthusiasm:

Such a union would at once decisively settle the question of races: it would enable all the Provinces to co-operate for all common purposes; and, above all, it would form a great and powerful people, possessing the means of securing good and responsible government for itself, and which, under the protection of the British Empire, might in some measure counterbalance the preponderant and increasing influence of the United States on the American continent.[3]

It was small wonder, then, that the concept's reappearance in the 1860s, this time backed by the great majority of the powerful and influential in English Canada and pushed enthusiastically by the British government, provoked a crisis. Again, ghosts walked upon the Plains of Abraham, and the spectre of assimilation appeared out of the past. Macdonald, the leading English-Canadian politician, was known to favour a sweeping legislative union—a union in which all provincial governments would be abolished, a union with a single central government, a union in which the English-speaking could have complete majority rule. If this was not practicable, Macdonald preferred a central government as strong as possible and provincial governments as weak as possible. What place would there be for French Canada in such a state? Surely, to leave the Union and enter such a Confederation with the English provinces would mean disaster.

Probably, French Canada would not have considered this course of action without George Etienne Cartier. Just as, without LaFontaine, the Union could not have been formed, so without Cartier, Confederation would have been impossible. Cartier was a businessman and a Patriot; he was a French Canadian loyal to his people and religion, and a Canadian who planned for a transcontinental Canada. He was the only French-Canadian member of the Standing Committee on Railways, and from 1851 on, he was its chairman. Cartier was both idealistic and pragmatic. He was fond of this jingle:

L'heure viendra.
Sachons l'attendre.
Bientôt nous pourrons la saisir.
Le courage fait entreprendre
Et l'adresse fait réussir.[4]
(The time will come.
Know how to await it.
Soon we shall be able to seize it.
Courage leads to undertakings,
Cleverness makes them succeed.)

Cartier was born into a well-to-do merchant family. He was educated in the traditional French manner of the classical colleges and the law. In 1838, he joined the *Fils de Liberté* and fought at Wolfred Nelson's side at Saint-Denis. With the defeat of the Patriots, Cartier fled to exile in New York State. Like many others, he returned disillusioned and convinced of the futility of rebellion. He settled down to practise law in Montreal and became a strong supporter of LaFontaine and the Union. Through the quiet 1840s, his interests turned increasingly to railways. He reasoned that Canada could not prosper through rebellion, nor backward agriculture, but only through a large vision of transcontinental trade. Montreal must look not to riots in the streets for its salvation, but to the rich trade of the interior. To compete with the enterprising Yankees of New York (whom he had grown to distrust and dislike), all Canadians would have to unite in a great national endeavour. His vision was breathtaking, yet practical:

> In the present age it is impossible for a country to enjoy great prosperity without railways … Let us resolve to have our railways in order to join them to those of an enterprising people separated from us by an imaginary line, by a line which becomes only too visible, alas, when we contrast our apathy and our laziness with the incessant activity, the feverish energy, and the enterprising spirit of our neighbours … The prosperity of Montreal depends upon its position as entrepôt of the commerce of the West … We cannot conserve it if we do not have the best means of transport from the Western waters to the Atlantic by our canals and by this railway … I then invite those who are present to come and take our shares according to their means—first of all for their own profit, and then out of patriotism … I address myself to Canadians of all origins: Americans, French, and English, let us be united and march together towards our destiny.[5]

Cartier, who fought under Papineau, became the heir of LaFontaine and the partner of Macdonald. In 1867, he was the man of the hour, on whom the resolution of the French-English crisis depended. It took all the vision, all the skill, and, yes, all the patronage he could command, to bring French Canada into Confederation. Even then, the thing was barely done and the margin of safety was narrow. The enemies of the Confederation scheme in Quebec—those who cried that it was assimilation in new clothes—were numerous, and they were articulate. They had much logic and history on their side, and they appealed to the passions of the people. Cartier responded by telling his fellow citizens that they had no realistic choice except to join Confederation, but in doing so, they would become part of a great nation. The Patriot's dream of *une nation canadienne-française*, was only a dream. It was for the young and the orators, but it was not the stuff of practical politics. An independent French state could never exist, but a transcontinental Canada could be achieved. And it would be a magnificent nation.

Cartier believed that without Confederation, the provinces of British North America would fall one by one into the American Union. This would mean assimilation for French Canada, the submergence of the nationality in the egalitarian, democratic, Protestant melting pot of the south, the loss forever of the monarchical, hierarchical, ordered Roman Catholic society of Quebec. Cartier accused those who opposed Confederation of being annexationists. In his persuasive Confederation speech, he outlined the choice before Canada:

> ... The question reduces itself to this—we must either have a confederation of British North America or be absorbed by the American Union. Some are of the opinion that it is not necessary to form such a confederation to prevent our absorption by the neighbouring republic, but they are mistaken ... The English provinces, separated as they are at present, cannot alone defend themselves ... When we are united, the enemy will know that if he attacks any province, either Prince Edward Island or Canada, we will have to deal with the combined forces of the Empire.[6]

Given the strength of the United States, it was for British North America a case of unite or perish.

If, without Confederation, there could be no French Canada, what were the prospects for the French in Confederation? Cartier rejected emphatically the danger of assimilation. The new state, he maintained, would be composed of a diversity of peoples:

> ... Some have regretted that we have a distinction of races, and have expressed the hope that, in time, this diversity will disappear. The idea of a fusion of all races is utopian; it is an impossibility. Distinctions of this character will always exist ... The objection that we cannot form a great nation because Lower Canada is French and Catholic, Upper Canada English and Protestant, and the Maritime Provinces mixed ... is futile ... In our confederation there will be Catholics and Protestants, English, French, Irish, and Scotch, and each by its efforts and success will add to the prosperity of the Dominion, to the glory of the new confederation. We are of different races, not to quarrel, but to work together for the common welfare.[7]

In Cartier's day, there was reason to hope that the West would be settled by French as well as English. When Manitoba, for instance, entered Confederation in 1870, it was more French than English. It was thought also that the domain beyond, of the fur traders in the Prairies, then known as the Northwest Territories, would also develop a significant French population.

The French Canadians had a much better chance for growth and survival in Canada than in the United States. There were the written guarantees from the British Crown concerning their culture and religion in the *Quebec Act*. In the new state, there would be similar guarantees and a division of powers between the central and provincial governments. Cartier argued that the federal system would protect the minority:

> ... There is no reason to fear that it will ever be sought to deprive a minority of its rights. Under the federal system, which leaves to the central government the control of questions of general interest, to which differences of races are foreign, the rights of race and of religion cannot be invaded. We will have a general parliament to deal with questions of defence, tariff, excise, public works, and all matters affecting individual interest. I will therefore ask those defenders of nationality who have accused me of bartering fifty-eight counties of Lower Canada ... how can injustice be done to the French Canadians by the general government?[8]

No government could interfere with their basic rights of language and religion.

What of Quebec's real power in the central government? Here, clearly, French Canadians would be in a minority. This was the soft spot in Cartier's case: the French could get only what their numbers made possible and no more. Cartier assumed that they would therefore act together as a bloc. United, their voting power would be too strong for any government to ignore them. They would be part of every government in Canada, and each Cabinet would contain French-Canadian members. It would be a matter of political infighting for Quebec's politicians to decide how many. With Macdonald, Cartier knew just how many he would get. Creighton writes of the formation of Macdonald's first Cabinet:

> The real difficulty was not in Ontario at all, but in Quebec ... Quebec would have to be content with one seat fewer than her sister province ... Cartier was ready to agree that Quebec could have only four cabinet ministers; but he would not consider for even a minute the suggestion that the French-Canadian membership should be reduced by one. Whatever happened, he and Hector Langevin and Jean Charles Chapais must be ministers.[9]

Their numbers would not be equal to the English-speaking ministers', but they would be there in sufficient force to be reckoned with.

Was it enough? Cartier's enemies, the *Rouges*, did not think so. "How can it be expected," cried Aimé Dorion, "that the French population can anticipate any more favourable result from the general government ... Experience shows that majorities are always aggressive, and it cannot be otherwise in this instance."[10] Henri Joly, deputy from Lotbinière, called Cartier a traitor who had sacrificed his people to his own political ambition.[11] And J.F. Perrault called Confederation the political suicide of the French race in Canada—a "scheme of Confederation [whose] ...real object is nothing but the annihilation of French influences in Canada."[12] The fear was that the day might come when the English majority alone would form the Cabinet, and the French would be excluded. This was possible, Cartier conceded, but not probable. There were many pressures Quebec could bring to bear to avoid it. At any rate, the chance had to be taken.

The vote in Lower Canada was 27 to 21 for Confederation. There were six more French Canadians for it than against it. Cartier had his hour of triumph; Macdonald had his partner; and Confederation had its chance.

At the beginning, then, of our national life in 1867, there were two founding peoples exhibiting two contrasting attitudes. English-speaking Canadians were enthusiastic and optimistic. They envisaged nothing but gain from the union of all the provinces. Here was the chance to build a strong transcontinental nation in British North America. Here was the chance to build a single unit, where before there had been five weak and divided provinces and that impossible deadlock with the French. Here was the chance to build a nation to take her place proudly among the nations of the world. Really, they preferred a legislative union to a federation, but believed that it would come in time. French-speaking Canadians, on the other hand, were dubious and pessimistic. They viewed Confederation as the lesser of two evils; it was better than being absorbed into the United States. It probably offered them their best chance for survival. They hoped for French expansion into the West, for full French representation in every Cabinet, for full bilingualism in the federal government. Canada was in the beginning one thing to the English and another to the French.

Would the English version of one nation or the French version of two nations within a single state take hold? In Ottawa, the Parliament buildings were illuminated on the night of July 1, 1867. The dark, green lawns were crowded with spectators who had come to look at the lights and celebrate the launching of the new nation. Macdonald and Cartier went home tired, leaving the celebrations to others. In myriad small villages and hamlets across the land, fireworks lit up the black skies. In Montreal, celebrating Canadiens thronged the streets, and in Hamilton, huge bonfires lit up the crest of the Mountain. All Canada was on holiday. Only the future could answer the tense question that lay at the heart of Confederation.

English and French Canadians held radically different views of the Confederation agreement. These are placed in striking opposition in Chapter 15, The Confederation Debate.

NOTES

1   Donald G. Creighton, *John A. Macdonald,* vol. 1, *The Young Politician* (Toronto, 1952), 340–41.

2   Smith to Dorchester, 7 November 1788, Smith Papers, New York Public Library.

3   *Lord Durham's Report on the Affairs of British North America,* vol. 2, Text of the Report, ed. C.P. Lucas (Oxford, 1912), 309.

4   Benjamin Sulte, *Mélanges historiques,* vol. 4, *George-Etienne Cartier* (Montreal, 1919), 15.

5   George Etienne Cartier (speech given in Montreal in 1846 regarding the Montreal-Portland railroad), qtd. in J. Tassé, *Discours de Sir Georges Cartier, Bart.* (Montreal, 1893), 2.

6   John Boyd, *Sir George Etienne Cartier, Bart., His Life and Times: A Political History of Canada from 1814 until 1873* (Toronto, 1914), 216–17.

7   Ibid., 222–23.

8   Ibid., 223.

9   Creighton, *The Young Politician,* 473. It is recommended that students read the epilogue of *The Young Politician* in full.

10 Hon. Antoine Aimé Dorion, member for Hochelaga, *Parliamentary Debates on the Subject of the Confederation of the British North American Provinces, 3rd Session, 8th Provincial Parliament of Canada* (Quebec, 1865), 264.

11 Paraphrase of speech by Henri Gustave Joly, member for Lotbinière, Ibid., 358.

12 Joseph F. Perrault, member for Richelieu, Ibid., 597.

5 ❧ The Crisis of Louis Riel, 1869–1885

The new nation was only two years old when the issue of French-English relations again had to be faced. And strangely enough, it arose not in old Canada of the East, but in the new lands beyond the Confederation. Retrospectively, continental expansion in North America looks like an easy process, a simple peopling of the wide-open spaces. But, in fact, it was far from being an automatic process of bringing in immigrants, and it was far from inevitable that they would reach the Pacific coast. Westward expansion raised the fundamental question in concrete terms: What kind of nation would finally be created?

Was the West to be half-French and half-English? Or was it to be all French—the land of the Métis, the fur trader, and Aboriginal nations? Or should it become all English, the land of the agricultural settler? In 1869, just two years after the achievement of Confederation, events in the Red River Colony forced an answer from the reluctant, procrastinating government. What Ottawa really hoped was that the tenuous bonds of the Union in the old settled areas would not be strained unduly, and that if ignored, the problem would go away.

In the decades before Confederation, the Canadian West had been a primitive wilderness—challenging, forbidding, and empty. It was peopled only by about ten thousand Métis, descendants of the fur traders and their Native wives, and by their pure-blooded Native allies. Since the early traders had been chiefly French, more of the Métis were part-French than part-English. But they were really neither French nor English; they were Canada's original "Third Force." They felt they were a new nation in their own right and that the West belonged to them.

The buffalo hunt was a traditional annual event in the life of the semi-nomadic Métis. In spring and fall the people planted and harvested their crops on narrow strips of land laid out along the Red River in the old French style. In winter they fished and trapped furs; in summer they hunted the buffalo, following the great herds across the Prairies. The buffalo hunt was the mainstay of their economy, yielding food, shelter, and trade goods. It even provided them with a rudimentary form of government. This description has been given of the hunt:

> The great annual hunt started early in June. Armed men on horseback, women and children on foot or riding in cumbersome Red River carts, moved out of the settlements along the river to the appointed rendezvous ... sometimes as many as two thousand *métis* ... The organization of the hunt usually took several days. First, the men assembled in open meeting and elected a governor and several captains, whose orders they agreed to obey without question ... Next, a carefully chosen band of scouts was sent out far ahead

of the main body to look for buffalo; and lastly, the women and children piled tents and equipment into the Red River carts and struck out across the prairie in the direction which the scouts, now far out of sight, had taken. Sometimes the scouts were lucky and spotted a herd of buffalo almost at once ... and the hunt was on. The governor of the hunt signalled the beginning of the "killing" run with a wave of the arm and a shrill "Ho-ho!" The *métis* horsemen approached the herd at a slow trot; then when the herd stampeded, at a reckless gallop. They swept back and forth through the confused turmoil ... shooting with deadly accuracy ... Considering the risks involved, the casualties were few. The *métis* were superb horsemen, the ponies they rode sure-footed as mountain goats.[1]

How magnificent! And in 1869 how anachronistic—for the last buffalo herds were being pushed farther and farther west by encroaching settlements. The day was fast approaching that would see them in their last refuge, the foothills of Alberta. If the buffalo were becoming a thing of the past, would their hunters also vanish?

Just as the Golden Age of the Métis was drawing to a close, the new Confederation was looking west with a hungry eye to the lands that had lain empty so long. In 1869, these lands, owned but not really controlled by the Hudson's Bay Company, were transferred to the Dominion. This event triggered the rebellion in the Red River Colony, and fifteen years later, in 1885, a second rebellion along the banks of the Saskatchewan.

The facts of the Riel Rebellions are simple, though it is still unclear who was at fault. In 1869 and 1870, Louis Riel led the Métis to form a provisional government to protest against the takeover by Canada without adequate safeguards for their rights, especially to the titles of their farms. During the provisional government's brief tenure of office in Red River, its officials executed one Thomas Scott, an Ontario Orangeman, for refusing to bow to its authority. Enraged by this act, Ontario bitterly condemned the "French half-breeds." Fifteen years later, the Métis, who by then had moved with their Native allies farther west to the Saskatchewan River country, resisted further attempts by Ottawa to bring them under the Canadian government's authority. At Duck Lake, Fish Creek, and Cut Knife, once again led by Riel, they fought the volunteer militia that had been rushed out from the East on the CPR; at Batoche the Métis were decisively beaten, and surrendered.

The commander of the militia, Major-General Frederick Middleton, filed this report after the clash at Batoche:

> We found a large camp of women and children, natives and half-breeds, on the bank of the river below Batoche's House, and a good many camped round our bivouac for the night ... On inspecting the scene of action after

it was over, I was astonished at the strength of the position and at the ingenuity and care displayed in the construction of the rifle-pits ... In and around these pits were found blankets, trousers, coats, shirts, boots ... one or two shot-guns and one good rifle. It was evident that a detachment of Rebels had lived in these pits, day and night, and it was easily understood, by an inspection of them, how perfectly safe the holders of these pits were from the fire of our rifles, and especially from the Gatling and artillery. These pits were also judiciously placed as regards repelling a front attack, but by attacking their right (which was their weakest point) and driving it in, we turned and took in reverse all their entrenchments, along the edge of the prairie ground, and thus caused a rout which ended in a "sauve qui peut". As it was getting dark, and my men were tired out, I did not attempt to pursue. We found 21 of the Rebels dead on the ground in the vicinity of the houses, and 2 dead men on the river bank ... Also five wounded, of whom 2 were belonging to Riel's Council, two of whom were also amongst the killed.[2]

The Métis had on their side knowledge of the land and skill in guerilla warfare; the militia had technology and discipline. Middleton wrote in mid-May 1885:

The Half-breeds were continually coming in with white flags to give themselves and their arms up, some by themselves and some with the priests. I have a list of the worst of the Rebels, and I dismiss those not in it, with a caution to return to their houses, and a warning that if hereafter any charge is brought against them they are liable to be arrested. I have now 13 prisoners, two of them being members of Riel's Council ... I sent out parties of mounted men, under Major Boulton, to scour the woods. In the afternoon two scouts, Armstrong and Hourie, who had been sent out with Boulton and had moved away by themselves, came upon Riel who gave himself up, producing my letter to him in which I summoned him to surrender and promised to protect him until his case was considered by the Canadian government. The scouts brought him into my camp, and I made a prisoner of him.[3]

After his capture, Riel was brought to Regina to be tried for treason. His trial was the most famous, the most significant, and the most controversial in the history of Canada's courts, for the whole Dominion considered itself his jury.

Perhaps the simplest explanation of the Riel Rebellions can be found in the "frontier vs. civilization" thesis of George F.G. Stanley.[4] According to Stanley, the Métis and Native people were primitives who resented and fought the encroachments of the civilized white settlers. There were observers at the time who would have agreed with him. For example, Bishop Grandin wrote in 1887: *"Ils [the Métis] n'étaient pas assez préparés à cette civilisation qui tout à coup est venue fondre sur eux … Je pourrais dire que c'est là toute l'explication de la guerre civile."*[5] (They were not sufficiently prepared for this civilization that suddenly descended upon them … I could say that this was the entire explanation for the civil war.) But today we must ask, Was this all? Was it just a matter of a revolt of Aboriginal peoples, of resistance to white advance, so common on the North American frontier?

The Riel Rebellions could be given political significance. The government of Canada had attempted to extend its control into the West. There it had encountered an independent people who already possessed their own government and the organization of the buffalo hunt, and who, under Riel, had transformed this into an actual civil government in Manitoba. Riel's provisional government had a president, a secretary, a council, and a general assembly, and its authority was generally recognized. Its flag flew over the headquarters in Fort Garry. Its leaders negotiated intelligently with both Canadian authorities and American annexationists. The Métis were no "mere savages" but a nation in their own right, who bid for recognition and independence.

An economic interpretation might also fit the facts. The Métis were in part an agricultural people, practising subsistence farming and living on the edge of famine. They believed that their lands were threatened by the crews of surveyors sent out by the government of Canada. They believed that the buffalo hunt was threatened by the advance of Ontario settlers. The Rebellions were, then, a struggle between the wealthy society of old Canada, based on trade, manufacturing, and specialized mechanized agriculture (the haves) and the poor society of new Canada (the have-nots).

Finally, considering the geographical and regional factors, the Rebellions might be viewed as the first protest of the West against control by central Canada. It was the West's first stand for its own destinies and interests as distinct from those of the East, of the metropolitan centres of Montreal and Toronto, the funnels that were sucking in the wealth of the Prairies. The Métis were the first, but by no means the last, to protest that Ottawa ignored the interests of western Canada. W.L. Morton, historian of western protest movements, traced the radical Progressive movement on the Prairies in the 1920s back to the days of Riel. He maintained, in *The Progressive Party in Canada*, that the Métis were the first champions of the West against the East, and that this was their significance in history.

There is disagreement among historians as to who should accept responsibility for the conflict. Was Ottawa the culprit—or were the Métis? Probably each was to blame, but English-speaking Canada more often defended the Macdonald government, while French-speaking Canada defended the Métis. The battles fought in the West have been refought in the archives many times. On the one hand, it can be said that the Métis were impatient, quick to anger, and unduly suspicious of outsiders. They were a people on the defensive, unable and unwilling to change with the times. They preferred the glory and glamour of the buffalo hunt to the slow, steady routine of agriculture. They were eager to ride off on horseback, but slow to accept the discipline of organized society. They chose rebellion, the quick, simple solution of armed conflict, not negotiation— the long, patient, talking out of problems.

On the other hand, the government acted too slowly. To John A. Macdonald, events in the primitive West were of secondary importance. He was Minister of the Interior, but first he was Prime Minister. He had little time and less inclination to answer petitions from the territories, even from the white inhabitants. And "Old Tomorrow," as he was called, procrastinated, hoping that in time, the problem would go away. When the outbreak of violence in the West forced his immediate attention, Macdonald displayed contempt for the Métis. They were "half-castes," he said. "If you wait for a half-breed or an Indian to be contented, you may wait for the millenium!" Ottawa acted, then—slowly, ineffectually, and with prejudice against the inhabitants of the Plains. Whatever interpretation is given to the events of 1870 and 1885, the result is clear: the whole Dominion was involved. Because Louis Riel's blood was mostly French, in old Canada his cause set French against English and Quebec against Ontario. The first phase of the crisis, in 1870, was solved according to the French view of Confederation, and the second, in 1885, according to the English view. The second crisis, more than the first, created almost unbearable national tension.

In 1870, the Red River colony was admitted into Confederation by the *Manitoba Act*. This piece of legislation was George Etienne Cartier's pride, for it embodied his dream of a new Quebec in the West. Shortly after its passage, Louis Riel was elected a member of Parliament from the new province. He did not go to Ottawa, however, fearing that his activities as head of the now disbanded provisional government would ensure his arrest.

The *Manitoba Act* was a bicultural solution arrived at after long negotiations between the delegates from Red River and the ministers in Ottawa. It embodied the chief provisions of the bill of rights put forward by the Métis themselves: self-government for the new province, security for existing land tenure, French language and separate school guarantees, and official bilingualism. There was to be a French-English partnership in Manitoba. In numbers, the province was half-English and half-French, and the *Manitoba Act* assumed that it would continue thus.

By 1885, however, English-speaking Manitobans had outnumbered French, and the Métis had taken refuge on the banks of the distant Saskatchewan. The long shadow of an English-speaking West linked to the English majority in old Canada hung over the trial of Louis Riel, now charged with treason for his role in both rebellions. He became a symbol of the nation's turmoil: to the French a martyr, to the English a justly prosecuted rebel. Not only his fate, but the fate of the nation, was in the balance when the court opened in Regina on July 20, 1885.

The makeup of the court was highly political and ethnic. The presiding officer was an English-Canadian magistrate and his assistant a French-Canadian justice of the peace. From a panel of thirty-six jurors, a six-man jury of English settlers and merchants was chosen. The prosecution were Conservatives, B.B. Osler of Toronto and T.C. Casgrain of Quebec; the defence were Liberals, F.X. Lemieux, Charles Fitzpatrick, and J.N. Greenshields. The Crown's charge was treason. They argued that Riel was a British subject, a resident of Canada, and a sane man who had led a revolt against the government. The defence pleaded that Riel was insane and hence incapable of treason. Unfortunately for the defence, the medical evidence was contradictory. Dr. Wallace of Hamilton said that Riel was capable of distinguishing between right and wrong, but was "of unsound mind"; Dr. Jukes pronounced him sane; others testified that he had insane moments. The difficulties of the defence were compounded by Riel's speech to the court at the end of the trial, in which he denied the plea of insanity, the only way of saving his life. His speech was eloquent and moving, but not entirely rational.

A study of Riel's trial leads to only one sure conclusion: his fate was decided elsewhere. True, the jury in Regina found him guilty and recommended mercy. The magistrate sentenced him to hang, and the government delayed the sentence through three stays of execution. But the issue was decided in the last event by public opinion, which exerted pressure on jurors, magistrate, and government. Because the pressure was stronger from English Canada, Louis Riel had to hang. And French Canada had to accept it. If there had been a way out, John A. Macdonald, the consummate politician, would have found it. As it was, Macdonald decided that Riel "shall hang, though every dog in Quebec bark in his favour."

Contemporary comments reveal the depth of feeling involved. The editors of the Toronto News declared on May 18, 1885, before the trial had begun, that Riel should be strangled with the French flag, "the only service which that rag can render in this country." General Strange, an officer who had led the militia against Riel, wrote:

> How sad and silly it all seems—after sending those brave battalions to the front—to start in with this childish twaddle about hanging a cur of a self-interested conspirator who has twice brought this country to rebellion and at least let loose savage Indians to murder White Men and even Priests. The idea that because a criminal is half-French it is to stop the sword of justice is outrageous. I would rather join a war of extermination between French and English than to submit to live in a Country where such monstrously insolent pretensions were put forward by a part of the population.[6]

The French case was stated with equal passion as a *nationaliste* movement arose to champion the dead Riel and to defend his people against any further outrages. *La Presse* of Montreal declared, "There are no more Conservatives nor Liberals nor Castors. There are only PATRIOTS AND TRAITORS." In November 1885, Honoré Mercier, the new Parti National leader, addressed a mass meeting in the Champs de Mars:

> Riel, our brother, is dead, victim of his devotion to the cause of the Métis of whom he was the leader, victim of fanaticism and treason—of the fanaticism of Sir John and some of his friends, of the treason of three of our people [the three French-Canadian cabinet ministers in Ottawa] who sold their brother to keep their portfolios. In killing Riel, Sir John has not only struck a blow at the heart of our race, but above all he struck the cause of justice and humanity, which represented in all languages and sanctified by all religious beliefs, begged mercy for the prisoner of Regina, our poor brother of the North-West.[7]

By January 1887, Mercier had led his party to a sweeping victory at the polls in Quebec. Old political allegiances in the province were shaken as French Canadians united in one party to oppose the united English.

A century later, Riel had become a hero of the West, its defender against the wicked East. His life was treated sympathetically, even by English biographers, and his death was viewed as a tragedy.[8] His statue could be seen on the grounds of the Manitoba Legislature, a tribute to his role as the province's founding father. In 1979, his life and cause were portrayed on nationwide television.[9] He became something of a national hero, as well as an ethnic and regional one, a champion of the underdog.

But in 1885, his death brought about division, the two peoples united against each other in the worst crisis Canada had yet faced. The partnership of 1867 and 1870 was strained to the breaking point. But out of the depths of national despair, out of the fragmentation, came new hope. The three French-Canadian Cabinet ministers did not resign their portfolios. Their presence meant that the Conservative Party was still bicultural. Wilfrid Laurier, a rising young Liberal politician, also remained within his party. Each major party could still claim to represent both peoples. Laurier spoke to the whole nation, reminding them of the spirit of Confederation:

> ... Our country is Canada, it is the whole of what is covered by the British flag on the American continent ... What I claim for us [French Canadians] is an equal share of the sun, of justice, of liberty; we have that share, and have it amply; and what we claim for ourselves we are anxious to grant to others. I do not want French Canadians to domineer over anyone, nor anyone

to domineer over them. Equal justice; equal rights ... Cannot we believe that in the supreme battle on the Plains of Abraham, when the fate of arms turned against us, cannot we believe that it entered into the designs of Providence that the two races, enemies up to that time, should henceforth live in peace and harmony? Such was the inspiring cause of Confederation.[10]

Eleven years later, he became the first French-Canadian Prime Minister, the clearest possible proof that the nation was willing to try again.

To some, Louis Riel was close to a saint; to others, he was the devil incarnate. For the clash of views on the enigma of the Métis leader, see Chapter 16, Assessments of Louis Riel.

NOTES

1   Edward McCourt, *Revolt in the West* (Toronto, 1958), 22–24.

2   Department of Militia and Defence of the Dominion of Canada, *Report upon the Suppression of the Rebellion in the Northwest Territories, and Matters in Connection Therewith in 1885* (Ottawa, 1886); Report to the Minister of Militia, 32–33.

3   Ibid., 33.

4   George F.G. Stanley, *The Birth of Western Canada* (Toronto, 1960), viii.

5   Ibid., viii.

6   T.B. Strange to H.G. Joly, 10 December 1885, Archives seigneuriales de Lotbinière, Leclercville, Québec.

7   Robert Rumilly, *Histoire de la Province de Québec,* vol. 5 (Montreal, 1940–62), 123.

8   E.B. Osler, *Louis Riel: The Man Who Had to Hang* (Toronto, 1961); George F.G. Stanley, *Louis Riel* (Toronto, 1963); Hartwell Bowsfield, *Louis Riel: The Rebel and the Hero* (Toronto, 1971).

9   Janet Rosenstock and Dennis Adair, *Riel* (novelization based on the CBC screenplay by Roy Moore) (Markham, 1979).

10 U. Barthe, *Wilfrid Laurier on the Platform* (Quebec, 1890), 527–28.

6 ⚜ THE IMPERIALIST CRISIS, 1896–1914

The years between 1896 and 1911 in Canada's history belong to Wilfrid Laurier. They were the years in which he proved that a French Canadian could succeed as Prime Minister. Laurier had qualities of greatness—nobility of spirit and strength of will, gentility and toughness. His official biographer, Oscar D. Skelton, stressed the noble side of his character, describing him as "the finest and simplest gentleman, the noblest and most unselfish man it has ever been my good fortune to know." John W. Dafoe, editor of the Winnipeg *Free Press*, a friend of Laurier, but also a critic, gave a more balanced judgement. "The final appraisement … will perhaps put Sir Wilfrid higher than Professor Skelton does and yet not quite so high; an abler man but one not quite so preternaturally good," Dafoe wrote, "a man who had affinities with Machiavelli as well as with Sir Galahad."[1]

It was the Rebellion of 1885 that gave Laurier his chance. Before the Rebellion, he was respected in Parliament and admired for his eloquence; he was appreciated in the inner circles of the Liberal Party for the assistance he gave to the party leader, Edward Blake; but beyond that, he was unknown. Then the execution of Louis Riel changed the course of Canadian politics, undermined the Quebec base of Conservative strength that was Cartier's legacy to his friend Macdonald, and paved the way for the Liberal Party in Quebec and for Laurier in the Liberal Party. These events were not immediately foreseen in 1885, but Laurier's speech in the Commons on the hanging of Riel, not Macdonald's or Blake's, attracted the attention of the nation. It came to be believed that only he, a French Canadian of national stature, could bring the two peoples back together.

Laurier became Leader of the Liberal Party in June 1887, a position he held until his death in February 1919. By selecting a French Canadian, the Liberal Party proved its faith in Confederation, and in a sense, overcame the bitterness of the Riel Rebellions. Despite doubts and hesitations, he was chosen leader of a party which at that time found most of its support in English and Protestant Ontario, among the descendants of the Clear Grits. Dafoe has described the Ontario prejudice and how Laurier's charm and his "good French mind" dispelled it:

> … Still under the influence of the George Brown tradition of suspicion of Quebec, they felt uneasy at the transfer of the sceptre to Laurier, French by inheritance, Catholic in religion, with a political experience derived from dealing with the feelings, ambitions, and prejudices of a province which was to them an unknown world … The Ontario mind was under the sway of that singular misconception, so common to Britishers, that a Frenchman by temperament is gay, romantic, inconsequent, with few reserves of will and

perseverance. Whereas the good French mind is about the coolest, clearest, least emotional instrument of the kind that there is. The courtesy, grace, charm, literary and artistic ability that go with it are merely accessories ... But, whatever the uncertainties of the moment, they soon passed. Laurier at once showed capacities which the Liberals had never before known in a leader ... The party sensed almost immediately the difference in the quality of the new leadership; and liked it. Laurier's powers of personal charm completed the "consolidation of his position", and by the early nineties the Presbyterian Grits of Ontario were swearing by him.[2]

He was to the Liberals what John Diefenbaker was to the Tories in 1957: a saviour to lead them out of the wilderness of Opposition.

Careful planning lay behind Laurier's campaign in the election of 1896. "Elections," said Israel Tarte, chief Liberal organizer, "are not won by prayers." In English Canada, the issue was the Manitoba Schools Question; in French Canada, it was Laurier himself.

The Manitoba Schools Question marked a further chapter in Canada's westward expansion, and like the Riel Rebellions, provided grounds for more conflict between English and French. Since its beginnings in 1870, the province of Manitoba had, through Ontario immigration, become increasingly Protestant and Anglo-Saxon. Agitation arose over demands for repeal of clauses in the *Manitoba Act* sanctioning a dual school system and for the institution of a common public school to suit the English Protestant majority. The government of Manitoba, under the premiership of Thomas Greenway, passed a series of laws designed to accomplish just that. The French minority in the provinces appealed to the federal government to disallow the Greenway laws and to protect the Roman Catholic schools from extinction. After much hesitation, the Conservatives decided to come to their aid and pass the necessary federal "remedial" legislation. Going into the campaign of 1896, they hoped that Quebec would support them on these grounds, under strong pressure from the bishops, and that English Canada, remembering the hanging of Riel, would still produce enough seats to form a majority. The calculation looked good, even though Macdonald was no longer at the helm of the party.

The Liberals, taking a tremendous gamble, decided to oppose remedial legislation. They would support the public school system in Manitoba, thereby pleasing English and Protestant Canadians everywhere, and negotiate as Laurier said, "by sunny ways," for the rights of the minority. But would not French Canadians be antagonized by such a course? "Make the party policy suit the campaign in the other provinces," said Tarte. "Leave Quebec to Laurier and me." They gambled that the loyalty of the French to Laurier would be strong enough to overcome the bitter pill of the Manitoba schools. And they were right. Laurier swept French Canada and changed the face of Canadian politics.

It was the Quebec base, captured by Laurier from the Conservatives, that carried him through the next decade and a half. Cartier's belief that no stable government could be formed in Canada without the support of the French bloc was proved correct. The Quebec Conservatives, the Bleus, deserted their party and voted for Laurier; their old allegiance weakened before the prospect of a French-Canadian Prime Minister in Ottawa. In 1900, Quebec again went nearly solidly Liberal. In 1904, at the height of his power, Laurier once more swept Quebec, and he carried English Canada with a majority double that of 1896. In 1908, he achieved a fourth victory, though there was a decline in his popular vote in Quebec, and outside the province, his majority was only four. In 1911, a combination of circumstances united his enemies, the Nationalists in Quebec and the Conservatives in English Canada, against him, but that is another story. As the score is reckoned in the changeable political world, Laurier was successful, and his success demonstrated the spirit of compromise at the base of Confederation.

The great issue of Laurier's day was imperialism, and it, like westward expansion, was fraught with peril for Canada. What was to be Canada's place in the British Empire? An answer was forced on the nation by the rise of the imperialist movement in England and in English Canada. As Prime Minister, it was Laurier who had to find a solution that would be acceptable to both English and French Canada. He walked a tightrope. "In the end," Dafoe wrote, "Sir Wilfrid fell; but his Imperial policies lived … For his services in holding their future open for them, every British Dominion owes the memory of Laurier a statue in its parliament square."[3]

Imperialism triumphed in Great Britain in the later days of Queen Victoria. A tremendous feeling of pride in the Anglo-Saxon race and its imperial achievements went to British heads as they contemplated in panelled drawing rooms the map of the world with the Empire marked in red. Alfred, Lord Tennyson wrote:

> Sons be welded each and all
> Into one Imperial whole,
> One with Britain heart and soul!
> One life, one flag, one fleet, one throne! Britons, hold your own.[4]

In his book *The Expansion of England,* John Robert Seeley declared, "The history of England is not in England but in America and Asia." England, in his view, was no longer just an island off the coast of Europe, but "a great homogeneous people, one in blood, language, religion and laws, dispersed over a boundless space."[5] It was as if, having possessed an empire for centuries already, the British had just noticed its existence. And having noticed it, they almost regretted having granted it so much freedom. Benjamin Disraeli, Britain's Prime Minister, felt that self-government should have been:

... accompanied by an Imperial tariff ... by a military code which should have precisely defined the means and responsibilities by which the colonies should be defended, and by which, if necessary, this country should call for aid from the colonies themselves ... by the institution of some representative council in the metropolis.[6]

This heady atmosphere pervaded the Imperial Conferences that Laurier attended as Canada's representative. Laurier related to O.D. Skelton what it was like to be in London:

One felt the incessant and unrelenting organization of an imperialist campaign. We were looked upon, not so much as individual men, but abstractly as colonial statesmen, to be impressed and hobbled. The Englishman is as businesslike in his politics ... as in business, even if he covers his purposefulness with an air of polite indifference. Once convinced that the colonies were worth keeping, he bent to the work of drawing them closer within the orbit of London with marvellous skill and persistence. In this campaign, which no one could appreciate until he had been in the thick of it, social pressure is the subtlest and most effective force ... It is hard to stand up against the flattery of a gracious duchess. Weak men's heads are turned in an evening, and there are few who can resist long. We were dined and wined by royalty and aristocracy and plutocracy and always the talk was of empire, empire, empire.7

What exactly did the British imperialists want from Canada and from Laurier? The first revelation came with the outbreak of the Boer War in 1899. In July, Joseph Chamberlain wrote from the Colonial Office asking for a Canadian contribution as "proof of the unity of the Empire." A spirit of approval sprang up in the English-speaking provinces, particularly in Ontario. From Lord Minto, Governor General, and from General Hutton, British commander of the Canadian forces, the pressure for a contribution mounted. Only Quebec remained unmoved, opposing any contribution to the Anglo-Saxon cause in faraway Johannesburg. Henri Bourassa, Laurier's young French lieutenant, a grandson of Papineau, electrified the country and the Commons with a passionate denunciation of the imperialist "game":

British Imperialism ... is a lust for land-grabbing and military dominion. Born of the overgrowth of British power, bred by that stupid and blatant sense of pride known as *Jingoism*, it delights in high-sounding formulas:
— *"Britannia, rule the waves!"* ... *"Britons never shall be slaves!"* ...

having undertaken more responsibilities than she is able to stand ... the new Britain of Mr. Chamberlain is in sore need of soldiers and sailors to prop the fabric raised by her frantic ambition ... she turns in distress to her colonies ... Under miscellaneous names and variegated uniforms—Royal Rifles, Mounted Infantry, Strathcona Horse ... they extort from us whatever they may get in the shape of human material for their army; even if they have to dangle before our eyes a few paltry advantages to be thrown as a sop to us whenever we get tired of this deadly game. In short, MILITARY CONTRIBUTIONS FROM THE COLONIES TO GREAT BRITAIN, in men and treasure, but mainly in men, constitute British Imperialism.[8]

In English Canada, he declared, "both parties run for the prize of 'loyalty'—each side claiming the credit of having done the most for Great Britain."[9]

English Canada said "yes" to the imperialist request, and French Canada said "no." Between them, Laurier tried to hold the balance and sought the narrow ground of compromise. He refused to send an official contingent, but passed an order-in-council authorizing the equipping and transporting of 1,000 volunteers. In the end, Canada sent some 7,300 men to South Africa and spent some $2,800,000 in their support. Laurier's compromise pleased English and French moderates and drove the extreme imperialists and the extreme nationalists into opposition together. Canada came through the first crisis raised by her relationship with Great Britain. This would be more difficult in 1917 and 1944.

Laurier's triumph in achieving the Boer War compromise was solid and enduring, and it pointed the way for the future. But compromise, moderation, and reason eventually yielded to extremism, emotionalism, and intransigence when after nine years, he was swept from office by a combination of imperialists and nationalists. For nine years, he controlled the tension at the heart of the nation and prevented it from getting out of hand. He not only governed Canada well, but saw with clear vision the final solution to the problem of the imperial relationship. "We are under the suzerainty of the King of England. We are his loyal subjects," Laurier said in Toronto, "but the King of England has no more rights over us than are allowed him by our own Canadian Parliament. If this is not a nation, what then is a nation?"[10]

Laurier sought the broad, middle way to self-respecting nationhood: the tie with Britain had to be maintained to please English Canada, and independence of decision had to be gained to satisfy French Canada. He looked forward to an Empire in which Canada's status would be equal to that of Britain—an Empire bound by loyalty to the common Crown, but with each part fully self-governing in its own Parliament. Still, it would be many years before Laurier's dream would come true.

But in 1909, time was running out for him. Henri Bourassa broke with Laurier over the Boer War compromise. He became the leader of a nationalist movement in Quebec that was directed against imperialism and against Laurier, who, in its view, was "too soft" on the issue. He became the hero of the younger generation in Quebec, voicing their secret hopes and aspirations. Between Laurier and Bourassa, it was partly a clash of personalities and partly one of issues. Laurier said of Bourassa, "He has one capital defect, he does not know how to keep within bounds." Bourassa, he felt, became intoxicated with his own words. Laurier's reason contrasted with Bourassa's emotion; his compromises with Bourassa's intransigencies. Laurier's politics were tepid; Bourassa's were piping hot.

In 1903, La Ligue Nationaliste was formed by the young and enthusiastic backers of Bourassa. It placed itself on record for autonomy—political and economic—within the framework of the Empire. Speaking in the Théâtre National in Montreal, Bourassa said that he desired no break with England, but if there had to be a choice between such a break and the servile dependence demanded by imperialism, he favoured separation. The French, he said, were bound by the Confederation pact to defend only Canada's frontiers, not those of Britain's far-flung Empire. He accused Laurier of selling out his own people and of promising Britain that they would be sent anywhere at any time. Some English Canadians, he told the crowd, are more loyal to Britain than to Canada. Canada should be the first loyalty of all its citizens, French and English alike. By 1909, drawing crowds as large as those listening to Laurier in Quebec, he urged the formation of a third party—neither Rouge nor Bleu—to unite English and French in an independent Canada. Fanned by Bourassa's white-hot words, this movement grew rapidly and undermined Laurier's base of power in Quebec.

Clifford Sifton, Minister of the Interior, broke with Laurier over the Autonomy Bills in 1905. Laurier's chief lieutenant in English Canada, an ardent public school supporter from Manitoba, Sifton refused to sanction the guarantee of separate school rights in the new provinces of Saskatchewan and Alberta, which were fast filling up with settlers. Sifton said that the West was to be peopled by many nationalities and educated into a single Canadianism through the public school, not fragmented by separate schools. It was to be one nation with one language, not a multiplicity of tongues. The Toronto *News* was quick to accuse Quebec of threatening English Canada:

> It is an intolerable situation for English Canadians to live under French domination ... It is infinitely deplorable that the government remains in power by the massive vote of a section of the Canadian people speaking a foreign language and maintaining an ideal foreign to the dominant race in this country.[11]

The breaks with Bourassa and Sifton were signs of increasing tension between English and French Canadians and the narrowing of the tightrope Laurier had walked since the Boer War. The final crisis came in 1908 and 1909 when Britain asked for contributions of dreadnoughts to the British navy. This request opened old wounds, not entirely healed since the Boer War. Should Canada contribute? How should she contribute—in ships or men or money? Should she add to the British navy or develop her own? Every aspect of the problem held implications for French-English relations and was therefore fraught with peril.

Laurier offered a compromise in the form of the Naval Service Bill of 1909. Canada was to have her own navy under the control of the Canadian government; in time of war, it could be placed under imperial control with the consent of Parliament. Service in the navy would be voluntary, unlike the militia, and plans were outlined to build five cruisers and six destroyers. Bourassa denounced the bill in *Le Devoir* as a capitulation to imperialism:

> Let the notion occur to a Chamberlain, a Rhodes, a Beers ... of causing a conflict in South Africa or India ... or on the banks of the Black Sea ... We are involved, always and regardless, with our money and our blood ... It is the most complete backward step Canada has made in half a century. It is the gravest blow our autonomy has suffered since the origin of responsible government.[12]

If it passed, he declared, Canadians could be sent anywhere at any time to fight imperialist wars.

Robert Borden, the Leader of the Conservative Opposition, bitterly complained that the bill was too slow in coming, too inadequate, and too niggardly. It set up a "tin-pot" navy, he declared, when an immediate emergency contribution of dreadnoughts from Canada to the British navy was urgently needed. Between the Nationalists and the Conservatives an alliance of convenience was formed. They shared nothing beyond contempt for Laurier, both having longed for many years to see his defeat. In the election of 1911, they struck with their combined forces. Sir Hugh Graham, arch-imperialist in Montreal and publisher of the Montreal Star, took out subscriptions to Bourassa's *Le Devoir*. Politics, as cynics note, can make strange bedfellows.

The Naval Bill was not the sole reason for Laurier's defeat in 1911. It was but one factor among many that put him on the defensive. In St. John's, Newfoundland, Laurier spoke to the crowd, no longer joyfully and eloquently, but with a certain pathos and the tiredness that came from struggling to compromise in a nation that had turned against compromise.

I am branded in Quebec as a traitor to the French, and in Ontario as a traitor to the English. In Quebec I am branded as a Jingo, and in Ontario as a Separatist. In Quebec I am attacked as an Imperialist, and in Ontario as an anti-Imperialist. I am neither. I am a Canadian. Canada has been the inspiration of my life. I have had before me as a pillar of fire by night and a pillar of cloud by day a policy of true Canadianism, of moderation, of conciliation.[13]

In 1911 the Laurier government was old and tired. The country wanted a change. J.W. Dafoe wrote with remarkable perception:

... The Laurier administration ... came in with the good wishes of the people and for nearly ten years went on from strength to strength ... then its strength began to wane and its vigour to relax. Its last few years were given up to a struggle against the inevitable fate that was visibly rising like a tide ... The Laurier government died in 1911, not so much from the assaults of its enemies as from hardening of the arteries and from old age. Its hour had struck in keeping with the law of political change.[14]

Laurier, said Dafoe, accepted the blow of 1911 "with the tranquil fortitude which was his most notable characteristic."

It was quite a blow. The majority in the Commons was exactly reversed, the Conservatives holding now 133 seats to the Liberals' 88. The Conservatives' victory was so sweeping that they could hold office without their Nationalist allies, who were 11 seats short of Laurier in Quebec. The new government was to be based, not like Laurier's on Quebec with English-Canadian support, but on English Canada with some French-Canadian support. It was Robert Borden's government, strong in English Canada, that voted an emergency contribution to the British navy in 1912 and led the nation into war in 1914.

What Borden, Bourassa, and Laurier thought and said about the thorny problem of the Canadian navy can be found in Chapter 17, The Challenge of the Middle Way.

NOTES

1 John W. Dafoe, *Laurier: A Study in Canadian Politics* (Toronto, 1963), 24.

2 Ibid., 31–32.

3 Ibid., 61–62.

4 From poem written for the opening of the Indian and Colonial Exhibition by the Queen [Victoria], 1886.

5 J.R. Seeley, *The Expansion of England* (London, 1883), 171.

6 C.A. Bodelsen, *Studies in Mid-Victorian Imperialism* (New York, 1925), 121.

7 Dafoe, Laurier, 46–47.

8 Henri Bourassa, Great Britain and Canada (Montreal, 1902), 4–5.

9 Ibid.

10 Dafoe, *Laurier,* 54.

11 *News* (Toronto), 8 November 1899.

12 *Le Devoir,* 7 January 1909.

13 O.D. Skelton, *Life and Letters of Sir Wilfrid Laurier,* vol. 2 (Toronto, 1965), 142.

14 Dafoe, *Laurier,* 44.

7 ❧ THE CONSCRIPTION CRISIS, 1917, 1942–1944

The nationalist-imperialist clash of Laurier's day was but a prologue to the Crisis of Conscription. This issue was raised not in one world war but in two. The question of the survival of the nation was never put in more immediately compelling terms than in the crises of 1917 and 1942–44. For French-English relations, Canada's participation in the world wars was the cardinal issue in the first half of the twentieth century.

Britain's declaration of war on Germany produced a spirit of national unity and even enthusiasm as Parliament met in a special war session on August 18, 1914. Prime Minister Borden spoke of the necessity of sacrifice "not for love of battle, nor for lust of conquest … but for the cause of honour … to uphold principles of liberty." And Laurier, now Leader of the Opposition, assured the government of his support:

> We are British subjects, and today we are face to face with the consequences which are involved in that proud fact. Long have we enjoyed the benefit of our British citizenship; today it is our duty to accept its responsibilities and its sacrifices. We have long said that when Great Britain is at war, we are at war; today we realize that Great Britain is at war and that Canada is at war also[1] … I have declared more than once that if England were in danger … it would be the duty of Canada to come to her aid in the full measure of her resources.[2]

But it proved easier to utter fine sentiments in 1914 than to sustain the long haul required by two, three, and an unthinkable four years of war. By 1916 and 1917, the first legions Canada had sent abroad were decimated by casualties, and volunteers needed to replace them were becoming increasingly scarce. In January 1916, 30,000 men signed up; by April 1917, 5,000; and by August, only 3,000—not enough to maintain the forces in the field, let alone increase them. The voluntary system broke down. It became in fact a kind of "conscription by cajolery" as recruits were pressured to "volunteer" for overseas service. And still it was not enough. By 1917, it was taking four months' enlistments to make up for one month's losses at the front.

The problem of total numbers masked a graver one hidden in the enlistment statistics: the disparity in numbers between English and French recruits. The British-born in Canada were the strongest supporters of the war; the English Canadians came next; and the French Canadians lagged behind. After March 1918, no further official figures were released, and through the whole course of the Second World War, none could be obtained. The truth was that French Canadians did not consider the war their concern. They were not given a chance. The blunders of Sam Hughes' Department of Defence, such as the use of English as the sole language of command, the practice of allowing overwhelming numbers of English Canadians in the officer corps, and the breakup of the original French-Canadian regiments, look ludicrous in retrospect. But even if these blunders had not been committed, it is doubtful whether the average French Canadian would have identified himself with Britain's cause at Vimy Ridge and Passchendaele. Never in any sense a military people, French Canadians were little inclined to fight in a foreign land for a foreign cause.

Henri Bourassa was the natural spokesperson for French-Canadian doubts. He questioned the theory, so passionately held in English Canada, that the Kaiser was solely responsible for the war. It was a reasonable question, but hardly the right one to ask in the fiercely loyal atmosphere of 1914. Canada, Bourassa continued, should not pledge all-out aid, but just that which accorded with her resources. He was, of course, totally opposed to conscription, and as early as October 1914, he denounced misguided generosity:

> Instead of spending one hundred to one hundred and fifty million to enlist and maintain for months, perhaps years, a great number of men badly clad, badly shod, and undisciplined, they could have, with a fifth of this sum, organized a suitable contingent of soldiers, well-disciplined and perfectly equipped.
>
> Instead of making a gift, at one swoop, to very wealthy England of millions of bags of flour and great piles of cheese—which rot today on the docks of Liverpool because the English do not know what to do with it while millions of Belgians starve and thousands of Canadians have scarcely enough to eat, they could have organized ... Canada's economic and agricultural production ...[3]

On occasion, Bourassa disparaged the Anglo-Saxon character. He accused the British of "obtuseness developed by insular isolation," "alcoholism," "pride and domination over weak peoples," "cupidity," and "brutalities."

English Canada came to hate the very name of Bourassa. On one occasion, when he tried to speak, his words were drowned out. An English-speaking sergeant climbed onto the platform, handed him a Union Jack, and demanded that he wave it. "I shall not do so under threats," replied Bourassa, and the audience rose, howling, to its feet. The curtain dropped, and Bourassa fled the mob. The French were no less guilty of violence. A soldier who insulted Bourassa in Montreal was beaten. In April and May of 1917, troops passing through Quebec City were pelted with rotten vegetables, ice, and stones. In June, crowds marched night after night through the streets, yelling "A bas Borden!" and "Vive la révolution!"

Against the background of violence in the streets and in the press, the national war policy had to be worked out in Parliament. Here power was held by the Borden government, formed largely, but not wholly, from the English-speaking provinces, while the Laurier Opposition drew its members chiefly from French Canada. Behind Borden, a conscientious and stolid, if unimaginative, Prime Minister, there was the extremism of Arthur Meighen, author of the Conscription Bill. Meighen judged the issue as a rational exercise; he was as insensitive to the feelings of French Canada as Bourassa was to those of English Canada. His biographer, Roger Graham, describes his manner in the great debate:

> ... Here again ... he [Meighen] shouldered the heaviest burden of debate ... In Committee he gave a masterly exhibition of parliamentary prowess, demonstrating ... that in that particular phase of the battle he had no peer. The ready, accurate answer, the crystal-clear explanation of a complicated point, the retort courteous or crushing as the moment demanded—these were ever on the tip of his tongue. His mind working with the speed of lightning, his mordant wit flashing like a sword, he took on the enemy almost single-handed as they doggedly stormed the bridgehead of conscription. They did not pierce his armour; they hardly even dented it.[4]

Meighen would sacrifice men to the abstract "honour of Canada" as he conceived it. He was as heartily despised in French Canada as Bourassa was in Ontario.

In 1916, Borden went to Europe and was much impressed by the urgency of the situation at the front. In January 1917, he asked for a National Registration of all able-bodied men. His demand was met with suspicion and hostility in Quebec and in the farming communities of Ontario and the Prairies. Once registered, would the men next be conscripted? Sir Robert said "no"; the Quebec Nationalists said "yes." And as the Recruitment Crisis grew throughout 1917, the prediction of the Nationalists came true. Borden moved after much soul-searching toward the policy of conscription, convinced that it was vital to the national war effort. Reluctant to go it alone, he approached Laurier, told him the policy had to be conscription, and asked him to join in a coalition government.

Laurier refused—probably the most consequential "no" in Canadian history. Why did he refuse? A frequent answer is pressure from Bourassa, who was thundering against him in Quebec. "To prevent the designs, by no means established, of William the Autocrat," cried Bourassa, "shall we permit Robert the Headstrong—even with the co-operation of Wilfrid the Conciliator—to play with our lives ... ?"[5] Laurier wrote to Lomer Gouin, the Liberal Premier of Quebec, "As to conscription, there can be no hesitation ... If we were to hesitate at this moment [and join the Government] we would hand the province over to the extremists." Concerning conscription, Laurier declared, "All my life I have fought coercion." It was the harshest choice of Laurier's long career—his own people or the Liberal Party's unity. He chose his people, and Dafoe, one of many English-speaking Liberals who joined the Union Government in its patriotic crusade of 1917, wrote bitterly:

> ... Laurier ... feared Bourassa with a fear which in the end became an obsession ... Laurier feared him because if Bourassa increased his hold upon the people ... he would be displaced from his proud position as the first and greatest of French Canadians. Far more than a temporary term of power was at stake. It was a struggle for a niche in the temple of fame. It was a battle not only for the affection of the living generation, but for a place in the historic memories of the race ... as the unquestioned, unchallenged leader of his own people.[6]

Laurier had sacrificed Canada to Quebec. The Toronto *Daily News* printed the map of Canada with Quebec outlined in black. –"The Foul Blot on Canada," the caption read.

Without Laurier, the Conscription Bill passed the Commons, 102–44. The western Liberals supported the Conservatives, and a coalition Cabinet was formed. The Union Government, as it was called, went to the people on the issue of conscription. It fortified itself with the *Wartime Elections Act*, which permitted the men overseas to vote; enfranchised the mothers, wives, and sisters of enlisted men; and disenfranchised conscientious objectors and enemy aliens naturalized since 1902. The results were predictable. The Unionists carried English Canada with an overall majority of 71. In Quebec, they won only three seats, all in predominantly English areas of Montreal. The Laurier Liberals swept Quebec but carried only ten seats west of the Ontario-Quebec border. The split between French and English was almost complete. Majority rule triumphed over the clear objection of the minority. Could such a nation endure any longer? In the depths of despair, the Francoeur motion was introduced in the Quebec Legislature. Quebec, the resolution said, "would be disposed to accept the breaking of the Confederation Pact of 1867 if, in the other provinces, it is believed that she is an obstacle to the union, progress, and development of Canada."[7] It was put forward and it was voted down.

Historians disagreed on interpretations of the dramatic events of 1917. The Whig School endorsed Laurier's stand. Conscription, they maintained, was a catastrophe brought on by the Borden government. It was neither necessary nor successful; it could not be enforced; it provoked bloody riots such as those on Easter Sunday in Quebec City, where the cavalry drove back the crowd with axe-handle bludgeons. It filled the woods with deserters and defaulters. And it created a rift between English and French Canada that lasted for a generation. Not so, argued Tory historians. Conscription in their view was necessary to reinforce the army at the front and to sustain the great offensive of 1918. It succeeded in producing the 50,000 men needed and it upheld

Canada's place among the nations of the world. It was not politically expedient. It represented the ruin of the Conservative Party in Quebec. But had the will of the majority been ignored, there would have been a greater threat to national unity. No nation can long survive if the minority dictates its course; the majority has to rule.[8]

The Conscription Crisis reappeared in 1942 and 1944. The plot was the same, the stage was the same, but the actors were different. The nation had learned a little since its ordeal by fire in 1917. This time there was a consummate politician at the helm, a man renowned for flexibility and compromise. Mackenzie King had replaced Borden, but unlike Borden, he had a French-Canadian lieutenant, Louis St. Laurent. George Drew, an imperialist, was in power in Ontario, and Maurice Duplessis, a nationalist, was in power in Quebec—the political descendants of Meighen and Bourassa. But only the first round in the Conscription Crisis, that of 1917, fought out in the press, in Parliament, and in the streets, went to the extremists. The second round, in 1942 and 1944, saw the triumph of the moderates in the tradition of Baldwin-LaFontaine and Macdonald-Cartier. The fabric of Confederation torn in 1917 was mended in 1944.

One suspects that Borden enjoyed the glory won by Canadians on the battlefields of Europe despite its cost to national unity. On the other hand, King hated war. For him, there was no glory in it—only unrelieved tragedy. He sought to avoid its reality as long as possible and to defer the inevitable. In the 1930s, he refused, like Laurier before him, to commit Canada to armed preparations within the Empire, and as late as 1937, he described Hitler as "a simple sort of peasant." When war came in 1939, he did not endorse it in ringing phrases as Borden had done, but specifically rejected any "spectacular, headlong policy."[9] Canada's contribution, King said after the logic of Bourassa, must be based on her geographical location, the ethnic composition of her people, her economic development, and her "internal preoccupations and necessities." Not a word about the glories of British civilization. King saw the war as a dangerous political process for Canada, but flattered himself that he alone could bring her through.

The war debate in 1939 revealed the Prime Minister in the centre of moderate opinion, favouring a contribution in line with the nation's resources. It showed also where opposition would originate—with the nationalist extremists, who demanded neutrality, and with the imperialist extremists, who urged conscription. Behind him King had the powerful alliance of Ernest Lapointe and later Louis St. Laurent and the support of the moderates. Lapointe, in an eloquent address to Parliament, pledged to English Canada Quebec's participation in the war and to French Canada the government's promise of no conscription:

> ... It is impossible, practically, for Canada to be neutral in a big war in which England is engaged ... No government could stay in office if it refused to do what the large majority of Canadians wanted it to do ... For

the sake of unity we cannot be neutral in Canada ... the whole province of Quebec—and I speak with all the responsibility and all the solemnity I can give to my words—will never agree to accept compulsory service or conscription outside Canada ... I am authorized by my colleagues in the cabinet from the province of Quebec ... to say that we will never agree to conscription and will never be members or supporters of a government that will try to enforce it.[10]

Thus the policy was set, and the nation entered the war. King was returned to power in 1940, when his party won 178 seats, the largest majority since Confederation, including a virtually solid Quebec with 58 seats. Opinion polls in the Argenteuil constituency showed the majority behind his moderate policies:

For conscription	15%
For co-operation and participation within Canada's means without conscription	65%
For no participation	20%[11]

King's slow and careful advance to conscription showed that his concern was not with Canada's honour, to be vindicated in one fell swoop, but with her national unity, to be earned through long days and months. Canada, he was wont to complain, was such a difficult country to govern.

The government waited until 1942 to ask to be released from its pledge against conscription in 1939. Did this mean conscription? King replied that it meant "conscription if necessary, but not necessarily conscription." A plebiscite was held to determine popular sentiment. Its results surprised no one: Quebec voted 72 percent "no"; the rest of Canada voted 80 percent "yes." Acting on these results, King introduced Bill 80 into the Commons, giving the government the power to introduce conscription if it deemed it necessary. The bill passed, 158–54, the Conservatives voting with the government and 45 French-Canadian Liberals voting against it. In what King's biographer, Bruce Hutchison, has called "The Crisis, Stage One," P.J.A. Cardin resigned from the Cabinet on the grounds that the promise of 1939 had been broken.

"The Crisis, Stage Two" came in 1944. Colonel Ralston, Minister of Defence, went—like Borden before him—to Europe to inspect the troops at the front. In Brussels, he heard that men wounded two, three, and four times were being sent back into the line. He returned convinced that conscription was essential to maintain the Canadian forces. Through October, the longest October in Canada's history, the Cabinet debated the Battle of the Figures. The conscriptionists argued that the 16,000 men needed immediately could not be obtained from the home service recruits without compulsion; the anticonscriptionists argued that they could be. King delayed and delayed the decision and finally called for Ralston's resignation. He replaced him with General McNaughton, highly respected in the Royal Canadian Army, hoping that the magic of his name would persuade Canadians to volunteer as recruits. On November 8, King himself went on the radio urging Canadians to sign for overseas service. November dragged on, and still the men did not come forward. Meanwhile, plans were being made for the great offensive against the Continent.

King delayed until further delay became impossible. Morale in the army was disintegrating. McNaughton could not raise enough recruits to meet the need, and King feared that the generals were about to refuse to continue to serve unless conscription was brought in. Hutchison has called this fear King's "terrible secret." It was probably just a product of his overwrought imagination, but it helped accomplish something. King turned to Louis St. Laurent, told him of the threatened *coup d'état*, and asked him to support conscription. The interview between the two men was a fateful one:

> The calm man from Quebec was incredulous. Civil government threatened by a military putsch? It was impossible. Yes, said King, but true. There could be no doubt about it. He had McNaughton's word ... There was only one possible thing to do. The Government, by yielding to the demand for conscription, could maintain its outward direction of events ... As St. Laurent listened in silence, King felt himself reeling, with his secret, on the lip of bottomless chasm and black night. Whether St. Laurent believed King, only St. Laurent knows. Whether King believed himself ... or was acting a part unbelievable and grotesque, only King knew ... We have only King's own version of this strange meeting, the version he repeated with rising passion and conviction until his death ... In the few minutes granted him, St. Laurent must have realized that if he opposed conscription further there might or might not be military disintegration, as King feared, but in either case, the Government, the party, and the nation would fly apart before the day was out ... He consented to immediate conscription. In that consent, he had saved the Government, the Party, and perhaps the nation.[12]

King, by asking, proved himself greater than Borden; St. Laurent, by consenting, proved himself greater than Laurier. The majority had its rule and the minority its rights.

To this day, historians question the effectiveness of the conscription bill, and indeed, whether Canada really did have conscription in 1944. King's P.C. 8891 authorized the conscription of 16,000 home service recruits for overseas service and gave the Minister of Defence the power to draft more if the need arose in the future. Was this conscription? Yes, of some men, for a limited time; and no, not of all eligible men for general purposes. King's bill passed the Commons 143–70, the Conservatives and the Nationalists voting against the government for opposite reasons. The Conservatives' own bill for total conscription failed 170–44, and the Nationalists' bill for no conscription failed 168–43. Save for the extremists, English Canada and French Canada gave credit to the government for doing its best.

The argument over conscription filled volumes in Hansard. It was one of those rare issues on which every man had his opinion and none could be indifferent. See Chapter 18, The Conscription Dilemma.

NOTES

1   O.D. Skelton, *Life and Letters of Sir Wilfrid Laurier,* vol. 2 (Toronto, 1965), 161.

2   A.D. De Celles, *Discours de Sir Wilfrid Laurier,* vol. 2 (Montreal, 1920), 79–80.

3   Qtd. in Robert Rumilly, *Histoire de la Province de Québec,* vol. 19 (Montreal, 1940–62), 81.

4   Roger Graham, *Arthur Meighen,* vol. 1, *The Door of Opportunity* (Toronto, 1960), 128–29.

5   Henri Bourassa, *Conscription* (Montreal, 1917), 38.

6   John W. Dafoe, Laurier: *A Study in Canadian Politics* (Toronto, 1963), 96.

7   A. Savard and W.E. Playfair, trans., *Quebec and Confederation: A Record of the Debate of the Legislative Assembly of Quebec on the Motion Proposed by J.-N. Francoeur* (n.p., 1918).

8   See A.M. Willms, "Conscription 1917: A Brief for the Defence," *Canadian Historical Review* 37, no. 4 (December 1956): 338–51.

9   Bruce Hutchison, *The Incredible Canadian* (Toronto, 1952), 231.

10   Canada, *House of Commons Debates* (1939), 68.

11   Ibid., 82, 88.

12   Hutchison, *The Incredible Canadian,* 374–75.

8 ⚜ THE CRISIS OF THE QUIET REVOLUTION, 1960S

With the end of the Second World War, Canada was freed from the conscription problems of "Britain's wars" but not from further crises in French-English relations. In the 1960s, the stage for the seventh crisis was set not by events in far-off imperial chambers, for which the responsibility could perhaps be shifted to others, but by events at home. They were summed up as the "Quiet Revolution" or the "Not-So-Quiet Revolution," a crisis between the old order and the new in Quebec, which created, in turn, a crisis for the rest of Canada. The province experienced a tremendous awakening, a leap into the twentieth century, a drive to catch up with English Canada. This meant demands for more money, more power, and even special status within Confederation. The new Quebec was more difficult for English Canadians to live with than the old.

Maurice Duplessis, Premier of Quebec from 1936 until 1959 (with one term out of office between 1939 and 1944), symbolized the old order. His Union Nationale regime was nationalistic, pro-clerical, conservative, and as its critics pointed out, corrupt. One year, during the budget debate, the Opposition protested that ridings that had returned their members were excluded from funds for road maintenance. Duplessis rose with a smile and said, "The budget of the province is not big enough to meet all needs. We must therefore serve our friends first. If I had a loaf of bread that was too small to allow me to share it with both my friends and my enemies, I would share it exclusively with my friends."[1] He believed that he was indispensable, that his policies were in the best interests of Quebec, and that any means required to promote them were justified by the end. He explained, "I have no family. My only responsibility is to the welfare of Quebec. I belong to the province."

Duplessis and his political machine won victory after victory until the last triumph in 1956, when he secured 72 seats to the Liberals' 20. He was supported by all classes in Quebec society—rural and urban, upper and lower; he always received close to 50 percent of the French vote in the cities and well over 50 percent in the country. Only the English-speaking sections of Montreal registered any significant opposition, and this was curiously confined to voting day. On other occasions, they, and their business leaders in particular, were willing to support him.

Duplessis's death in 1959 symbolized the passing of the old order. The Union Nationale was defeated in the election of 1960, and the former Premier's name became a term of abuse. The reformers of the Quiet Revolution saw Duplessis's terms in office as a black and backward time in the history of the province. In English Canada, he was pictured as a sort of monster, half-fascist and half-scoundrel, with whom no respectable Anglo-Saxon politician ever had dealings. It was not until the Parti Québécois came to power in the late 1970s that his contribution was recognized. His statue was removed from its dusty covers and placed on public view, and a favourable series dramatizing his life appeared on television. The Péquistes admired his fight for greater independence of action for Quebec and the isolationist bent to his nationalism.

In 1960, the Liberal government of Jean Lesage was elected on a comprehensive program of reform. The reformers charged that Duplessis had sold the wealth of the province to outsiders, to English-Canadian and American capitalists. He had encouraged these "foreign" investors and even obligingly harried labour unions that had stood in their way. In 1959, Jean Drapeau, who later became famous as the mayor who attracted Expo '67and the Olympics to Montreal, complained:

> What remains to us? Agriculture, small-scale manufacturing, a small portion of banking, or retail trade and of construction. For the rest, we are more and more employees ... of large English-Canadian, English and American companies. We are tending more and more to become a proletarian people.[2]

Seeking greater economic freedom, the leaders of the Quiet Revolution touted the slogan *"Maîtres chez nous."* This phrase was popularized by René Lévesque, a television personality who became Minister of Natural Resources in the Lesage government.

The reformers moved in two directions. One was toward a takeover of foreign investment, and the other was toward encouragement of the Quebec investor. Arguing that power was the basis for industrial development, the government nationalized the private company Shawinigan Water and Power, making it part of Hydro-Québec. The second direction led to the creation of La Société Générale de Financement, a public agency dedicated to raising capital within Quebec itself. In each of these endeavours, the government intervened in the economy, seeking to control it for the benefit of French Canadians.

Closely related to the drive for more economic power was a push for educational reform. Traditionally, education had been controlled by the Roman Catholic Church. The classical curriculum prepared students for the professions, such as teaching and law, but left them ill equipped to compete in the world of Anglo-Saxon business. In 1960, Brother Pierre-Jérôme wrote a scathing critique of clerical education, which he blamed for Quebec's backwardness. In his view, the system created a race of *"joual* speakers," a phrase that played on the colloquial pronunciation of cheval:

> Of course, joual-speakers understand each other. But do you want to live your life among joual-speakers? As long as you want merely to chat about sports and the weather ... joual does very well. For primitives, a primitive language is good enough; animals get along, with a few grunts. But if you want to attain to human speech, joual is not sufficient.[3]

In 1961, the Parent Commission was established under the chairmanship of the Right Reverend Alphonse-Marie Parent, vice-rector of Laval University, to recommend reforms. It declared that the educational system of the province embodied "organized confusion," with its separation of public and private, and Roman Catholic and Protestant, schools. In 1965, the government's Bill 60 aimed at modernizing the whole system, particularly in teacher training; at introducing more scientific and technical courses into the curriculum; at removing religion from its dominant place; and at establishing greater governmental control through a Department of Education. Bill 60 created controversy, but while it was being debated, changes went quietly on. The old texts in mathematics, where children practised addition by finding the sum of "two hosts [communion bread] plus two hosts" were replaced by texts without religious references. The old histories, in which the Church and the miracles of the saints held center stage, were also replaced. A strong drive for more drastic changes arose under the auspices of the Mouvement laïque de langue française. This group demanded a neutral school system, which would eliminate all religion, Roman Catholic and Protestant. On New Year's Eve 1965, Paul-Emile Cardinal Léger, Archbishop of Montreal, declared that the Church would not oppose the establishment of some neutral schools, hitherto unknown in Quebec.

This much accomplished, the public now turned to the issue of language, another area within the province's educational system that required reform. In 1969, the Union Nationale government's Bill 63 provoked a mass outcry. It attempted to solve the language conflict in the Montreal suburb of St. Leonard's, where there were many new Italian immigrants, by guaranteeing English-language education to anyone who wanted it.

Through the Quiet Revolution, the aspirations of the new generation were at least partly expressed. In the 1960s, youth had numbers on its side throughout the Western world, but particularly in Quebec. A demographic bulge thrust the Quiet Revolution forward; those who were not satisfied with its achievements went on to become separatists. During the Depression, when elsewhere in Canada the birth rate had fallen sharply, there was no corresponding decline in Quebec. It recorded 26.8 births per thousand to English Canada's 21.0 between 1930 and 1935. It continued to lead English Canada in nine years out of every ten until the early 1960s. This meant that by the 1960s, there were more young adults in Quebec than in other provinces; Canada's oldest province historically was its youngest demographically.

This large generation was aggressive and eager for education, employment, power, and change—more so than their parents had been. They wanted a larger place in Quebec and in Canada. They also outnumbered their children. The birth rate in Quebec dropped dramatically in the early 1960s—so much so that by 1963, it had dropped below Ontario's, and by the end of the decade, Quebec had the lowest birth rate in Canada.

Before this critical decade, the old French Canada simply wanted to survive. Now the new French Canada wanted to triumph. *L'épanouissement* replaced *la survivance*.

Jean-Jacques Bertrand, a leading figure in the post-Duplessis Union Nationale, put the matter thus:

> Today, in 1963, French Canada no longer wishes merely to endure. It wants to grow, to flourish. It feels cramped within structures devised for another age. It has an uneasy sense of constraint. It dreams of proving itself in all fields and sees in Confederation, soon to be a century old, an obstacle to its progress.[4]

The new Quebec demanded a new place in Confederation, more money, more constitutional powers to complete its internal revolution, and a higher status that would tip the balance of federal-provincial relations more in its favour. The province also began to act internationally, sending its own official representatives abroad to deal directly with France and other French-speaking nations. Quebec was changing more rapidly than any other part of Canada. Hence, it was Quebec (not English Canada) that was asking for a re--examination of the terms of union. The old Quebec had handled relations with Ottawa and English Canada largely by saying "no" and turning its back. Quebec's new leaders were less isolationist as far as the rest of the nation was concerned, but they were also more demanding.

English Canada often replied with an irritated "What does Quebec want?" and "Is that really necessary?". Often, by the time it got around to making what it considered a large concession, French Canada had formulated a greater demand. A time gap was revealed in the dialogue between the two peoples that lent urgency to the crisis. Would English Canada respond quickly enough—before the separatists took over from the moderates of the Quiet Revolution? Pierre Sévigny, a member of the Diefenbaker Cabinet, described the situation within his party:

> In the minds of a few English-speaking Cabinet ministers, the fairly indecisive struggle that had taken place on the plains of Abraham in the month of September 1759 had once and for all time settled the fate and future of Canada ... The victors had gained their prerogatives now and for all time ...
>
> The myth of the defeat for all that was French in Canada I for one could not accept. I said so whenever I had a chance. Time and again I pleaded with my colleagues to listen to my arguments for a master plan that would, once and for all, correct the past but ever-present anomaly in the relationship between English and French Canada ... My Quebec colleagues shared my views.
>
> What we wanted was simple enough. We were asking for a distinctive Canadian flag; the recognition of "O Canada" as the Canadian anthem;

the repatriation of the Canadian Constitution; the creation of a Canadian decoration to honour Canadian valour … a fuller degree of bilingualism within the ranks of the civil service … the correction of a few anomalies such as the absence of bilingual cheques in many Government departments.

After long and lengthy discussion, it was agreed that the granting of bilingual cheques might be acceptable … but before the full and official acceptance the inevitable happened. A senior member of the Commons … and a true prototype of the Tory soul in Canada, rose from his seat and asked if bilingual cheques were not "too much, too soon."

To Quebec and to the Quebec ministers, the cheques were an anomaly. Like such earlier measures as the abolition of appeals to the British Privy Council, simultaneous translations in the Commons, the cheques had the appearance of a concession reluctantly handed out by a victor to a fallen enemy.[5]

What did Quebec want? Here we will present three points of view from the wide spectrum of opinion in Quebec in the 1960s. There was a large body of moderate opinion, a radical extreme on the left, and a conservative position on the right. The moderates wanted changes in the *British North America Act* that would reform it in Quebec's favour, extending the province's powers and freedom of action. The radicals would overthrow the Constitution and start anew as an independent state. The conservatives would work for gains within the existing system.

The leading politicians of Quebec—Jean Lesage, Paul Gérin-Lajoie, Daniel Johnson, and Jean-Jacques Bertrand—and leading journalists such as André Laurendeau and Gérard Pelletier represented moderate opinion. They sought recognition of a special status for Quebec within Confederation, arguing that it was not simply a province like the others and should therefore be treated on an equal basis with English Canada. The Canadian ideal, which they insisted was that of a bilingual and bicultural nation, had to be more conscientiously pursued. This could be done through the revision of policy decisions and of the Constitution itself. The moderates put forward various suggestions in the years following 1960, which Laurendeau called "Year One of the Revolution." Jean-Jacques Bertrand proposed an "Estates-General of the French-Canadian nation." He made this criticism of the *BNA Act:*

The problem may be stated thus: how are we to provide, in present-day conditions, for the harmonious co-existence in Canada of two nations which are different, but which share many common interests, namely the English-Canadian and the French-Canadian nations … Here, in the Quebec legislature, whenever we deal with matters of revenue, of economic control, or of cultural development, we come up against institutions that are constitutionally ill-defined or ill-adjusted to our particular needs. Far from encouraging harmony and co-operation between Canadians of the two cultures, the 1867 Constitution ... multiplies occasions for uneasiness and conflict. Canadian federalism, as it exists today, provides for no institution charged and equipped to study and smooth away difficulties arising out of the relations between the two principal ethnic groups in the country ... In the absence of any body charged with revitalizing the relations between Canadians of the two cultures, our French-speaking citizens, in the eyes of some people, are merely one minority among others.[6]

He then indicated the choices before Quebec: integration or assimilation, logical but repugnant; the status quo with all its defects; a remodelled federalism as the product of the discussions of the Estates-General; or a confederacy such as Germany or Switzerland or the United States under the early Articles of Confederation. His own preference was for a new federalism that would:

(1) permit the State of Quebec fully to assume its role as the authority responsible for the national existence and cultural development of the French-Canadian people;

(2) guarantee the essential rights of the English- and French-oriented minority in Quebec and of the French minorities in the other provinces; and

(3) ensure legal and practical equality for the two nations at the federal level.[7]

A revised Constitution, therefore, would contain explicit recognition of the two-nation concept, grant more power to Quebec, and offer guarantees for French and English minorities, but none for the "Third Force."

Those forming the radical left were impatient with the constitutional schemes of the moderates. Marcel Chaput, author of the early "separatist Bible," Pourquoi je suis séparatiste, wrote of the options facing French Canada:

Since I naturally owe my first allegiance to French Canada, before the Dominion, I must ask myself the question: Which of two choices will permit French Canadians to attain the fullest development—Confederation, in which they will forever be a shrinking minority, doomed to subjection ... a people without a future, shut up in the vicious circle of destructive bilingualism ... or the independence of Quebec, their true native land, which will make them masters of their own destiny?[8]

To Chaput, independence did not mean economic deprivation, isolation, stagnation, or any of the other horrors that its opponents conjured up, but "liberty, fulfillment of the nation, French dignity in the New World."[9] In 1960, the first significant separatist group, the RIN (Rassemblement pour l'Indépendance Nationale) was founded. Some radicals looked to the use of force to achieve independence; they exalted the cult of revolutionary hatred and Communist ideology. One of them, André Major, wrote, "Hatred is not evil when it opens the way to man's freedom."[10] The reaction of one young radical to the death of a man by sabotage in Quebec was, "It wasn't important—he was English."

There existed a third, much more conservative, point of view. It was expounded by Pierre Elliott Trudeau, one of the "Three Wise Men" who went to Ottawa to support Pearson in the 1965 election and to promote the Quiet Revolution there. Trudeau maintained that Anglo-Saxon imperialism had been a bogey to frighten French-Canadian school children. The English, he said, had never really been in a position to ride roughshod over French wishes; they had made many compromises and in a most undictatorial way, had often resigned themselves to the inevitable. These were facts that Quebec nationalists conveniently ignored as they went about looking for dragons to slay. He ridiculed French-Canadian nationalism, calling it a "sorry story" that had too long distracted the province. There was little danger of assimilation at this late date, he argued, for "the die is cast in Canada." Neither group could assimilate the other; each was here to stay. The French should therefore put aside their nationalistic obsessions, forget the bogies of the past, live normally, and put their own house in order under the existing Constitution. Reform should begin at home, and the search for "foreign" scapegoats in English Canada should cease.[11]

What was the rest of Canada's response to this ferment in Quebec? The Royal Commission on Bilingualism and Biculturalism was appointed to report on public feelings from coast to coast and to make recommendations. They wrote in their Preliminary Report:

> All that we have seen and heard has led us to the conviction that Canada is in the most critical period of its history since Confederation ... We do not know whether the crisis will be short or long. We are convinced that it is here. The signs of danger are many and serious.[12]

Confederation itself was at stake, and unless major changes were made, the crisis would worsen rather than go away as past crises had done.

From the "anglophone" side (in the terminology of the Commissioners), a new view of democracy that did not seek to reduce it to a simple game of numbers by invoking the law of the majority, would have to develop. Governance by a numerical majority might work in unicultural or even in multicultural nations, but in a bicultural one, it was divisive and dangerous. The concept that Canada was "one nation" and its citizens "unhyphenated" (to use Diefenbaker's words) had to be set aside. The anglophone majority must act as if it were not a majority. The Commissioners recalled the words of Macdonald: "Treat them [francophones] as a nation and they will act as a free people generally do—generously. Call them a faction and they become factious."[13] Above all, anglophones had to accept the idea of a partnership between equals and act accordingly.

The Commissioners called for an equally difficult change of attitudes on the part of francophones. They should cease to act as a beleaguered minority. They should "restrain their present tendency to concentrate so intensely on their own affairs, and to look so largely inward." They needed to cast aside the type of thinking that put *la nation française* above all other considerations and look to a larger Canadianism. They should forget the Conquest mentality and stop blaming anglophones for their own failures. They would then be capable of working in a partnership of equals. Changes in the national psychology, such as the Commissioners were calling for, were not easy to effect. Given a change in attitudes, however, problems could be solved by an exercise in national tolerance and concessions from both sides. "We believe," the Commissioners wrote, "that Canada will live and thrive if there can be a satisfactory matching between the minimum of what French-speaking Canadians consider as vital, and the maximum that English Canadians will accept."[14] From the bargaining would come a healthier Confederation for the second hundred years. At that time, any other alternative seemed unthinkable.

The *Official Languages Act* was a concrete result of the Commission's work. It was passed in 1969 with wide support from all parties in Parliament. The act stated that the two languages were to enjoy "equality of status and equal rights and privileges as to their use in all the institutions of the Parliament and Government of Canada." It also recommended that government services be provided in both languages, including the courts; that bilingual districts be set up where there was at least 10 percent bilingualism; that a Commissioner of Official Languages be appointed to hear grievances; and that appointments to the public service enlarge the number of bilingual employees. "We are fighting against time," Prime Minister Trudeau warned. "The country [later he corrected this to mean the government and Public Service] has to be bilingual by a certain date, or French-speaking Canadians will lose faith."

The Canadian Institute of Public Opinion found that most Canadians agreed with steps to strengthen bilingualism:

> As you may know a number of steps have been taken in Canada to strengthen bilingualism, that is the use of both English and French in certain civil service areas, on signposts, on package information, and in other ways. In general do you think this is a good thing for the future of this country, or not a good thing?

	Good Thing	Not A Good Thing	Can't Say
National	59%	31%	10%
Maritimes	53%	38%	9%
Quebec	83%	11%	6%
Ontario	53%	34%	13%
The West	45%	44%	10%

Source: Canadian Institute of Public Opinion. Results published July 19, 1972.

When questioned about their reasons, those who approved mentioned national unity, the two founding languages, and the necessity of accepting the French fact. Those who disapproved said this was an English-speaking country and that bilingualism meant conflict, a waste of money, and discrimination against other ethnic groups.

In the House of Commons on June 6, 1973, a resolution on the principle of bilingualism passed with an overwhelming majority. The vote was 214–16, with Robert Stanfield, the Conservative leader, and David Lewis, the New Democratic Party leader, supporting the government. Opposition came from the 15 members of the Créditiste Party (who abstained) and 16 Conservatives (14 from western Canada and 2 from eastern Ontario), who voted against the resolution after a speech by Diefenbaker against hyphenated Canadianism.

The person appointed to handle the practical problems arising from the implementation of the new policy was Keith Spicer, the first Official Languages Commissioner. A bilingual anglophone, Spicer was to investigate complaints from the public and from civil servants in 150 federal departments, agencies, and Crown corporations. In an annual report to Parliament, he described his technique as beginning with "smiling tactfulness" and "gentle reminders" and ending with "stinging denunciations." Most of his work was concerned with assisting the advance of French in the Public Service:

> Federal services available (and taken for granted) anywhere in Canada in English still too frequently are denied as exorbitant for French-speaking Canadians. And the 82 percent English-speaking bastion of the Public Service cannot by any fair assessment be regarded as beleaguered. To seek promotion, or even work, with most federal agencies as a unilingual French-speaking Canadian remains incomparably more difficult than for unilingual English speakers: in 1971, of the 66,675 jobs filled by the Public Service Commission and departments, little over 8 percent allowed for a unilingual French-speaking incumbent; nearly 80 percent, about ten times as many, required English only. Our language reform, for all its past and current advances, is not yet a revolution.[15]

Imposing bilingualism on the Public Service was a daring experiment. Canada was a country made up of two unilingual peoples. In 1961, the percentage of bilingual Canadians was 12.2; in 1971, it was 13.4. Only 5 percent of the English-speaking population were bilingual, compared to 33 percent of the French. This meant that careers in the Public Service would be limited to a very small group, mainly francophone. Historic, economic, and sociological factors militated against anglophones learning the second language, though they might enroll their children in French-immersion schools. At a press conference in December 1972, Treasury Board President Bud Drury was asked which language was used in Cabinet meetings. "English," he said, though French was "permitted." Trying to please two fundamentally unilingual peoples could have its moments as one columnist noted:

> Consider the ridiculous—Mr. Spicer's satisfaction that French-speaking and English-speaking guests in Montreal are getting equal treatment. He intervened when French-speaking guests complained that an English language daily newspaper was left outside their hotel rooms in the morning. Now, nobody gets a paper, and Mr. Spicer is satisfied that Anglophones and Francophones are on an equal footing. [16]

The decade of the 1960s began with the Quiet Revolution in Quebec and ended with the drive for bilingualism in Ottawa. It seemed, for a time, that a consensus had been achieved by the moderates in Parliament and that they represented the majority of Canadians. The *Official Languages Act* defined a partnership more precisely than did the original clauses in the *BNA Act*. The election of a French-Canadian Prime Minister meant Quebeckers would have a sympathetic ear in Ottawa. Trudeau himself provided an example of a man who did not shut himself up in Quebec but looked on the whole of Canada as his country. The support he received in 1968 from English Canada, as well as French Canada, was a good sign. It appeared that the seventh crisis was not only passing; it was being resolved. Canada's two peoples were coming together in a single bilingual entity, led by a man who belonged to both.

The demands of the new Quebec and the reaction of English Canada as seen by journalists, politicians, intellectuals, and ordinary citizens are illustrated in Chapter 19, Thoughts on the Quiet Revolution.

Notes

1   Pierre Laporte, *The True Face of Duplessis* (Montreal, 1961), 53.

2   Jean Drapeau, *Jean Drapeau vous parle* (Montréal, 1959), 84.

3   Jean-Paul Desbiens (Frère Pierre-Jérôme), *Les Insolences du Frère Untel* (Montréal, 1960), 29.

4   Speech to the Quebec Legislature, 8 May 1963.

5   Pierre Sévigny, *This Game of Politics* (Toronto, 1965), 206–9.

6   Frank Scott and Michael Oliver, eds., *Quebec States Her Case* (Toronto, 1964), 114–15.

7   Ibid., 123.

8   Ibid., 52–53.

9   Ibid., 48.

10   *Liberté*, March-April 1963.

11   *Cité Libre,* April 1962.

12   The Royal Commission on Bilingualism and Biculturalism, *A Preliminary Report* (Ottawa, 1965), 133.

13   Ibid., 138.

14   Ibid., 137.

15   The Commissioner of Official Languages, *The Second Annual Report 1971–1972* (Ottawa, 1973), xiii.

16   Charles Lynch, in the *Ottawa Citizen,* 1 February 1973.

9 &. THE CRISIS OF SEPARATISM, 1970–1980

The 1960s ended on a note of optimism. There were achievements to look back on—the reforms of the Quiet Revolution, the *Official Languages Act,* the drive toward federal bilingualism. With a large Liberal majority in Ottawa and general approval across the country, a new Liberal government led by Robert Bourassa took power in Quebec. But a series of dramatic events beginning in the fall of 1970 brought an end to the optimism. Acts of terrorism, kidnapping, assassination, and—six years later— the election of a separatist government in Quebec sent shock waves throughout Canada. The breakup of the country was proposed and debated, campaigned for and planned. The 1970s became a crisis decade that overshadowed all past crises in French-English relations.

The election of April 29, 1970, gave Quebec a new Premier who seemed to have all the qualities for success. Robert Bourassa had been educated at the universities of Montreal, Oxford, and Harvard; he was married into the wealthy Simard family and had the support of the province's Establishment, English and French; he had youth as well as experience, having been the Opposition finance critic and Lesage's protégé; he gave every impression of competence, efficiency, and strength. His election victory appeared convincing in terms of both seats and popular votes:

Parties	Seats	Popular Votes
Liberals	72	42%
Parti Québécois	7	23%
Union Nationale	17	20%
Ralliement Créditiste	12	11%
Others	0	4%

The results were closely watched, as this was the first time a separatist party of significance had run. At its head was René Lévesque, who had left the Liberal Party in October 1967, when it refused to accept his manifesto favouring sovereignty for Quebec within a common market association with Canada. By October 1968, he was the Leader of the Parti Québécois, which had been formed from splinter groups. It took this party eight years and three tries to achieve power, and in 1970 this was still far in the future. Just three days before the election won by Bourassa, the Royal Trust sent a group of nine Brinks trucks full of securities out of the province. A cartoon in the Toronto *Globe and Mail* (April 30) showed the armed convoy heading back to Montreal, convinced that the separatist danger was over.

Nearly four out of five Quebeckers had voted against the Parti Québécois. On the other hand, more than 20 percent had voted for it. And within the voting pattern, there was a disturbing split between French and English. Lévesque commented on this after losing his own seat in the riding of Laurier:

> *Question (Canadian Press):* How do you interpret the election results? Some saw massive approval for federalism in the election.
>
> *Answer:* First a fact that is terribly flagrant. It's that 95 percent of the Anglophone bloc—I studied enough polls, including Laurier—voted Liberal … Even little old ladies on stretchers were hauled out in the end-of-regime panic, as if it were the end of the Roman Empire. They got them out and they manipulated them to the hilt …
>
> There's another striking thing about the election. It's that the defeated candidates we are most sorry about, men like Parizeau and Morin … were often defeated only by the vote of the anglophone ghetto. They had bigger French majorities … than those who were elected. In other words they got a bigger percentage of the French vote than those who won. That's the disturbing second fact considered from the point of view of the possibilities of the democratic process…. Things could get pretty damned serious if the will, becoming clearer and clearer of an ethnic majority, is blocked by an ethnic minority within Quebec.[1]

The defeat of the Parti Québécois suggested to extremists that Quebec's independence might not be achieved by peaceful means. Some radicals favoured the use of force and banded together to form the clandestine organization Le Front de libération du Québec, or the FLQ, as it became known. They began a campaign of violence fuelled by hatred that culminated in the October Crisis. James Cross, the British Trade Commissioner, and Pierre Laporte, the Quebec Minister of Labour and Immigration, were abducted. With the support of Jean Drapeau, the Mayor of Montreal, and Claude Ryan, the editor of *Le Devoir,* Premier Bourassa appealed to Ottawa for armed forces to help the local police cope with bomb threats and the prospect of mass street demonstrations. More than a thousand soldiers arrived in Montreal as Prime Minister Trudeau invoked the *War Measures Act* to deal with the state of "apprehended insurrection within the province of Quebec."

The next day, the body of Pierre Laporte was found. James Cross was finally released alive on December 4, and his kidnappers went into exile in Cuba. Altogether 468 people were arrested, of whom 408 were released without charges. There had been no other political kidnappings in Canadian memory and only one other political assassination—that of D'Arcy McGee, the Irish Father of Confederation, who was shot by a Fenian on Sparks Street in Ottawa a hundred years earlier. Never before had the *War Measures Act* been declared in peacetime, but the federal government had overwhelming support for its action (89 percent from English Canada and 86 percent from French Canada approved).

The shock of the October Crisis was enormous. It was followed six years later by a second shock—the defeat of the Bourassa government, of which so much had been expected. The Parti Québécois was elected on November 15, 1976, the first time a secessionist party had ever come to power in a critical central province, one of the two giants of Confederation. The turnover between 1973 and 1976 was startling:

Parties	Seats		Popular Votes	
	1973	1976	1973	1976
Liberals	102	21	54%	34%
Parti Québécois	6	71	30%	41%
Union Nationale	0	11	5%	18%
Ralliement Créditiste	2	1	11%	5%
Others	0	1	0%	2%

The Parti Québécois had a clear majority for a full five-year term, and it was pledged to hold a referendum on independence sometime before the end of that term in office. The crisis of separatism was to continue for years.

Why had this happened? After six years in power, the Liberal Party came to be seen as betraying the Quiet Revolution, as no longer being interested in reform. It was perceived as the party of the Establishment, indulging in patronage, tying itself too closely to business and financial circles, antagonizing the unions, and ignoring the desires of the nationalists. By contrast, the Parti Québécois represented the "state middle class": predominantly French speaking, young, educated, unionized, employed in the public sector, and eager for power. Henry Milner, a Péquiste professor, analyzed the delegates to party congresses this way:

> Several commentators remarked on the make-up of the approximately one thousand delegates to the PQ's 1969 congress. For example, forty percent had university degrees while another twenty percent had completed CEGEP or classical college. Both the *La Presse* and *Le Devoir* reporters described the typical delegate as a thirty-year-old teacher or semi-professional male from Montreal. The combined figures allow us to conclude that at least sixty-one percent of the delegates came from the new middle class (including students). This percentage has remained more or less constant through subsequent congresses. For example, the typical delegate at the 1973 congress was described as "thirty-five-year-old male, married ... , he attended university or

at least college and earns more than $8,000 annually. Teacher, professional, or white collar worker, he joined the party before 1970 but is at his first congress."[2]

Few had ties with the private sector or management; many were union members (the Quebec Federation of Labour endorsed the PQ in the 1976 election). The PQ was young, nationalistic, and leftist. At its head was René Lévesque, who always ran ahead of his party and ahead of other party leaders in popularity polls.

What did the PQ victory mean? It was understood that a vote for the party did not mean a vote for independence. A study in November 1976 showed that only half of those who voted PQ were also in favour of independence (about 20 percent). Nevertheless, the party hoped that in time and with the levers of power at its disposal, it would be able to win over the majority to its way of thinking. The Péquistes believed that the longer they stayed in power, the greater their chances of winning a referendum would become. Studies showed that the percentage in favour of some form of independence had been increasing since 1962. In that year, 8 percent were in favour, 73 against, and 19 undecided; by 1977, 32 percent were in favour, 52 against, and 16 undecided. Within these totals, English Quebeckers were always at least 80 percent against, while French Quebeckers were divided, about 46 percent against and 48 percent for.

The PQ sometimes gave the impression of a government guided by opinion polls. In the spring of 1979, it commissioned a series of personal interviews with 102 questions on the various options and wordings of the status question for Quebec.[3] The goal was to find the concept that had the best chance of winning. In September, Claude Morin, Minister of Inter-governmental Affairs and a gradualist in his approach, made public the results of the polling with the comment that it revealed a "clear improvement" in "public comprehension" of sovereignty-association (a concept that always brought a better response than straight independence). "The first elementary rule of strategy is to accept reality," he said.

The question that was finally to appear on the referendum ballot was long and complicated:

> The government of Quebec has made public its proposal to negotiate a new agreement with the rest of Canada, based on the equality of nations: this agreement would enable Quebec to acquire the exclusive power to make its laws, administer its taxes and establish relations abroad—in other words, sovereignty-association including a common currency. Any change in political status resulting from these negotiations will be submitted to the people through a referendum: ON THESE TERMS, DO YOU AGREE TO GIVE THE GOVERNMENT OF QUEBEC THE MANDATE TO NEGOTIATE THE PROPOSED AGREEMENT BETWEEN QUEBEC AND CANADA?
> YES   NO

The wording of the question was approved by the National Assembly 68–37 in March 1980 after a thirty-five-hour televised debate. At their June convention the previous year, the PQ had promised a second referendum, after the negotiations, to ratify or reject the terms. Asked what they would consider a moral victory, party spokespeople said anything in the 40 percent range (that would indicate support from half the French-speaking voters). If they lost badly, Quebec would lose its bargaining power. "Even worse," said Morin, "English Canada would die laughing."

Having the Parti Québécois in power presented a critical challenge to Prime Minister Trudeau. It seemed that Quebeckers were not satisfied, despite all the efforts on their behalf to promote the interests of French Canadians and the French language in Ottawa. Perhaps it was not enough. In 1979, M.F. Yalden, the Official Languages Commissioner, noted in his *Annual Report* that French was still the "closet language" of the Public Service and that "francophones have yet to be persuaded—deep down—that they are welcome in Ottawa."[4] The PQ could point to their Charter of the French Language, Bill 101; it made bilingualism appear irrelevant and Ottawa a sideshow when the main action was in Quebec City. And what of English Canada, which had accepted bilingualism in the Public Service on the understanding that this was what Quebec wanted? That policy had always been a gamble in a country populated by two fundamentally unilingual peoples.

Trudeau and Lévesque each drew strong support from Quebec. Yet apparently, no two men were further apart ideologically. They had been in conflict for years before either came to power, and after November 1976, they opposed each other as heads of governments. Their arguments had started long ago around Gérard Pelletier's dining table. One of their interchanges happened there when Lesage was in power in Quebec:

> Lighting another cigarette, he [Pelletier] walked back through the kitchen to rejoin the four men [Jean Marchand and André Laurendeau were also present] around the remains of a late supper in his dining room. René Lévesque was still talking.
>
> The butt of a cigarette smouldered between his thin lips. He gestured absent-mindedly toward Pelletier for another, lit it from the remnant pinched between his thumb and forefinger, and inhaled quickly without interrupting the tempo of his argument.
>
> His thin face glistened. In the overhead light of the dining room, the dark lines and sallow pouches made him look much older than his forty years. But he talked with the enthusiasm of a university student, not the deliberation that one might have expected from a senior member of the Quebec cabinet. And he talked. And talked.

Only Pierre Trudeau, the wealthy law professor from the University of Montreal, with the triangular, almost oriental face, was adept at locating the vulnerable spots in that seemingly impenetrable flow.

There had been some doubt, the previous autumn, that the Friday night meetings of the group would continue at all after Trudeau had goaded Lévesque almost to physical violence during an argument about the Quebec government's plan to borrow $300 million to nationalize the province's hydro-electric companies … Nothing had made Lévesque angrier than Trudeau's claim that the takeover was motivated largely by nationalist sentiment and political tactics … . Whenever Lévesque felt that he had conclusively proved his case, Trudeau sniffed his way back to the insinuation that it was all a costly exercise in nationalism in the classic Quebec pattern. Wasn't nationalization merely bread and circuses for voters who were starting to look critically at the Lesage government after only two years in office? Lévesque had exploded. He had told Trudeau that his ironic, Socratic pose was nothing but a joke. Trudeau had retorted that it was impossible to have a serious discussion with a small-fry party hack.[5]

While Lévesque was publishing An Option for Quebec, Trudeau wrote the series of articles that became Federalism and the French Canadians. Lévesque left the Liberal Party and Trudeau joined it. Lévesque came to fear assimilation and the falling French birth rate; he looked to the protection of sovereignty, coupled with the idea of an economic union—"divorce after a century together, then a remarriage that is a growing success."[6] Trudeau disagreed, denouncing separation as a step backward, a dead end: "Separatism a revolution? My eye. A counter-revolution; the national-socialist counter-revolution."[7] In his view, Confederation was not a failure for French Canadians; they had never tried to make a success of it. They should stop the English-speaking majority from treating them as simply another ethnic minority. They should make their presence felt in Ottawa, that English capital with an English Public Service and an English army. They should reach out to the minorities in other provinces. They should take up the challenge of Canada as their homeland from sea to sea.[8] As Prime Minister, Trudeau sought to lead the French out of their historic isolation by enlarging their role in Ottawa and enlarging the federal presence in Quebec. An enormous new complex of federal office buildings at Place du Portage in Hull symbolized his intention to bind the nation together. Now Trudeau, like Laurier, was challenged by the nationalists in his own province. Could he defeat them or would Quebec follow Lévesque out of the union?

The one certainty seemed to be more uncertainty and more tension until the promised referendum came. Was the country going to break up? Proposals to meet the crisis came forward. One of these came from the Task Force on National Unity, appointed on July 5, 1977. It was to tour the country, much as the earlier "Bi and Bi" Commission had done, hear opinions in all the provinces, and make recommendations for change. The Commissioners, a group of eight leading citizens, including John Robarts and Jean-Luc Pépin, rejected the idea of special status for Quebec. Instead, they proposed "restructured federalism," which would raise all the provinces to a position of constitutional equality with the federal government. In addition, they would be represented directly in a "Council of the Federation," composed of delegations headed by Premiers.[9] Culture would be left to the provinces, trusting that their good sense and good will would ensure the fair treatment of their minorities. Linguistic guarantees, such as section 133 of the BNA Act, which protected the English minority in Quebec, should be removed. "We support the efforts of the Quebec provincial government and of the people of Quebec to ensure the predominance of the French language and culture in that province," the Commissioners wrote.[10]

But the recommendations of the Task Force pleased no one. The federal government was loath to part with any of its powers. A.R.M. Lower, a constitutional critic, said that the Task Force would turn Canada into "ten principalities"; like Humpty Dumpty, once smashed, it could never be put back together again.[11] The minorities, both English and French, felt threatened. The separatists scorned the report on principle, claiming it was just another unacceptable half-way measure. "Being part of a federation without wanting to be subject to the restrictions it imposes is at best a political absurdity, and at worst, gross misrepresentation," wrote Morin. He insisted that the choice had to be Quebec or Canada; as for the middle way of the Pépin-Robarts Report, it was a waste of time, energy, and money.

Another proposal was put forward by Claude Ryan, Leader of the Liberal Party in Quebec. He explained his approach in an interview conducted by *Maclean's* magazine in January 1980:

> *Maclean's:* Is nationalism an important emotion for you?
> Ryan: I won't cry at the sight of the fleur-de-lis. I won't cry over the maple leaf either. I'm fond of Canada because it stands for a lot of good things in the world today but not to the point that I would cry about it.
> *Maclean's:* Would you cry if the country ceased to exist?
> Ryan: Everything would depend on the circumstances. If it were to occur after everyone had done his very best to keep it together and had come to the conclusion objectively that we could not continue, we would have to accept the facts. But if it were to break up before we had attempted everything in our power, I would be the sorriest of men.[12]

Ryan's ideas were contained in a document entitled "A New Canadian Federation" that became known as the "Beige Paper." It suggested giving residual powers to the provinces;

replacing the Senate with a Federal Council of provincial legislatures; restricting the unlimited spending powers of the federal government and its emergency powers; giving a Charter of Liberties that would take precedence over any federal or provincial laws; establishing two official languages in Ontario, New Brunswick, Quebec, and Manitoba; and a host of other items.[13] In reality, these proposals involved more internal changes for the English-speaking provinces than Lévesque's separation, which would lead to the provinces' pursuing their own destinies alone.

How did Canadians outside Quebec feel about separation? According to public opinion polls, a large majority wanted Quebec to stay within Confederation. They would make concessions to try to persuade the province to remain, but they were against unlimited concessions and special status. A Gallup Poll in 1977 showed the majority of English Canadians against special status, while two-thirds of French Canadians favoured it. The *Canadian Magazine* in January 1977 showed only 28 percent of English Canadians in favour of extending bilingualism as a strategy for saving Confederation, while 56 percent of French Canadians were for it. Opposition to extending bilingualism was 58 percent in the Atlantic provinces and 76 percent in British Columbia. The farther west, the greater the pessimism and unwillingness to accommodate.

What would Canada be like without Quebec? The experience of other federations losing a member was not encouraging. Ronald L. Watts looked at the consequences:

> Generally speaking, once the complete independence of one unit in a federation has been conceded, other units have raised similar demands, which have often led to further disintegration. Moreover, the resentments aroused at the time of separation or dissolution have tended to persist and to discourage the subsequent creation of a looser form of association between the territories concerned. Whenever secession has occurred it has inevitably been accompanied by sharp political controversies not easily forgotten. In addition, the unscrambling of a federation requires the allocation of assets and liabilities among the successor states and rarely has it been possible to achieve this without adding further to the resentments felt by one or both sides.[14]

One could only speculate about the results of Quebec's secession. Because of its size and geographical location, Ontario could take the lead in a new federation of English-speaking provinces, maintaining links with the Maritimes through the St. Lawrence corridor. But would the others follow? Could out-of-the-way Ottawa possibly remain the capital in a rump Canada? Would the Maritimes not prefer a special relationship with the United States or an independent "Atlantica," a union such as they had discussed in 1864? The Parti Acadien believed that the differences between

Acadia and Quebec could be reconciled in an independent French state; they would separate from the Maritimes. What about the Prairies? Would there be a common front among the three provinces or would Alberta go it alone with its new-found wealth? And what of British Columbia? Would there be enough collective will in Canada or would several states fill the vacuum?

How would Quebec itself fare? Although separatist Quebeckers put economics second to culture, in 1977 they waged a "battle of the balance sheets" with the federalists. Did Quebec gain or lose by Confederation? In a 220-page report, *Economic Accounts of Quebec*, Rodrigue Tremblay, the Quebec Minister of Finance, argued that the federal government took in $4.3 billion more from Quebec than it paid to the province. The federal government retorted that the Quebec minister had misconstrued the figures, inflating revenues derived from the province and ignoring numerous expenditures made there. The Ontario government joined the fray, noting in a paper accompanying its 1977 budget that Quebec had received $6 billion over the preceding ten years, "a rock-bottom and incontrovertible measure of Quebec's financial gain." In a general way as a redistributor of wealth, the federal government collected funds from the rich provinces and gave to the poor ones. Quebec was close to the break-even point, shifting from a "have" to a "have-not" province in the mid-1970s and hence gaining federal funds. Symbolic of the change was the relative decline of Montreal, losing ground to its ancient rival, Toronto, as the economic and financial capital of the country. Many believed that the advent of the PQ government hastened the transfer of head offices like those of the Sun Life Insurance Company out of the province. Another sign of the times was the demise of the Montreal Star in October 1979, the English-speaking community in Montreal no longer being strong enough to support both it and the *Gazette*.

Lévesque had never advocated total independence for Quebec. From the beginning he had suggested a tandem idea, "sovereignty-association." In *An Option for Quebec* (1968), he proposed a five-year treaty to cover the transition period, during which, among other things, the currency would remain the same. A long-term agreement would set up a common market, a secretariat and permanent committees, a court or arbitration, joint councils of ministers, and parliamentary exchanges.[15] The details were spelled out in the PQ White Paper *Quebec-Canada: A New Deal* (1979).

What could go wrong along the way? Many things. Economic depression was a distinct possibility. Civil war could not be ruled out, though it was unlikely that English Canada would block separation by violence if that was what Quebec truly wanted. Quebec could go in peace, although there might be border clashes or confrontations within the province itself. The new boundary might be disputed, a possibility discussed by Hugh Thorburn in *Must Canada Fail?*

French Canada and Quebec are not one and the same; and there could well be agitation from Quebec to permit parts of New Brunswick and Ontario to join the new country. English-speaking communities near the border may well seek to join the neighbouring provinces. There is also the long-standing dispute with Newfoundland over the Labrador boundary, which was determined by the Judicial Committee of the Privy Council in the Twenties but it is still contested by Quebec. Then the Hudson's Bay territory in the north which was added to Quebec in 1912 could well be claimed by Canada if Quebec became independent.[16]

Donald Creighton, a leading English-Canadian historian, said that if Quebec wanted to leave Confederation, it should go with what it had when it entered in 1867 and no more. (The province had entered the union with 495,189 km² of territory; by 1980 it had 1,356,797 km².) If the boundary was debatable, what of the division of the armed forces, the Public Service, the national debt, the currency, the use of the port of Montreal, and the St. Lawrence Seaway?

The referendum to decide the fate of the nation in the greatest crisis of its history, the decade-long crisis of separatism, came in the spring of 1980. After the debate on the question, the National Assembly divided into two "umbrella" committees, one for the oui and one for the non. Each was voted $1.1 million in public funds and each was legally and officially nonpolitical. But in reality the *oui* was *Péquiste* and the *non* was Liberal. The *oui* forces were well organized, and at the beginning of their campaign, exuded self-confidence. Their members shared a common nationalistic outlook, which gave them a greater sense of unity than the *non* forces. They started strongly, after what was considered a winning performance in the March debate. The *non* forces were more diverse, including federal Liberals, provincial Liberals, Progressive Conservatives, and Union Nationale supporters, and gave the impression of being on the defensive. The campaign was to be 35 days in length and the vote by the 4.3 million eligible citizens would be held on May 20, the day after the Victoria Day holiday.

Quebec became the most polled place in the country, the focus of its attention. New readings of public opinion were constantly taken by a host of public and private groups. In the winter there was a non majority; after the March debate, the two sides were even; in early May a non majority turned up again. The federalist slogans were oriented to the status quo—for example, *"J'y suis, j'y reste—pour ma sécurité"* or *"pour ma prosperité."* The PQ looked ahead: *"C'est ce qu'on veut!"* To this suggestion the federalists said, *"Non merci"* and *"Plus j'y pense ... plus c'est non."* Always notable was the large number of undecided voters and those who refused comment. Many were afraid of antagonizing friends, losing business and government grants, and splitting families. Famous "no comment" voters included Montreal Mayor Jean Drapeau, unwilling to lose either federal or provincial grants (or both), and the entire *Canadiens* hockey team.

Federal Liberals took part in the campaign; Jean Chrétien acted as their leader. He was viscerally anti-Péquiste, referring to the PQ as a "gangrene on the thumb—it should be cut out before it infects the whole arm." He said, "I have no problem with my identity. I am from Quebec and I am a citizen of Canada." Prime Minister Trudeau appeared three times. He challenged Lévesque on the question of accepting a *non* vote:

> Mr. Lévesque and the Quebec government have been spending a lot of time these past weeks telling the people of Quebec if they vote for sovereignty-association the rest of Canada will have no choice but to negotiate. Now we ask them to tell us what they will do if Quebec votes No. Would Mr. Lévesque renounce any aim of making Quebec an independent state? Would he sit down and negotiate a renewed federalism? Or would he say, heads I win, tails you lose? In my game if you vote Yes it's Yes but if you vote No you'll have another referendum.[17]

Trudeau received a standing ovation from his Montreal audience and there was a spontaneous singing of "O Canada," a characteristic of *non* rallies. His last speech, coming a week before the referendum, contained a promise for a constitutional conference in July if there was a *non* vote. Some called it his "finest hour."

Women played a crucial part in the campaign. The PQ was considered the political base for Quebec feminists, and the Public Works Minister Jocelyn Ouellette told a crowd of West Quebec women that separation was like women's liberation. Women who wanted their rights should vote *oui*. The polls, however, suggested that 56 percent of Quebec women would vote *non*. At one point, Lise Payette, a PQ member of the National Assembly, declared, "Two groups will have refused Quebec its liberty—anglophones and women." She called women who supported the *non* side "Yvettes" after a textbook character who was a household drudge. They responded with declarations of pride to be "Yvettes" and sang "Hello, Dolly" at their rallies. It was an intense and important scramble for the women's vote, 52 percent of the electorate.

English Canada listened to Quebec's internal dialogue with great concern but did not try to intervene. Support for the federalist side was overwhelming, but there was consensus that the question must be decided by Quebec itself. The chief statements came from provincial premiers. Allan Blakeney of Saskatchewan was the first to refuse sovereignty-association. He said that Westerners would see no economic sense in such a deal and that a *oui* vote would encourage them to say "goodbye and good luck." The four western premiers, Blakeney, Lyon of Manitoba, Lougheed of Alberta, and Bennett of British Columbia, met at Lethbridge, Alberta, and issued a communiqué rejecting sovereignty-association. The Ontario Legislature held a week-long debate in which it unanimously approved a resolution against sovereignty-association and called on Quebec to join the rest of Canada in drawing up a new Constitution. As voting day approached, a common front against Lévesque's idea was forming in English Canada. Senator Eugene Forsey, the leading constitutional expert on the English-Canadian side, sharply condemned it:

> Sovereignty-association is a horse that won't even start, let alone run. If Mr. Lévesque came to Ottawa to negotiate sovereignty-association, a government of Canada, of whatever party, would simply have to tell him the thing can't be done ... You can no more negotiate sovereignty-association than you can negotiate sour sugar, dry water, boiling ice or stationary motion.[18]

Lévesque himself referred to it less and less and talked about equality instead. "This inequality [between Quebec and Canada] must be corrected," he said, "and this is the heart of the debate between the yes and the no." He seemed at times to be merely asking for more bargaining power. Perhaps Quebeckers who had always had doubts about complete independence were now drawing back from the modified version also. Doris Lussier, a PQ member, spoke frankly: "It's the assurance of association that removes the fear of sovereignty. We have to play on that sentiment whether we like it or not. The only way to achieve independence is never to talk about it." Ryan warned that the policy of the PQ was *l'étapisme*. They could not be trusted; sovereignty-association was the first step to complete independence.

Fears surfaced in the campaign. The fear of losing their identity as French Canadians in an Anglo-Saxon sea was basic to the referendum proposal. A demographic scare was implicit in figures projecting Quebec dropping from 27 to 23 percent of Canada's total population by the year 2000. (In actuality, by 2001, it had dropped to 24 percent.) The minorities were afraid of independence, as were the old economic élite. "For sale" signs dominated the streets of Westmount. What about federal pension cheques? Would they continue if Quebec voted *oui?* Would taxes increase? Chrétien noted that the average Quebecker already paid higher taxes than other Canadians, and in an independent Quebec they would pay $900 more to have the same services as now, including subsidized oil.

Just how final would the results of the referendum be? There had been other referenda in Canadian history, but none on so fundamental an issue. Various provinces had voted on public ownership of power companies, prohibition, daylight saving time, and in the case of Newfoundland, entry to Confederation. There had been two federal votes, one in 1898 on prohibition and one in 1942 on conscription. But a referendum itself had no constitutional validity. No government was bound to follow one; it could accept or reject the results as it saw fit. In addition, the wishes of the people might not be well expressed. Though it was a government-sponsored opinion poll, decision makers might be stumped by the results. What turnout was necessary? What margin of victory constituted a clear expression? What safeguards existed for minorities? Would opinion change later on the same question?

May 20 dawned a bright and sunny day. Quebec voters turned out in large numbers. Some 84 percent of those eligible made their way to the polls, non-French voters in greater proportion than French. The results were anxiously watched in the two camps and across the country. At 7:55 p.m., within an hour of the polls closing, Radio-Canada announced a *non* victory. By the end of the evening, its magnitude was evident. Fifty-nine and a half percent, or 2,171,913, had voted *non,* against 40.5 percent, or 1,478,200, who had voted *oui.* Ninety-four ridings had a *non* majority and 16 a *oui.* Most of the *non* ridings were in the west, the south, and the southeast up to the Gaspé; the *oui* ridings were in the north, Abitibi-East, Roberval, Dubuc, Saguenay, and Duplessis. In ridings that were 90 percent French, 53.7 percent voted *non;* in ridings that were less than 50 percent French, 81.9 percent voted *non.*

The detailed voting pattern was assessed by an "exit" poll (as voters left the booths) by students of the Carleton University School of Journalism. In a sample of 935 voters, 52 percent of the French voters voted *non* and 48 percent *oui,* while 96 percent of the non-French voted *non* and only 4 percent voted *oui.* Men voted 54 percent *non* and women, 66 percent *non.* People aged 18 to 25 voted 46 percent *non;* the 26–40 group voted 57 percent *non;* the over-40 group voted 73 percent *non.* It was a convincing victory for the *nons,* based on a small majority of the French (some argued that the French vote was equally split) and overwhelming support from the minorities. It rounded off to the 60 percent that Ryan, the leader of the *nons,* had defined as decisive.

Referendum Day 1980 vindicated the historic hope that Canada had a future and Quebec within it. Premier Lévesque called on his followers to accept the results, as they had been democratically obtained. "Now the ball is in the federalist court," he said. It had been a long, emotional campaign, with tears of joy and sorrow shed by both sides, for neither had a monopoly on caring. The rest of the nation had watched and waited until finally Quebec itself had rejected the separatist solution.

The eighth crisis in the nation's history ended with the non vote. Its final resolution would come when the country approached a renewed Canadian federalism. The national will had risen above the divisive question. Now the old qualities of compromise, conciliation, tolerance, and discussion again had a chance. Would English Canada go back to sleep as the PQ had predicted? Or would there be an unprecedented push for constitutional reform?

Prime Minister Trudeau had written years earlier, "Of all the countries of the world, Canada has the eighth oldest written constitution, the second oldest one of a federal nation, and the oldest which combines federalism with the principles of responsible government."[19] With the *non* vote he had asked for, the long-awaited moment was at hand. He could attempt what Laurier had only dreamed of—to bring the *BNA Act* home and to transform it here, not in Britain. It appeared that Canada's search for a nation was not to end in separation, even in the mild form of sovereignty-association. Quebec had said *non* to that and *oui* to a new form of national unity, yet to be defined. Renewals of faith were heard everywhere on the morning of May 21, 1980. The future looked bright for post-referendum Canada.

The events and the clash of ideas in the decade-long crisis of separation, beginning with the October Crisis of 1970 and ending with the referendum of 1980, are illustrated in Chapter 20, Oui·ou Non?

NOTES

1   *Ottawa Citizen*, 22 August 1970.

2   Henry Milner, *Politics in the New Quebec* (Toronto, 1978), 158.

3   The PQ used the advice of Jacques Broussard of the University of Montreal and the services of the Centre de Recherche sur l'Opinion Publique (CROP).

4   The Commissioner of Official Languages, *The Annual Report 1978* (Ottawa, 1979), 20 and 17.

5   Peter Desbarats, *René: A Canadian in Search of a Country* (Toronto, 1976), 3–6.

6   Réne Lévesque, *An Option for Quebec* (Toronto, 1968), 95.

7   Pierre Elliott Trudeau, *Federalism and the French Canadians* (Toronto, 1968), 212.

8   Ibid., 5.

9   The Task Force on Canadian Unity, *A Future Together: Observations and Recommendations* (Ottawa, 1979), 97.

10 Ibid., 51.

11 *Ottawa Citizen*, 29 March 1979.

12 "Claude Ryan's National Dream," *Maclean's*, 14 January 1980, 19.

13 The Liberal Party of Quebec, *A New Canadian Federation* (Montreal, 1980).

14 Ronald L. Watts, "Survival or Disintegration," in *Must Canada Fail?* ed. Richard Simeon (Montreal, 1977), 57.

15 Lévesque, *An Option for Quebec*, 35–56.

16 Hugh Thorburn, "Disengagement" in *Must Canada Fail?* ed. Simeon, 210–19.

17 *Ottawa Citizen*, 2 May 1980.

18 *Maclean's*, 12 May 1980.

19 Trudeau, *Federalism and the French Canadians*, 131.

10   THE CONSTITUTION CRISIS, 1982–1992

Few would have foreseen what actually happened in post–1980 referendum Canada. For the moment, there was general relief and acceptance. The results seemed decisive, but a second and startling referendum came in Quebec fifteen years later. Would the search for identity and definition never end? In all, thirty years were consumed in the struggle over the role of Quebec in Canada and, more broadly, in the quest for a new Constitution. And all of this conflict took place in a remarkably calm and peaceful way.

Three major attempts at reform were made, in addition to several minor ones. First came patriation of the *Canada Act* with its Schedule B, the *Constitution Act* (formerly the *British North America Act (BNA Act)* of 1867), then the Meech Lake Accord in 1987, and finally the Charlottetown Accord in 1992. The latter two came close, but failed to be accepted when proposed to the legislatures and the public.

Success depends a great deal on the method used, but what method would most likely have led to success as Canada struggled to reach agreement between the federal government, the provincial governments and their legislatures, and the people themselves? This type of consent between all parties, endorsed by a referendum, may perhaps be the best way to make a Constitution. However, it is also the least likely to succeed, especially when stretched over three years and changing political players. The bar is too high. As Voltaire said, "The best is the enemy of the good." Besides, including the people and informing them was the least of the politicians' concerns, and it was the last thought on their minds.

Another possible method is to have the executive unilaterally establish the Constitution. But in a federal state, the central executive must consult its counterparts in the provinces. In all cases, there was a strong measure of political agreement, but never the agreement that was sought. There were seemingly endless discussions, committees, consultations, disagreements, and objections until reality and sheer weariness called a halt to the proceedings. Often one province would object; in one case, one individual (Elijah Harper, an Aboriginal MLA in Manitoba's legislature) prevented his province from acceding to the accord. By the late 1990s, the Constitution Crisis had drifted and died without resolution or satisfaction or separation.

The patriation of the old *BNA Act* came first, and it achieved the best results. The method used in this case was consultation by the central government with the provinces. Under the old order, the provinces could rely on the British Privy Council for favourable rulings against the Dominion government, playing on the British imperial custom of "divide and rule." In other words, the British government would support the provinces against Ottawa to keep power in London. But times had changed.

What was the Constitution Crisis all about? The pressures essentially came from Quebec. Increased intervention by the federal government in provincial jurisdictions since the Second World War and a decline in the French language led to an increase in nationalism and demands for constitutional change—and even for outright independence. Quebec's leaders sought greater protection for their language, culture, and powers, as well as a veto over constitutional amendments by the anglophone majority. They found some support in other provinces, which also wanted to halt increasing encroachments by the federal government. For his part, Prime Minister Pierre Trudeau knew that Ottawa could only be a loser in any reorienting of powers. However, he had long believed in the need for a charter of rights and freedoms because he felt that Canada's new multiethnic population no longer automatically understood the unwritten concepts of rights and freedoms inherited from Britain. He also promoted the notion of an amending formula that required the support of at least seven of the ten provinces and 50 percent of the population by the most recent census.

So the constitutional process started with Trudeau's unilateral initiative from the top, reflecting his personal views and individualistic liberalism. It passed to bilateral discussions with one premier at a time and moved on to multilateral discussions with a group of premiers at a government conference centre on Meech Lake, north of Ottawa. Finally, in a populist phase, it called for the people's involvement. The chief tool would be a referendum, whether in one province or throughout the ten provinces.

Meeting in Ottawa during the first week of November 1981, the premiers were concerned that patriation would weaken them against Ottawa. They met every morning "behind closed doors," and they had an agreement that each would consult the others before modifying his position. Suddenly, however, Premier René Lévesque sided with Trudeau on the issue of a referendum on the charter and a veto for Quebec and Ontario only. The "Group of Eight" (Saskatchewan, Nova Scotia, B.C., Alberta, Manitoba, Quebec, P.E.I. and Newfoundland) opposed these new positions.

How could Lévesque side with Trudeau, his known opponent? Had he betrayed the premiers from English Canada and isolated his own province? Was he trying to sabotage the deal? Premier Lougheed of Alberta insisted that Lévesque had been informed on all issues. Lévesque, on the other hand, said that he had been kept in the dark. Then, on November 4–5, 1981, during the "night of the long knives," the other provinces repositioned themselves and came to their own agreement with Ottawa. Thus was born a mystery and a myth of Quebec nationalists. Lévesque's comment on November 5 (Guy Fawkes Day) to La Presse was enigmatic: "This provides us with a respectable and extraordinarily interesting way out of this whole imbroglio." In Trudeau and Our Times, Stephen Clarkson and Christina McCall note that on that night, November 4 to 5, when Trudeau issued his referendum challenge, Lévesque agreed, because he thought he could win a referendum in Quebec, stating, "'Okay, I'd like to fight the Charter.'" Trudeau announced to reporters the launching of a "'new Quebec-Canada alliance.'" Lévesque confirmed what Trudeau said, by announcing that a referendum would be "an honourable way out for Quebec." But Lévesque had broken the cardinal Gang of Eight rule that the dissidents should never change position without advance consultation. The anglophones feared that Lévesque had joined with Trudeau just to sabotage the process, since as a separatist, he could not possibly sign any deal.[1]

The next year, in spite of Quebec's not signing on, the *Constitution Act* was signed by Queen Elizabeth II with its Charter of Rights and Freedoms and amending formula. Quebec was legally bound, but its government regarded the act as politically illegitimate. It insisted that twenty-two demands be met before it would consider itself to be governed by the *Constitution Act*.

New governments were elected in Quebec (Robert Bourassa's Liberals in 1985) and in Ottawa (Brian Mulroney's Progressive Conservatives in 1984). Their goal was to "bring Quebec into Confederation." Mulroney was determined to use his record majority to obtain Quebec's endorsement of the *Constitution Act,* and his Quebec lieutenant, Lucien Bouchard, a former separatist, decided to take the *"beau risque"* to make it work.

Bourassa presented five conditions to be met:

1. Quebec recognized as a "distinct society,"
2. more power over immigration.
3. appointment of Quebec judges to the Supreme Court,
4. limits on federal spending powers, and
5. recognition of Quebec's veto over constitutional amendments.

He had been assured that the other premiers would be flexible, and they did indeed agree on the Meech Lake Accord in 1987. In this agreement, however, Aboriginal claims were not considered. The leaders gave themselves three years; by 1990 their proposals had to be passed by each provincial legislature, as well as by the federal Parliament. Under the Constitutional Accord of 1987 (the Meech Lake Accord), the goal was rigid (pass it as is, no amendments), included a deadline, and could not be met without the unanimous consent of all the provinces.

Quebec was the first province to sign the Meech Lake Accord. It contained a "distinct society" clause to recognize Quebec's uniqueness and its government's need to preserve and promote that "distinct society." This created a problem for those who wanted a "Canada Clause" to make all provinces equal. There were fears that "special status," "asymmetrical federalism," and undefined powers to promote French culture would come with Meech. By 1989, New Brunswick, Manitoba, and Newfoundland had changed governments. The new premier of New Brunswick insisted on reviewing the whole accord.

Some Conservative members from Quebec, led by Lucien Bouchard, left the federal government to set up a pro-sovereigntist party, the Bloc Québécois. They were enraged that Mulroney was watering down some of Quebec's hard-won agreements concerning its "distinct society" in the Meech Lake Accord, making sometimes "gratuitous concessions" to the premiers during the discussions at Meech Lake. Finally, Premier Clyde Wells of Newfoundland failed to call a ratification debate in his legislature before the deadline and the accord died.

It all came to an end on June 23, 1990, just before St-Jean-Baptiste Day. Blue and white flags with the lily of prerevolutionary France flooded the province that was "not like the others." If Canada was rejecting the accord Quebec wanted, then Quebec would look after itself. In the Quebec National Assembly, the opposition Parti Québécois voted against Meech Lake.

For several years, political leaders licked their wounds, shunning the constitutional issue. Slowly, Bourassa and Mulroney realized they had to try to reach a deal. The Citizens' Forum (or "Spicer Commission") was set up to study public opinion (and let people sound off) about the issues of Canadian ideals and values, Quebec and Canadian unity, official languages, Aboriginal issues, cultural diversity, the Canadian economy, responsible leadership, and participatory democracy. In 1991, they produced a report which suggested strongly that Canadians were fed up with politicians who paid no attention to them. The "grassroots" were consulted further through travelling committees, informed briefs were taken into account by the government, and a referendum was recommended. Joe Clark was appointed minister responsible for constitutional affairs and chair of the Cabinet committee on Canadian unity. Following the lead of a private group, Dialogue Canada, he initiated a series of cross-country consultative conferences about the question of Canadian national unity.

Then, in August 1992, after negotiations in Charlottetown between the federal, provincial, and territorial governments and representatives for the Assembly of First Nations, the Inuit and Métis, the federal government launched the third major constitutional effort, the Charlottetown Accord. In a sense, the new challenge was to try to respond to the criticisms that governors and the general public had made of the Meech Lake Accord. Thus, the Charlottetown Accord included a "Canada Clause" that would recognize Quebec as a "distinct society" but that also recognized other key elements of the Canadian identity. Special attention was paid to Aboriginal peoples and the equality of all the constituent elements of the Canadian community. With regard to institutions, there would be an elected Senate, an entrenched Supreme Court, and a restructured House of Commons. The powers of the central government to encroach on provincial jurisdictions were to be limited, and there would be an obligatory federal-provincial conference at least once a year. Even the socioeconomic union was to be spelled out more clearly, with improved equalization and a defined common market.

With Bourassa on board, unanimous agreement was finally achieved on August 28, 1992, in the home of Confederation. It was agreed that a referendum question would be put to the Canadian people, who would have a matter of weeks to make up their minds. In Quebec, the provincial government would handle the question; outside Quebec, the federal government would run it. In both cases, the referendum question would be the same:

> "Do you agree that the Constitution of Canada should be renewed on the basis of the agreement reached on August 28, 1992?"

All the leaders agreed, texts were sent out to each household, and the people turned it down. Why?

The answer appears to lie in the old problems and in some new attitudes. First of all, it was easier to say "no" than "yes" because the "no" forces attacked certain sections or one clause or another, rather than the whole. The populist method created a sense of popular power and entitlement, a new attitude for Canadians. Women's groups and Aboriginals doubted whether the new accord would really help them. The 25 percent guarantee of Commons seats for Quebec fed anti-Quebec sentiment. Quebec and British Columbia had not been in favour from the beginning. Quebec nationalists claimed Bourassa had settled for too little. Trudeau also attacked it. At the same time, Preston Manning and the Reform Party were calling it the "Mulroney deal," playing on "abc" (anybody but the Conservatives) sentiment. This anti-Conservative feeling may have arisen from Canadians' anger at regional disparity, budget cutbacks, unemployment, interest rates, and the goods and services tax. People were more weary than ever before of Constitution making. There was a fixed deadline of October 26. There were more public consultations and the people were tired. There were more matters than ever before in the amending formula that required unanimous consent, that old idealistic goal. But perhaps more than anything, the leaders had left themselves with too little time to inform and convince the citizens, who once again had been taken for granted by the members of the élite.

The Charlottetown Accord was rejected by a majority of Canadians in a majority of provinces, including Quebec. In Quebec, the vote was 56.6 percent "no," and outside Quebec it was 54 percent "no." Ontario was closely divided, with 49.8 percent "yes" and 49.6 percent "no." The accord was rejected in British Columbia, Alberta, Saskatchewan, Manitoba, Quebec, and Nova Scotia. The turnout was 72 percent in Quebec, and outside that province, it ranged from a high of 76 percent in British Columbia to a low of 54 percent in Newfoundland. Maybe it was all too complicated— in which case, it was easier to say "no."

The Constitution Crisis ended in calm. Bouchard said that thirty years of struggle had ended in failure. In spite of this, however, Canada did have a reformed Constitution, the *Canada Act* of 1982. In quasiconstitutional legislation following the near-loss of the 1995 referendum in Quebec, the federal Parliament did give recognition to Quebec's distinct society, "lent" Quebec its veto power, and promoted some degree of decentralization. And Canadians had a greater understanding of issues such as unity and diversity, French and English, equality and special status, unanimous consent and a simple majority, unilateralism and populism—a long list. While the search for a definitive identity was still unresolved, there was an awareness that Canadians could live in peace and calmly agree to disagree. Perhaps that was the most important success of the long, drawn-out constitutional negotiations.

The events and negotiations relating to the Constitution Crisis are illustrated in Chapter 21, Constitutional Debate, Defeat, and Compromise.

NOTES

1   Stephen Clarkson and Christina McCall, *Trudeau and Our Times Volume 1: The Magnificent Obsession* (Toronto, 1990) 378-9.

11 ❧ THE CRISIS OF THE 1995 REFERENDUM

Quebec did not get what it wanted in the constitutional struggle with the rest of Canada (ROC). But it was difficult to discern what Quebec wanted. The answer, as recorded in the results of the 1995 Quebec Referendum, was ambiguous. To understand the meaning of the referendum, we must weave in the history, leadership, and politics of the day.

Quebec was not a nation-state. It lacked sovereignty. But it possessed the attributes of an "organic" nation, springing from its own people. It had an ethnic group, a common language, a dominant religion, a civil code, customs, a history, and other marks of distinct identity—in a discrete geographic area. What it lacked, however, was an independent government.

One Quebec motto, *"la belle province,"* suggested that it was the jewel in the crown of the Canadian provinces. Another motto, *"Je me souviens,"* pointed to its glorious, idealized past before the defeat of New France. The original context for this phrase resided in these words of the French-Canadian architect Etienne-Eugène Taché (1836–1912):

> *Je me souviens*
> *Que né sous le lys* [the symbol of France]
> *Je grandis sous la rose"* [the symbol of England].

But the "rose" line was forgotten in revisionist history, and only the *fleur-de-lys* appears on Quebec's official flag. Quebec has had a long-lasting nationalist movement, like that of Scotland, Wales, Catalonia, and the Flemish, to name a few. But it has always been a colony or an integral part of Canada.

The facts are there. Quebec's population is greater than that of 120 member-countries of the United Nations. Of more than 200 nations in the world, only 18 are geographically larger than Quebec. It is three times the size of its motherland, France, and five times larger than Japan. It is in the top twenty industrialized countries in the OECD and compares to Switzerland and Sweden. It is the seventh-largest exporter to the United States, just behind the United Kingdom. It is the third-largest producer of hydro-electric power in the world. It has the third-largest reserves of fresh drinking water in the world. Its forest area is the size of France. The list could go on.

Quebec's modernization began in the 1930s, accelerated in the 1960s with the Quiet Revolution, and continues to this day. The old traditions of light manufacturing based on cheap, unskilled labour were replaced with a new, high-technology economy concentrated in manufacturing and services. More workers were skilled, women entered the workforce, and francophones gained power. Bombardier and Quebecor became international private enterprises owned by Quebeckers. Quebec began to prosper as it had not done before. By 2000, exports of office, telecommunications, and transport equipment accounted for over two-thirds of the increase in Quebec's international exports, and Quebec was responsible for nearly half of all high-tech exports in Canada.[1] In 2006 Quebec's aerospace sector ranked sixth worldwide, with sales of over $11.4 billion.[2]

It should come as no surprise that the nationalist movement prospered more than ever as Quebec's economy grew stronger. The nationalists were not interested in decentralization through constitutional reform; they pushed for outright independence or sovereignty, with some kind of association with Canada. After Lévésque, Quebec had two striking leaders, Jacques Parizeau and Lucien Bouchard. Bouchard, portrayed as a Napoleonic figure (and not only by cartoonists), was the most powerful and charismatic figure. A skilled orator, he promoted a vision of Quebec sovereignty that was both romantic and pragmatic. He always proposed ties with Canada that would work in some way to Quebec's advantage. He became friends with Brian Mulroney at Laval University, then ambassador to France, an MP, and a Cabinet minister. He broke with Mulroney over compromises in the Meech Lake Accord. In 1990 he formed the Bloc Québécois (BQ), and in 1993 his party easily took 54 of Quebec's 75 seats in the federal Parliament. This made him the Leader of Her Majesty's Loyal Opposition. "Only in Canada," said some.

Bouchard explained: "The political problem with Canada is Quebec, and the problem of Quebec is Canada." Many spoke of one nation, others maintained that Quebec and English Canada were two different nations. The *raison d'être* of the BQ was to represent Quebec's interests in Canada's Parliament. They favoured a European Union format for Canada and Quebec, as in the Maastricht Treaty.

Bouchard had moved from the Parti Québécois to the Progressive Conservatives to the Bloc Québécois, and when the 1995 referendum came, he took over the leadership of the *"Oui"* forces from Jacques Parizeau. He became Leader of the PQ and Premier of Quebec. Always he sought maximum power for Quebec and himself. He became a national hero when he survived the flesh-eating disease (necrotizing fasciitis) in December 1994. He lost a leg but was undeterred for another two years. In the end, he resigned on January 29, 1996, saying, "The results of my work are not very convincing." Too many failed to take a chance on sovereignty and on his self-empowerment.

Jacques Parizeau was a well-known economist and René Lévesque's finance minister. He was a true separatist hardliner, a flamboyant and abrasive politician. He broke with Lévesque over compromises and became Leader of the PQ in 1987. He moved the PQ away from Lévesque's sovereignty-association proposals to a vision of full independence. In 1989 the PQ had 40 percent of the vote but only 29 seats. By 1994, with 45 percent of the vote, they gained 125 seats, and Premier Parizeau promised a sovereignty referendum on October 30, 1995.

But Parizeau's campaign for the *"Oui"* forces faltered. He made controversial remarks, he failed to define, he exaggerated, and he was a true believer in complete independence. One Bloc Québécois MP said he aimed a "Scud missile" at the party when he wrote the book *For a Sovereign Quebec*. It seemed to suggest that he would proclaim sovereignty immediately after a successful referendum. He was doing more harm than good to the party and the cause. He blamed the 1995 referendum's *"Non"* result on "money and the ethnic vote" and resigned the day after it was held. He had helped the opponents of Quebec's sovereignty: Jean Chrétien, Preston Manning, and Jean Charest all took advantage of the fears he aroused within and outside Quebec. Parizeau was clever but unwise. A catastrophe as leader, he illustrated how easily fear, rather than confidence, won in Quebec when it came to action instead of oratory on independence. He became a figure of fun.

The federal side was led by Jean Chrétien, a career politician who had started distributing Liberal pamphlets at the age of fifteen. Hard working, dedicated, and a true federalist, he was a fighter who resisted pressure from the "soft nationalists," who wanted more autonomy for Quebec within Canada. He became Minister of Justice in 1980, supported the *"Non"* forces in the referendum of that year, and became Prime Minister when the Tories collapsed in 1993. He faced the BQ as Official Opposition and Reform as the third party. He went on to win strong majorities in 1997 and 2000 against a badly splintered Opposition. He was known as "Trudeau's man," and showing total dedication himself, he insisted on party loyalty in his followers. He did better in combat than in easy times. On the eve of the 1995 referendum, he urged the people not to be fooled by ideas of a better Canada if Quebec separated, and a better Quebec if it were to separate. He said this was dangerous and false thinking.

Chrétien was blamed for the eventual narrowness of the referendum vote. He was accused of overconfidence, of doing little in the campaign and taking a *"Non"* victory for granted. He reacted to events, rather than promoting them. Very late, he promised to recognize a "distinct society," veto power over changes in Quebec's powers, and more decentralization. After the referendum, he led the passage of the Clarity Bill, which required that the wording of the question in any independence referendum would have to be clear (according to the judgement of the House of Commons) and that a clear majority would be needed before separation negotiations could begin. He also supported a federal court reference on the legality of secession. His government had been shaken by its near-miss in the referendum. In the summer of 2001, he trailed former Prime Minister Joe Clark in approval rating as a leader. But there was no credible alternative to his party.

Preston Manning went to Ottawa both to get the West into power and to promote radical conservatism with his Reform Party. He was the English-Canadian and especially the Western response to separatism. His theories were based on religion and individualism. Like Diefenbaker, he believed in "One Canada" and in himself as a nation builder, like Sir John A. Macdonald and Abraham Lincoln. He appealed to prejudice against Quebec and its language. Many of his ideas (such as initiative, recall, and referenda) were borrowed from the American Progressive movement circa 1900. He favoured an American-style Senate—equal, elected, and effective. Equality meant no special status for Quebec; for example, that province was to be no more favoured than Prince Edward Island. He wanted laissez-faire economics to be applied to all Canada's regions, and he wanted tax cuts, privatization, and more powers to be given to all the provinces and territories, including the veto against any constitutional amendments for British Columbia. Manning's self-appointed voice of Western protest helped wreck the constitutional process. He became Leader of the Opposition, and after the 1995 referendum, the Calgary Initiative in 1997 spelled out his position. Bouchard was gone.

From retirement, Trudeau opposed Meech Lake, Charlottetown, and the referendum. He wrote "J'accuse," a stinging attack on Bouchard, for his "stupid allegations" flowing "more from hallucinations than the science of politics." His influence helped the *"Non"* side, but his legacy in retaining Quebec in the Confederation was problematic. For instance, Quebec's discontent had grown when Trudeau repatriated the Constitution in 1982 without Quebec's agreement.

Province building in Alberta coincided with separatism in Quebec—and both stressed the prefix "con" in Confederation. Trudeau referred to Joe Clark as "the headwaiter for the provinces." The Albertan was a Red Tory who believed in the compact, or contract, theory of the Constitution. Significant powers over local affairs and guarantees for Quebec in language, religion, and education were favoured. If the terms of the original compact were violated by the central government, a province could withdraw. It should be a true confederation, rather than a federation or legislative union as envisaged by Macdonald. Clark's favourite phrase was "a community of communities," which meant devolution of powers. He, Mulroney, Broadbent, Lougheed, and the premiers were generally province builders, whose views collided with the national Liberals' centralization tendencies.

Mulroney, whose government had pushed the Meech Lake and Charlottetown accords, took no public part in the referendum. Once skilled in uniting Quebec and the West behind himself, he had become the most unpopular prime minister ever. But in Quebec, he was represented by the young and popular Jean Charest, who was Leader of the federal Conservative Party and a member of the *"Non"* Committee. In one memorable picture, Charest was seen waving his Canadian passport—a shot with similar implications to the one showing a huge Canadian flag being carried through the streets of Montreal on the shoulders of a crowd. He was an eloquent defender of

Canadian unity and was credited with saving the day during the 1995 referendum. He was a federalist with an appeal to the "soft nationalists" in Quebec. He survived the débâcle of the 1993 federal election, when the Progressive Conservatives lost all but 2 of their 151 seats, along with about half the votes they'd received in 1988 (going from 43 to 16 percent). Charest then became Conservative Leader in Quebec and later Leader of the Quebec Liberal Party.

The election of 1993 was a shock to the country's whole political system. The West and Quebec produced two parties based solely on regions: Manning's Reform Party and Bouchard's Bloc Québécois. Because of the concentration of their vote, they won many more seats than the traditional parties, which ran candidates in every riding. The anti-French and anti-English forces aroused by constitutional failures, led by Manning and Bouchard, crushed the Tories and the NDP, whose votes were "wasted" across the country. Manning's Reform Party won 52 seats, with 18.7 percent of the vote, while Bouchard's BQ won 54 seats with 13.5 percent. The PCs, with 16 percent, received only 2 seats, and the NDP, with 7 percent, won 9 seats . As a result of this, a few voices were raised for proportional representation. Canada's modified two-party system had become a multiparty one. The governing structure it engendered was called the "pizza Parliament."

The vote statistics of 1993 were repeated, more or less, in 1997 and 2000. The Liberal hegemony (177 seats and 41.3 percent of the vote in 1993, 155 seats and 38.5 percent in 1997, and 170 seats and 40.1 percent in 2000) made Chrétien a long-serving prime minister like Macdonald, Laurier, King, and Trudeau. The voters were choosing the only party that had the chance of winning and keeping the country together; they rejected the four remaining small or regional groups. Most of the government seats came from a split vote and a sweep in Ontario, but it also had a national reach. The Bloc and the Reform/Canadian Alliance surprised observers by their appearance and even more by their tenacity. They were the "two solitudes," whose attitudes of mutual contempt made for a House of fractious debates. Solitary but far from silent.

Just as the election of 1984 had shown a glittering national unity, the 1993 results revealed an alarming disunity and were the prelude to the 1995 Quebec referendum. The referendum campaign began shortly after the PQ assumed office in September 1994. They drafted a law for the second referendum, and public hearings then took place during the winter of 1994–1995. The bill was debated in the National Assembly and voted into legislation. The PQ had set the agenda and the dates. The referendum question was agreed upon by the "Oui" side—the PQ, the BQ, and the ADQ (l'Action Démocratique du Québec, led by Mario Dumont)—as a common project to achieve sovereignty and a formal proposal for a new economic and political partnership with Canada. It read:

Do you agree that Quebec should become sovereign after having made a formal offer to Canada for a new economic and political partnership within the scope of the bill respecting the future of Quebec and of the agreement signed on June 12, 1995?

It sounded like simply ratifying a fait accompli. Bouchard had taken over from Parizeau.

The timetable looked like a blueprint for a march toward sovereignty, which had gained popularity since the 1960s and especially in the 1990s. According to the nationalists' plans, if the negotiations with Canada failed, Quebec would be empowered to declare unilateral sovereignty immediately; one year was allowed for negotiations— not to be exceeded unless approved by the National Assembly. If it desired, the new state of Quebec could use the Canadian dollar and have access to external markets. There were to be joint institutions between Canada and Quebec—a council, an assembly, and a tribunal. Twenty-five percent of the assembly's seats would be reserved for Quebec, and the newly independent entity would have as many ministers as Canada. Decisions would require a unanimous vote, and Canada and Quebec would each have a veto. The tribunal would settle disputes, and its decisions would be binding.

The key figures on the "no" side were Daniel Johnson, the Quebec Liberal leader; Prime Minister Jean Chrétien; and Jean Charest, who at the time was Leader of the federal Conservatives. The Prime Minister took little part in the campaign until the last moment, leaving that work to Johnson and Charest. The referendum had moral, if not legal, authority, and its results were a near-disaster for the country. The final count was almost too close to call. Of the 4,757,509 who voted, there was a 1.16 percent majority, or 54,288 votes, for the "no" side. Cries of foul were heard, especially from the "no" side. Some 50,000 votes had been declared invalid and thrown out for a variety of reasons. Montreal's allophones (people who spoke French, English, and another, native, tongue) had almost all voted "no" with the anglophones and some francophones. From all over Canada people had gone to rallies in Montreal, to show Quebeckers they wanted them to stay in Confederation..

The province was split in half: 50.6 percent "no" and 49.4% "yes." The voter participation rate had been a staggering 93 percent on October 30, referendum day. This was even greater than the May 20, 1980, high turnout of 84 percent on May 20, 1980, when the results were a more convincing 59.5 percent "no" and 40.5 percent "yes." Fifteen years had passed, and 9 percent had swung their votes from "no" to "yes." Why?

The close result was partly the child of failed constitutional reform—especially the collapse of the Meech Lake Accord. It was taken as final proof that Quebec could never get enough power and security in Canada for its "distinct society." The terminology used to described Quebec's possible new status had also changed. Although the word "sovereign" was used in the referendum question, the terms "independence" and "separation" had been used in pre-referendum debates and publicity. They had infinitely softer, vaguer connotations. Polls consistently showed that many voters believed they could have sovereignty (whatever that meant) and remain in Canada just the same (they knew what that meant). Hence, the "soft" nationalists could have safety, as well as the nation-state of their dreams. The federal government let such notions gain acceptance as the PQ set the agenda on their own terms. By the time Ottawa realized what was going on, it was almost too late; and they responded, as people do in such cases, with too little, too late.

There was a basic ambiguity in Quebec's position. Its citizens did not want to decide between separation and remaining in Canada. Many genuinely wanted to be both Quebeckers and Canadians as Prime Minister Chrétien said he was. They wanted the best of both worlds, and they were largely left to decide on their own, as there was silence in the rest of Canada—perhaps because of fear of saying the wrong thing or of interfering in Quebec's decision. On both sides, then, there was fear, and in Quebec there was doubt. When in doubt, it is easier to vote for the status quo, especially if one is not being pushed. So in the end, a majority (however slim) did vote for the status quo.

The 9 percent who switched from "Non" to "Oui" between 1980 and 1995 were francophones who had deserted the provincial Liberals. They were targeted by the PQ and were listening to the ADQ, whose numbers were increasing. The disillusioned Liberals who had left the party may have been attracted by the ADQ because it was a new party that supported the Allaire Report. (The Allaire Report proposed a decentralized federal system and increased powers for Quebec.) Did they then feel relief or disappointment when they saw the results? Imagine the implications if there had been 10 percent of them ... or more.

What happened next was a surprise to those who had listened to the oratory and scrutinized the results. There was no secession, no civil war, no partition, no large exodus of refugees, no humanitarian crisis, and there were no executions. A few moderate steps were taken to respond to the grievances of Quebec and the West. These took the form of resolutions, acts, court referrals, and more discussions. For this was Canada, that unusual nation, seeking its identity, in most cases peacefully, while discussing both unity and separation.

One month after the referendum, Prime Minister Chrétien began to deliver on the commitments he made during the referendum campaign:

- to recognise that Quebec is a Distinct Society ...
- not to proceed with any constitutional change that affects Quebec without Quebecers' consent ...
- and to undertake changes to bring services and the decision-making process closer to citizens, initially in the field of labor-market training.

First, a simple parliamentary resolution declared Quebec a "distinct society." Chrétien said, "This is just the start of a process of change, not the final outcome. What is important is that those changes be innovative and realistic and respect the will of Canadians. The initiatives for change that I have announced today clearly go in that direction." Secondly, a bill was introduced in Parliament, proposing that Quebec, Ontario, the Atlantic, and the Western provinces be given a veto against any constitutional amendments—including changes to federal institutions like the Senate, the creation of new provinces, and the distribution of powers. The federal government was thus lending its veto to four regions of the country, and later British Columbia was included as a fifth region. Finally, the federal government withdrew from its apprenticeship-training system, cooperative education programs, and workplace training—clearly a devolution of powers.

The Chrétien government also made a court referral, asking for an opinion on the absolute right to unilateral sovereignty being claimed in Quebec. The Supreme Court ruled that Quebec did not have this right either under the Constitution or under international law. It noted that if Quebec voters demonstrated a clear desire for sovereignty, not just a simple majority, then there was an obligation for Ottawa and the other provinces to negotiate. But there was no guarantee that such negotiations would succeed or that the territory of Quebec would remain intact, for minorities within Quebec had to be respected. Internationally, there was no right to separation except for colonies and oppressed peoples, and this was not Quebec's case. This court decision marked the first time a democratic country had ever tested in advance the terms of its separation.

The *Clarity Act* of 2000 added to the Supreme Court's findings on the legitimacy of referenda on separation. There had to be a clear expression of the will of the people in that province on secession, not just on a mandate to negotiate. Canada's House of Commons would oversee the process to ensure that the views of all were taken into account, and it could determine whether any referendum question was in fact clear. The *Clarity Act* also addressed the issue of the size of the "majority" of valid votes in a referendum, the percentage of eligible voters voting, the views of Aboriginal people in the province, and other matters. In short, the secession of Quebec would not generate a civil war like the mid-nineteenth-century conflict in the United States, but it would be no simple matter. Lucien Bouchard had indicated that there would be a third referendum when "winning conditions" existed. It was "inevitable," he said. In that case, there would at least be negotiation principles in place, as outlined in the *Clarity Act*, which could help prevent open conflict.

Chrétien also urged the premiers to accept the Calgary Declaration, another attempt to heal the wounds of the 1995 referendum. In September 1997 it was approved by all the provincial premiers outside Quebec. This document, coming from the West, the business community, Preston Manning, and the Reform Party, represented an effort to unite the country. Quebec was recognized as having a "unique character," and the declaration also stated that powers Quebec received in future constitutional amendments should be automatically available to all the provinces. The West had taken the initiative and Manning was learning French. Plan A (the option of making Canada a more attractive place to stay) now existed, and it replaced Plan B (the terms of secession being spelled out in the *Clarity Act* if nothing could be obtained from Canada).

In February 1999 the "social union" agreement came into being. It supported the equality of all Canadians and commitments not to erect any new barriers to mobility. Within three years, according to this agreement, any residency-based policies that constrained access to postsecondary education or training in health and social services had to be eliminated. There was to be consultation and cooperation and avoidance of unilateral decisions that could undermine confidence in the social program partnership.

Thus, after the 1995 referendum, there were no bold actions, no meetings of a great tribunal to mediate between Quebec and ROC (the rest of Canada), no treaty to set up a joint currency. There was a simple feeling that, besides taking its unity mini-steps with the ever-cautious Chrétien, the country should move on to other things. What could be done to increase interprovincial and international trade? How could Canada meet the challenge of globalization? How should the ever-closer relationship with Washington be handled? It was time to look outwards.

Self-absorption and internecine struggles passed away in a wave of citizen fatigue. Students at the Laval University Law School had once focused on the 1981 "night of the long knives," when premiers of the provinces outside Quebec had come to their own agreement with the federal government about the Constitution—leaving Quebec out of the discussions. But now they saw the Charter of Rights and Freedoms attached to the constitution as an inspiring document and useful in court.

There might never be a final solution, a carved-in-stone identity, but the search could be put to rest for a while. Through ten crises, Canada was a work-in-progress. And, after all, in 1997, the United Nations had rated Canada the best country in the world.

Comments and documents relating to the 1995 Referendum Crisis are given in Chapter 22, Commentaries on Quebec and the 1995 Referendum.

NOTES

1   See "Economy—Forging Strong Links" on www.budget.finances.gouv.qc.ca/budget 2001 2002/en/maillon/economie.

2   See Quebec International Trade & Investment, Aerospace, on www.gouv.qc.ca/portail/quebec/?lang=en.

PART II
SOURCES AND DOCUMENTS

12 ❧ CONTROVERSY OVER THE PROBLEM OF THE NATION

INTERPRETATIONS BY FRENCH CANADIANS

Emile Paladilhe (1844–1926) composed "Comme Nos Péres." It praised the spirit and the character of the early French pioneers in North America and revealed pride in French Canada's past. The poet recommended the ancestral qualities of courage, endurance, loyalty, and religious zeal to his generation in the late nineteenth century.

Comme Nos Pères

Sortis de la vieille Armorique,
Nos pères, marins et soldats,
Pour peupler le sol d'Amérique
D'une race altière et stoïque,
Ont livré de rudes combats.
Ces preux à la robuste épaule
Voulaient, fiers de leur noble rôle,
Sur le rivage canadien,
A la gloire du nom chrétien,
Fonder une nouvelle Gaule.

Chorus
Comme eux, pleins de mâle fierté,
Poursuivons partout notre rêve
De progrès, de fraternité!
Travaillons et luttons sans trêve
Pour l'Honneur, pour le Droit et pour la Liberté!

Forts d'un zèle que rien n'altère,
Sans peur et sans fiel, nox aïeux,
Sous le brocart ou sous la haire,
Bravaient l'Iroquois sanguinaire
Au fond des grands bois ténébreux.
Partout ils portaient la lumière,
Et saluaient lac ou rivière
Au nom du Christ, au nom des rois;
Puis y plantaient une humble croix
Auprès d'une blanche bannière …

De ces lutteurs d'une autre France,
Aussi fervents que valeureux,
Nous avons gardé la constance,
Et, vibrants de leur espérance,
Nous saurons triompher comme eux.
Leurs croyances sont nos cuirasses,
Et sur nos bords, parmi les races
A qui Dieu voulut nous unir,
Resplendira notre avenir,
Si nous suivons toujours leurs traces …

Emile Paladilhe

L.O. David, one of the Rouge historians of late nineteenth-century Quebec, has left us his analysis of the French-Canadian character, its good qualities and its faults. The picture is a traditional one.

Comme peuple et comme individus, les Canadiens-français ont les qualités et les défauts de leur origine, mais modifiés considérablement par les circonstances de temps, de lieu, de climat, par leur contact avec le race anglo-saxonne. Ainsi, quoique l'esprit et le caractère français se manifestent clairement chez nos compatriotes, il est incontestable que nous sommes moins ardents, moins chauds, moins enthousiastes que nos cousins de France. D'un autre côté, nous ne sommes pas aussi froids, graves, solennels et pratiques que nos concitoyens d'origine anglo-saxonne. Nos qualités sont nombreuses. Notre population, celle de la campagne spécialement, a conservé tous les traits caractéristiques de ses ancêtres, des Français de cette époque. Elle est croyante, patriotique, morale, laborieuse et bienveillante.

Sa moralité ne peut être contestée, les statistiques criminelles l'établissent clairement. La proportion des crimes et des délits, dans la province de Québec en dehors des villes spécialement, est inférieure à celle de toutes les autres provinces. Elle aime l'ordre, la paix; elle respecte les lois et les chefs de l'Eglise et de l'état; elle fait la sourde oreille aux théories funestes du socialisme et de la libre pensée. Elle a un gros bon sens qui la protège contre les exagérations dangereuses, les extravagances ridicules. Depuis quelque temps, les journaux anglais se plaisent à lui reconnaître ces qualités et à proclamer qu'elle est pour le Canada un élément de force morale, une source d'idées saines et de bons sentiments.

Nous pouvons affirmer sans hésitation que les Canadiens-français sont doués d'un bon caractère, d'une nature douce, paisible, bienveillante, que leur jugement est sain, leur esprit droit, leur imagination vive et fertile. Ils ont un talent inné pour les beaux-arts, l'éloquence, la littérature, la poésie, la musique et la fine industrie— un talent bien français.

L.O. David, Les gerbes canadiennes (Montreal, 1921), 248–49.

Jean-Marc Léger expressed the French nationalist and separatist point of view in a series of articles in Le Devoir in October 1967. In his opinion, French Canada could not survive much longer without being assimilated by the Anglo-Saxon majority.

The truth is that we are a people in danger of death, and we now have, doubtless for the last time in our history, the opportunity for a genuine choice on the most essential point. It is childish to think that we can plan our collective future in the way one plans the various stages of building some industrial complex: that we might first try out the "special-status" solution for ten years or so, after which we would go on to the system of associate states for another decade and finally, if circumstances seemed favourable, proclaim our independence. It certainly would take less than ten years before French Canada would have to choose between life and death, between having a fatherland and consenting to a slow submersion in the Anglo-Saxon sea.

Far from being the daydream or the mad adventure that some would call it, independence is at the same time the only logical result of our situation and the absolute pre-condition for a natural life. Without its inspiration, the struggle for survival would be only a rear-guard action, an odious deception. If we can control our irrational reflexes of conservatism and false sentiment, we will recognize that the independence of Quebec and Canada represents (in a world of diversity and interdependence) a formula of dignity and reason and our great chance for organic co-operation. Tomorrow, English Canada would be grateful to Quebec for bringing it about.

For Quebec, in fact, independence is a vital necessity; for Canada, Quebec's independence is the prerequisite to a fuller development. For the two states this would provide a new and fruitful start. For we are a dead weight on English Canada, and we ourselves lead a mutilated existence. Canada in its present form is condemned to mediocrity. In a permanent atmosphere of mistrust, bad humour, and general dissatisfaction, what do we find? An endless series of delicate and crippled compromises, negotiations forever underway on age-old problems and new situations, a shocking waste of time, money, and talent in attempts to hold the pieces together and, above all, to preserve the illusion in the weaker of the two partners that he is "just as equal as the other." Does anyone believe that a country can survive and progress in the atmosphere that has prevailed for the last few years? And things are not about to improve, for the requirements of our time and the natural inclinations of the Anglo-Saxons will lead to increased centralization. And at every stage this will be less favourable for Quebec, until the day when its very name no longer expresses a distinct entity, for the Franco-Quebec nation will have become a minority in its own home.

Fifteen years of difficult discussions between ministers of justice and heads of governments were needed to reach a difficult agreement on the simple matter of amending the constitution—an agreement which Quebec was finally to discard. At the most optimistic estimate, Quebec would need twenty-five years of negotiations to obtain an *ersatz* special status (and by that time, in the year 2000, the probable English-speaking majority in Quebec, made up of Britons and anglicized New Quebeckers, would not even want such a special status) ...

If the people of Quebec, adopting the terms of the preamble to the American Declaration of Independence, should be asked to "declare the causes which persuade them to independence," they would be obliged to add to the "free right of peoples to self-determination" another reason: the slow suicide that membership in this federation means. Under siege for so long, our nation now is under attack: its economic position is continually worsening, not only in Canada as a whole but in Quebec itself. The masses of immigrants arriving in its territory add the weight of their numbers to the English-speaking minority (who would, without them, amount to eight or nine percent rather than twenty or twenty-one percent). The use of the French language, and its usefulness, recede continually, especially in Montreal. We are on the way to losing Montreal, if we have not already done so, and the rot in the metropolis, the cancer of French Canada, is an indication of what will happen tomorrow in all Quebec …

The tools of salvation can be found only in national independence.

Selections from articles by Jean-Marc Léger entitled "Sovereignty, Condition of Salvation," published in *Le Devoir* 2, 3, 24, and 25 October 1967.

Pierre Vallières was a separatist and a terrorist. He was arrested in New York City in September 1966 for his association with the FLQ. He was detained by the American police for a number of months before being deported. While in prison, he wrote the following passage:

To be a "nigger" in America is to be not a man but someone's slave. For the rich white man of Yankee America, the nigger is a sub-man. Even the poor whites consider the nigger their inferior. They say: "to work as hard as a nigger", "to smell like a nigger", "as dangerous as a nigger", "as ignorant as a nigger". Very often they do not even suspect that they too are niggers, slaves, "white niggers". White racism hides the reality from them by giving them the opportunity to despise an inferior, to crush him mentally or to pity him. But the poor whites who despise the black man are doubly niggers, for they are victims of one more form of alienation—racism—which far from liberating them, imprisons them in a net of hate or paralyzes them in fear of one day having to confront the black man in a civil war.

In Quebec the French Canadians are not subject to this irrational racism that has done so much wrong to the workers, white and black, of the United States. They can take no credit for that, since in Quebec there is no "black problem." The liberation struggle launched by the American blacks nevertheless arouses growing interest among the French-Canadian population, for the workers of Quebec are aware of their condition as niggers, exploited men, second-class citizens. Have they not been, ever since the establishment of New France in the seventeenth century, the servants of the imperialists, the white niggers of America? Were they not *imported,* like the American blacks, to serve as cheap labour in the New World? The only difference between them is the colour of their skin and the continent they came from. After three centuries, their condition remains the same. They still constitute a reservoir of cheap labour whom the capitalists are completely free to put to work or reduce to unemployment, as it suits their financial interests, whom they are completely free to underpay, mistreat and trample underfoot, whom they are completely free, according to law, to have clubbed down by the police and locked up by the judges "in the public interest," when their profits seem to be in danger.

Pierre Vallières, *White Niggers of America: The Precocious Autobiography of a Quebec "Terrorist"* (New York, 1971), 21–22.

Gilles Vigneault, an auteur-poète from the fishing village of Natashquan on the North Shore of the St. Lawrence, wrote the song "Mon Pays," which became popular in the 1960s. He refused to identify the subject as either Quebec or Canada, describing it simply as "a song seeking for identification and finding none."

Mon Pays

Chorus
Mon pays ce n'est pas un pays c'est l'hiver
Mon jardin ce n'est pas un jardin c'est la plaine
Mon chemin ce n'est pas un chemin c'est la neige
Mon pays ce n'est pas un pays c'est l'hiver

Dans la blanche cérémonie
Où la neige au vent se marie
Dans ce pays de poudrerie
Mon père a fait bâtir maison
Et je m'en vais être fidèle
A sa manière à son modèle
La chambre d'amis sera telle
Qu'on viendra des autres saisons
Pour se bâtir à côté d'elle.

De mon grand pays solitaire
Je crie avant que de me taire
A tous les hommes de la terre
Ma maison c'est votre maison
Entre mes quatre murs de glace
J'ai mis mon temps et mon espace

A préparer le feu, la place
Pour les humains de l'horizon
Et les humains sont de ma race

Mon pays ce n'est pas un pays c'est l'envers
D'un pays qui n'était ni pays ni patrie
Ma chanson ce n'est pas ma chanson c'est ma vie
C'est pour toi que je veux posséder mes hivers

Gilles Vigneault, *Avec les vieux mots* (Ottawa, 1964), 13.

Georges Dor, a broadcaster for CBC Radio-Canada, recorded the song "J'suis Québécois" after the 1970 October Crisis, during a concert in Montreal to protest the presence of federal troops. A shortened version was published two years later under the title "Je suis Québéquoi?" It shows the Quebecker's search for identity.

Je Suis Québéquoi?

Je suis Québéquois
je sais pas pourquoi
peut-être pour rien
peut-être pour rire
en attendant qu'on soit plus rien
en attendant qu'on puisse en rire
en attendant de plus être personne.
je suis Québéquoi qu'est-ce que ça me donne
je me demande souvent
bien souvent quoi … ?

Je suis Québéquois
je sais pas pour qui
peut-être pour elle
peut-être pour lui
peut-être aussi pour les amis
qui sont des Québéquois comme *ME*

des Québéquois d'un peu partout
de Québec ou de Rimouski
mais je me demande
souvent pour qui … ?

Georges Dor, *Poèmes et chansons d'amour et d'autre chose* (Montreal, 1991).

INTERPRETATIONS BY ENGLISH CANADIANS

In the late nineteenth century, English Canadians were sure of their British identity, proud of their Protestant faith, and fond of looking back with admiring eyes to their Loyalist forbears. William Kirby proudly called himself "the last of the Loyalists" and composed this verse to honour his ancestors.

The Hungry Year

The war was over. Seven red years of blood
Had scourged the land from mountain-top to sea;
(So long it took to rend the mighty frame
Of England's empire in the western world).
With help of foreign arms and foreign gold,
Base faction and the Bourbon's mad revenge,
Rebellion won at last; and they who loved
The cause that had been lost, and kept their faith
To England's crown, and scorned an alien name,

Passed into exile; leaving all behind
Except their honour, and the conscious pride
Of duty done to country and to king.

Broad lands, ancestral homes, the gathered wealth
Of patient toil and self-denying years
Were confiscate and lost; for they had been
The salt and savour of the land; trained up
In honour, loyalty, and fear of God:
The wine upon the lees, decanted when

They left their native soil, with sword-belts drawn
The tighter; while the women, only, wept
At thought of old firesides no longer theirs
At household treasures left, and all the land
Upset and ruled by rebels to the king.

Not drooping like poor fugitives, they came
In exodus to our Canadian wilds;
But full of heart and hope, with heads erect
And fearless eyes victorious in defeat.
With thousand toils they forced their devious way
Through the great wilderness of silent woods
That gloomed o'er lake and stream, till higher rose
The northern star above the broad domain
Of half a continent, still theirs to hold,
Defend, and keep forever as their own,
Their own and England's, to the end of time.

Annals of Niagara (Welland, 1896), 70–71.

Colonel George T. Denison, a proud British patriot, addressed the Sons of England in Toronto on the evening of 27 February 1891. He defined English Canada in terms of its Loyalist ancestry and recommended the loyalty, sense of law and order, honour, and courage under adversity of the Loyalists to their descendants.

There is an immense significance in the fact ... that the U.E. Loyalists, leaving all other possessions behind them, brought with them the Ten Commandments, the Bible, and the sacred vessels of communion, as the most precious relics of their old homes in the Thirteen Colonies ... In war, they proved themselves to be of the truest mettle; in peace, industrious, law-abiding and honourable, and it may be recorded that while during the course of the revolutionary struggle, not a few of the eminent men of the rebellion drew off and returned to their allegiance, it cannot be recorded that a single U.E. Loyalist, either for family, for property, or any consideration whatever, went over to the enemy ... The Pilgrim Fathers, a few in number, came to America leisurely, bringing with them all their goods and the price of their possessions, at peace and secure under charter granted by their sovereign. The U.E. Loyalists, unlike them, came bleeding with the wounds of seven years of war, stripped of every earthly possession, and exiled from their native land.

Colonel George T. Denison, Address to the Sons of England, *Empire* (Toronto), 27 February 1891.

Charles G.D. Roberts, in his patriotic History of Canada published in Toronto in 1897, repeated the common idea of his day that the American Revolution had "sifted" the Thirteen Colonies and left the best men for the north.

But the destiny that governs nations was working to great ends. It was decreed that of stern and well-tried stuff should be built a nation to inherit the northern half of this continent ... They brought to our making about thirty thousand people, of the choicest stock the colonies could boast. They were an army of leaders, for it was the loftiest heads which attracted the hate of the revolutionists. The most influential judges, the most distinguished lawyers, the most capable and prominent physicians, the most highly educated of the clergy ... were the Loyalists ... For having remained true to their allegiance they were hounded to the death as traitors. Canada owes deep gratitude to her southern kinsmen who, thus, from Maine to Georgia, picked out their choicest spirits, and sent them forth to people our northern wilds.

Charles G. D. Roberts, *A History of Canada* (Toronto, 1897), 195.

English Canadians looked back to the War of 1812 as the great vindication of Canada against the United States. Here, Canadians had demonstrated their courage under fire against great numbers. Here, the new nation had proved that it could not be overrun and defeated. "The Khan," a patriotic poet who chose an unusual pen name, wrote "The Frontier Way." J. Cawdor Bell, an amateur poet, composed the ditty "Grandfather's Gun of Eighteen-Twelve." Both poems ring with pride in the achievements of Canadians in the War of 1812.

The Frontier Way or CANADA IS NOT COMING

As I stood on the frontier way,
I heard the indignant people say,
"Who fought and bled to save our rights
At Chateauguay and Queenston Heights,
Who is it fills each silent grave
That marks the hill or dots the plain?
The dust of patriots true and brave,
Who if they lived would cry again
"You're welcome as the flowers of May."
To Queenston Heights and *Chateauguay!*

As I went up the frontier way,
I heard the patriot people say,
"No alien flag shall ever wave
Above the hero's honoured grave.
No alien heel shall e'er defile
Each green and grassy diadem;
No cunning tongue shall wean or wile
The shelter of our swords from them.
Their name shall never pass away,
From Queenston Heights and Chateauguay."

"The Khan" (Library and Archives Canada: Denison Papers, vol. 35: scrapbook).

Grandfather's Gun of Eighteen-Twelve

Some blowin'-adder paper men
Out over there in Yankeedom,
Say we're to them as one to ten,
And woe betide us if they come,
I've said before, 'twixt Christian lands,
It's time hard feelin's for to shelve:
But, Brock my boy, put in my hands
Grandfather's gun of eighteen-twelve.

She's not a beauty, but she did
Her duty in that ugly scrap;
That bay' net on her nozzle rid
Our Canada of many a chap
As thought we Canucks in the snow
Were only fit to chop and delve.
But here's what taught 'em 'twasn't so:
Grandfather's gun of eighteen-twelve.

J. Cawdor Bell (Library and Archives Canada: Denison Papers, vol. 35: scrapbook).

Donald Creighton, a leading historian in English Canada and author of the classic biography of Sir John A. Macdonald, expressed the federalist point of view in an article in Saturday Night in September 1966. Cultural matters, he wrote, were not uppermost when the Constitution was written. Nevertheless, the BNA Act offered the best protection possible for the French fact in North America.

For six years, ever since the lately deposed Premier Jean Lesage won power in the Province of Quebec, English Canadians have been subjected to what is undoubtedly the most extreme example of the political hard sell in their entire experience. For six long years, the advocates of French-Canadian "nationalism: have used every conceivable form of persuasion, compulsion, shock, and menace to compel English Canadians to buy a particular view of Confederation and of French Canada's place in it. This prolonged siege of promotion, like every other well-organized campaign of commercial pressure, has certainly had its conquests. A good many English Canadians, faced with this rapid, interminable flow of sales talk, have acted as simple, gullible, badly informed consumers often do: they have bought the product.

Like all successful promoters, the French-Canadian nationalists hit upon a completely novel approach, a gimmick, for their campaign. English Canadians had always known about French Canada and the problem of its relation with the nation as a whole. Our fathers and grandfathers had called this "the race question." But the phrase had an antiquated, nineteenth century look. It plainly wouldn't do as a modern slogan. Something much more up-to-date, more impressive, more vaguely "sociological" was obviously required. And, in a happy moment of inspiration, the French-Canadian theorists found it. They began to insist that "ethnic and cultural values" were, and ought to be recognized as, the fundamental values in Canadian society. They appropriated two fine, big words, "bilingualism" and "biculturalism," to describe the ideal at which Canadian society ought to aim ...

The acceptance of these values as basic implied a completely new way of looking at Canada and Canadian Confederation. It grotesquely exaggerated the importance of language and culture; it absurdly minimized the importance of everything else ... It didn't matter very much whether Canadian Confederation provided good government and promoted economic growth. It didn't matter very much whether Canada was united at home and respected abroad. All that really mattered was whether Confederation satisfied French-Canadian cultural needs and fulfilled French-Canadian cultural aspirations ...

No, the movement to reconstitute Canada in the interest of bilingualism and biculturalism can have only one probable outcome—the creation of a separate, or virtually separate, Quebec. This could happen in one of two ways—either gradually and tacitly through the present decentralizing policies of the federal government, or suddenly and openly as a result of a positive decision to break up the federal union. The process of decentralization could conceivably go so far that Canada would lose the power to cope with a serious political or economic crisis and would simply disintegrate under its pressure. Or alternatively, the campaign for French-Canadian nationalism could be carried to the point at which English Canada would finally decide, in disgust and indignation, that it had had enough.

Either of these outcomes is now possible. If present tendencies continue, one or the other may become the probable destiny of Confederation. The division of Canada into two unequal parts, English and French, would mean an uncertain and hazardous future for both; but it would carry a far greater and more fundamental danger for the smaller than for the larger of the two divisions. It might result in the political disintegration of English Canada; but for French Canada its consequences would be cultural as well, in the broadest and deepest sense of the word. Separation would leave French Canada a small, exposed, culturally indefensible community in a monolithic English-speaking continent. Separation would probably mean the loss of political independence for both English Canada and French Canada. It would also mean the rapid decline and eventual extinction of the French language in North America.

The French language has survived in North America for one reason only: because Canada has survived. The Fathers of Confederation reached a settlement which gave the French language the best chance it will ever have on this continent. And if we try to improve on that settlement, we do so at our peril.

Norman Sheffe., ed., Canadian/Canadien, Issues for the Seventies Series (Toronto, 1971), 8–16.

From Donald Creighton, "The Myth of Biculturalism or The Great French-Canadian Sales Campaign," *Saturday Night*, September 1966.

Earle Birney, an English-Canadian poet, expressed the twentieth-century search for national identity. The points of reference were French, English, and American, and the poet wondered if the nation would ever grow up.

Canada: Case History

This is the case of a highschool land
deadset in adolescence
loud treble laughs and sudden fists
bright cheeks the gangling presence
This boy is oriented well to sports
and the doctors say he's healthy
he's taken to church on Sunday still
and keeps his prurience stealthy
Doesn't like books (except about bears)
collects new coins old slogans jets
and never refuses a dare
His Uncle spoils him with candy of course
but shouts him down when he talks at table
You'll note he has some of his French mother's looks
though he's not so witty and no more stable
He's really much more like his Father and yet
 if you say so he'll pull a great face
He wants to be different from everyone else
and daydreams of winning the global race
Parents unmarried and living apart
relatives keen to bag the estate
schizophrenia not excluded—
will he learn to grow up before it's too late?
Ottawa 1945

Earle Birney, *Selected Poems, 1940–1966* (Toronto, 1966), 95.

Can. Hist.

Once upon a colony
there was a land that was
almost a real
country called Canada
But people began to
feel
different
and no longer *Acadien*
or French
and rational
but *Canadien*
and *Mensch*
and passional

Also no longer English
but Canadian
and national
(though some were less specifically Canadian
Pacific)

After that it was fashionable
for a time to be Internationable
But now we are all quite
grown up and fir-
-mly agreed to assert our right
to be Amer-
icans perhaps
or possibly
not Amer-
icans

except for the French
who still want to Mensch
1962

Earle Birney, *Near False Creek Mouth* (Toronto, 1964), 31.

13 ❧ REFLECTIONS ON THE CONQUEST

WHAT DID THE SURRENDER OF QUEBEC MEAN?

Written into the Articles of Surrender in 1759 were certain safeguards for the Roman Catholic faith. But not all the requests submitted by the French were granted.

The Capitulation of Quebec, 1759

Article VI

French Request

That the exercise of the Catholic, Apostolic, and Roman religion shall be maintained: and that safeguards shall be granted to the houses of the clergy, and to the monasteries, particularly to his Lordship the Bishop of Quebec, who animated with zeal for religion and charity for the people of his diocese, desires to reside in it constantly

British Reply

The free exercise of the Roman religion is granted, likewise safeguards to all religious persons, as well as to the Bishop, who shall be at liberty to come and exercise, freely and with decency, the functions of his office ..."

Article XXVII

French Request

... These people shall be obliged, by the English Government, to pay their Priests the tithes, and all the taxes they were used to pay under the Government of his most Christian Majesty.

British Reply

Granted, as to the free exercise of their religion, the obligation of paying the tithes to the Priests will depend on the King's pleasure.

Article XXX

French Request	British Reply
… His most Christian Majesty shall continue to name the Bishop of the colony, who shall always be of the Roman communion, and under whose authority the people shall exercise the Roman Religion.	Refused

Article XXXIV

French Request	British Reply
All the communities, and all the priests, shall preserve their moveables, the property and revenues of the Seignories and other estates, which they possess in the colony … and the same estates shall be preserved in their privileges, rights, honours, and exemptions.	Granted

Article XLI

French Request	British Reply
The French, Canadians, and Acadians of what state and condition soever, who shall remain in the colony, shall not be forced to take arms against his most Christian Majesty, or his Allies, directly or indirectly, on any occasion whatsoever; the British Government shall only require of them an exact neutrality.	They become Subjects of the King.

Reginald Coupland, The Quebec Act: A Study in Statesmanship (Oxford, 1925), Appendix A, 197–205.

Abandoned by France!

At the time of the Conquest, French Canadians felt a sharp and bitter sense of abandonment by France. Octave Crémazie, the leading poet of the nineteenth-century Patriotic School of Quebec, recaptured this sense of loss in his poem "Chant du Vieux Soldat Canadien."

Chant du Vieux Soldat Canadien

Pauvre soldat, aux jours de ma jeunesse,
Pour vous, Français, j'ai combattu longtemps;
Je viens encore, dans ma triste vieillesse,
Attendre ici vos guerriers triomphants.
Ah! bien longtemps vous attendrai-je encore
Sur ces remparts où je porte mes pas?
De ce grand jour quand verai-je l'aurore?
Dis-moi, mon fils, ne paraissent-ils pas?

…

Et le vieux soldat croit, illusion touchante!
Que la France, longtemps de nos rives absente,
Y ramène aujourd'hui ses guerriers triomphants,
Et que sur notre fleuve elle est encore maîtresse:
Son cadavre poudreux tressaille d'allégresse,
Et lève vers le ciel ses bras reconnaissants.

Octave Crémazie, *Poésies* (Montreal, 1925), 111–13.

After their desertion by their old mother country, the French Canadians came to realize that they had a destiny of their own in the New World. But to fulfill their destiny, they had to preserve intact their nationality and their religion, in a word, to survive.

Fête Nationale

Il est sur le sol d'Amérique
Un doux pays aimé des cieux,
Où la nature magnifique
Prodigue ses dons merveilleux.
Ce sol, fécondé par la France
Qui régna sur ses bords fleuris,
C'est notre amour, notre espérance
Canadiens, c'est notre pays.

Pour conserver cet héritage
Que nous ont légué nos aïeux,
Malgré les vents, malgré l'orage,
Soyons toujours unis comme eux.
Marchons sur leur brillante trace,
De leurs vertus suivons la loi,
Ne souffrons pas que rien efface
Et notre langue et notre foi.

Octave Crémazie, *Poésies* (Montreal, 1925), 150.

THE BARGAIN WITH THE ENGLISH—GOOD OR BAD?

Louis Fréchette saw the good side of the bargain in his poem "Le Drapeau Anglais." The British had kept their word. The French nationality and the Roman Catholic faith flourished under their banner, the best guarantee of French Canada's heritage. Good relations were possible between the two races.

Le Drapeau Anglais

Regarde, me disait mon père,
Ce drapeau vaillamment porté;
Il a fait ton pays prospère,
Et respecte ta liberté ...

Un jour, notre bannière auguste
Devant lui dut se replier;
Mais alors s'il nous fut injuste,
Il a su le faire oublier.

Et si maintenant son pli vibre
A nos remparts jadis gaulois,

C'est au moins sur un peuple libre
Qui n'a rien perdu de ses droits.

Oublions les jours de tempêtes;
Et, mon enfant, puisque aujourd'hui
Ce drapeau flotte sur nos têtes,
Il faut s'incliner devant lui ...

Louis Fréchette, *La légende d'un peuple* (Montreal, 1887), 195–96.

François Xavier Garneau, the founder of the French-Canadian school of historians, looked at the bad side. At the Conquest, he wrote in his Histoire du Canada, the French had had no choice but to submit to British rule to avoid assimilation by the Thirteen Colonies. In their hearts, they preserved hatred for all Anglo-Saxons.

Through a fear of jeopardizing their religion and nationality by entering into a confederation both Protestant and alien in blood—an apprehension not groundless, for the men of that confederation had already incorporated the French settlements of Louisiana—the clergy and seigniors resolved to resist every assault of the Anglo-Americans, and to retain our country for monarchic Britain, 3,000 miles distant; a patroness all the less likely, for that remoteness, to become perilously inimical to Canadian institutions ... They ever preserved in their hearts that hatred for the British race, wherever born or located ... and beyond.

F.X. Garneau, *History of Canada*, vol. 2 (Montreal, 1862), 360–61. Originally published as *Histoire du Canada* (Quebec, Impr. de N. Aubin).

SIR GUY CARLETON—HERO OR BUNGLER?

A.G. Bradley, writing in 1907, maintained that Sir Guy Carleton was a wise, generous, and far-seeing statesman. He maintained that the French Canadians should be allowed to keep their national institutions. It was due to Carleton, Bradley believed, that the French Canadians remained loyal at the time of the American invasion. They fought side by side with the British governor and his forces. In those dark days, Carleton saved Canada.

His jealousy for the honour of the British Crown and impatience of everything mean, dishonest or unjust that would cast a slur on it, was a leading note in his career. His kindness of heart was a byword, while his fair and liberal treatment of the king's new subjects, in accordance, as he thought, both with policy and justice, never wavered, though it often brought him temporary unpopularity with one side or the other. For this, however, or its opposite, Dorchester cared very little. Of strong personality and extreme independence of character, he was never swayed for a moment by what men might say or think of him; but his instincts were true and his heart was sound ... And this reputation, it should be remembered, was steadily maintained through two long terms of eight years apiece, so widely sundered that they almost represented two different generations of Canadians. No cases of undeserved hardship or neglected merit seem to have been too insignificant for Dorchester's attention ...

Against jobbery, whether in the grasping of fees, or in that odious and then too common custom of foisting incompetent deputies on the colony while politicians at home shared the plunder, he waged incessant war ... He desired to be fair to the French Canadians and thus frequently laid himself open to the accusation of a bias in favour of that nationality ... Above all, the trials of 1775–76 divided the sheep from the goats, and inclined a better feeling between the educated English and French who shared a common peril and fought side by side against a common enemy. It had been Dorchester's lot to govern Canada through periods of great political stress and in some moments of extraordinary peril. That he saved her to Great Britain in those years would alone entitle him to perpetual gratitude of Canada and of the Empire. But this achievement, conspicuous though it was, is very far from comprising the whole debt under which he has laid posterity. It was but a crowning incident in many years' record of less showy but valuable service.

A.G. Bradley, *Sir Guy Carleton* (Toronto, 1966). (Formerly *Lord Dorchester*, vol. 3, Makers of Canada Series (1907).)

A.L. Burt says that Bradley's view of Carleton is sentimental hog-wash, that his 1907 biography is "a work of adoration," which must be qualified by a new view of the facts. In Burt's view, Carleton made many mistakes, and if Canada was saved in 1775, it was due more to good luck than to good management. Carleton made two serious errors in judgement. His first was a misreading of the real nature of Canadian society; only the seigneurs were pleased with the Quebec Act, not the more numerous habitants. His second was an incredible bungling of the military opportunity presented by the weakness of the American forces. The truth was that he nearly lost Canada for the British Crown.

The Errors of the Quebec Act

In the practical application of the Quebec Act, Carleton made two fundamental errors that operated to defeat its purpose. One was his misconception of the nature of Canadian society. Although on various occasions he pointed out that the broad conditions of life on this continent made for democracy, he failed to see how these very conditions had produced in New France a society fundamentally different from that of Old France.

This difference has often been missed, even in our own day, but it is easily explained. With liberty forever beckoning through the trees and up the rivers beside their cottages, the habitants could not be ridden by feudal lords. The competition of the Old World was turned upside down in the New World. Here it was between seigniors for tenants, not between peasants for the land of the seigniors ... The habitants were devout Roman Catholics, but no slaves of the clergy. They absolutely refused to pay the tithe when a royal decree of 1663 introduced it at the same rate as in Old France ... Carleton ... fondly imagined that the habitants had been hewers of wood and drawers of water for the seigniors and the clergy and he sought to restore what had never existed in the country, a well-ordered society controlled through these leaders— who naturally fostered his illusion ... The seigniors were particularly delighted with Carleton's policy because he would make them what they had never been—the real lords of the land—and they were not discreet in their rejoicing at the prospect. This stirred uneasy feelings among the habitants, and they became more suspicious when they learned the nature of the new Council, to which Roman Catholics were now admitted by the Quebec Act ... Carleton picked seven Roman Catholics to represent the interests of the Canadian people. All seven were seigniors and the majority of them belonged to the haughtiest of their class, the wearers of the Croix de St. Louis.

A.L. Burt, *Guy Carleton, Lord Dorchester 1724–1808,* Canadian Historical Association Booklet no. 5, revised version (Ottawa, 1955), 5–6.

The Bungling of the American Invasion

A common mistake of reputable writers even today is to refer to Carleton as Sir Guy before he was knighted. He received that honour in July 1776 for successfully withstanding the siege of Quebec, an achievement that now appears to have been very much overrated. A close study of the siege reveals that from beginning to end the odds were so heavily against the Americans that Carleton would have deserved to be court-martialled had he lost the place. It is also wrong to say, as many still do, that by saving Quebec he saved Canada for the Empire. If by some mischance Quebec had fallen, the powerful army that arrived from Britain in May 1776 was well able to blow out any force that the Americans could have placed in that city ...

When the Americans saw the first ship of the approaching fleet, they fled in panic from Quebec ... Carleton had all the Americans in the country at his mercy; for, still ignorant of his overwhelming strength, they were reluctant to abandon Sorel until sixty British vessels approached it. He ordered General Burgoyne with 4,000 troops to follow the Americans up the Richelieu but not to press them until he himself, with the main army, cut off their retreat ... He was at Varennes, fourteen miles below Montreal, on the afternoon of Saturday, 15 June, and he could have reached his objective on Sunday while the Americans were still many miles below ... Carleton and his army did not arrive until the next day. If he had carried out his part of his own plan, he could have captured all the American forces in the country, and he could have seized all the shipping accumulated at St. Johns, which would have given him command of Lake Champlain. Carleton thus threw away not only a resounding victory that was in his hands but also the means of following it up that year by striking south with the powerful force that was sent to him at his own request to cut the rebellious colonies in two ... The military opportunity he threw away was lost forever.

A.L. Burt, *Guy Carleton, Lord Dorchester 1724–1808,* Canadian Historical Association Booklet no. 5, revised version (Ottawa, 1955), 7–9.

What Were the Terms of the Quebec Act?

And for the more perfect security and Ease of the Minds of the Inhabitants of the said Province, it is hereby declared, That His Majesty's Subjects professing the Religion of the Church of *Rome,* of, and in the same Province of *Quebec* ... may have, hold, and enjoy, the free Exercise of the Religion of the Church of *Rome,* subject to the King's Supremacy, declared and established by an Act made in the First Year of the Reign of Queen *Elizabeth* ... and that the Clergy of the said Church may hold, receive, and enjoy their accustomed Dues and Rights, with respect to such Persons only as shall profess the said Religion.

Provided nevertheless, That nothing herein contained shall extend, or be construed to extend, to the disabling ... (of) His Majesty, His Heirs or Successors ... from making ... such Provision for the Encouragement of the Protestant Religion, and for the Maintenance and Support of a Protestant Clergy within the said Province ...

And be it further enacted by the Authority aforesaid, That all His Majesty's *Canadian* Subjects within the Province of *Quebec,* the Religious Orders and Communities only excepted, may also hold and enjoy their Property and Possessions, together with all Customs and Usages, relative thereto, and all their other Civil Rights, in as large, ample and beneficial Manner ... as may consist with their Allegiance to His Majesty, and Subjection to the Crown and Parliament of *Great Britain;* and that in all Matters of Controversy relative to Property and Civil Rights, Resort shall be had to the laws of *Canada* for the Decision of the same ...

And whereas the Certainty and Lenity of the Criminal Law of *England,* and the Benefits and Advantages resulting from the Use of it, have been sensibly felt by the Inhabitants from an Experience of more than Nine Years, during which it has been uniformly administered ... That the same shall continue to be administered, and shall be observed as Law, in the Province of *Quebec* ...

And whereas it may be necessary to ordain many Regulations, for the future Welfare and good Government of the Province of Quebec, the Occasions of which cannot now be foreseen, nor without much Delay and Inconvenience be provided for, without intrusting that Authority for a certain Time, and under proper Restrictions, to Persons resident there:

And whereas it is at present inexpedient to call an Assembly; be it therefore enacted by the Authority aforesaid, That it shall and may be lawful for His *Majesty* ... to constitute and appoint a Council for the Affairs of the Province of *Quebec,* to consist of such Persons resident there, not exceeding Twenty-three, nor less than Seventeen ... to make Ordinances for the Peace, Welfare, and good Government of the said Province, with the Consent of his Majesty's Governor ...

Provided also, and be it enacted by the Authority aforesaid, That every Ordinance so to be made shall, within Six Months, be transmitted by the Governor ... and laid before His Majesty, for his Royal Approbation; and if His Majesty shall think fit to disallow thereof, the same shall cease and be void from the Time that his Majesty's Order in Council thereupon shall be promulgated at *Quebec*.

Reginald Coupland, *The Quebec Act,* Appendix B, 208–17.

DID THE QUEBEC ACT SECURE THE LOYALTY OF THE FRENCH CANADIANS?

Reginald Coupland argues that it satisfied French Canada and secured the northern half of North America for the British Empire, even though the southern half was irretrievably lost. If it had not been for the Quebec Act, the French Canadians might have joined the United States either in 1775 or in 1812. Coupland emphasizes the loyalty of the French Canadians.

... If it [the *Quebec Act*] had never been drafted, the result of the Government's other measures would have been the same. And if [Lord] North's ill-fated Government had done the wrong thing in Canada as well as in Massachusetts, if it had made such a settlement as the British minority in the province and their friends outside desired, it would not have altered a hair's breadth nor delayed a moment the inexorable outcome of its policy of coercion in the South. Nay, rather, it would have made matters worse in the end ... If British statesmen had treated Canada as Ireland had been treated, torn up the Treaty of Paris like the Treaty of Limerick, and cynically applied the familiar doctrines of religious intolerance and race ascendancy, the British government of Canada would surely not have lasted long. No one can be certain about the might-have-beens of history; but in this case the probability is very strong. The incorporation of the Canadians in the British Empire was very recent; they were still uncertain what the change would mean for them; and if once they had been convinced that it meant the restriction or suppression of their national life and, above all, of their religion, surely they would not have passively acquiesced in such a fate, but, when the time came, they would have risen, *seigneur* and priest and peasant together, joined forces with the "rebel" colonists, and for better or worse escaped with them from British tyranny. It was fortunate indeed, then, for the destinies of the British Empire that North and his colleagues made no such fruitless sacrifice of honour and justice, that they did not add that crowning folly to the rest. Without the *Quebec Act* they would still have lost the thirteen colonies. With it Canada at least was saved ...

After 1775 the history of Canada would probably have been merged in the history of the United States. But, as it was, while Saratoga and Yorktown created a new American nation, the defence of Quebec made it possible for Canada to remain outside it and build up a nation of her own ... And the foundations of it were laid when French and British fought side by side in the darkness and the driving snow of that December night [during the American invasion of Quebec] ...

... On the site of the Sault au Matelot barricade the inscription reads: HERE STOOD HER OLD AND NEW DEFENDERS UNITING, GUARDING, SAVING CANADA ...

Thirty years later [during the War of 1812] the loyalty of the French Canadians was again put to the proof. Once again the United States and France were in alliance against Britain. Once more Canada lay open to invasion. Once more, since Britain was now at death-grips with Napoleon in Europe, the regular garrison was absurdly small ... But the hierarchy remained loyal ...

In 1812 Bishop Plessis issued a *mandement* congratulating his fellow Catholics in Canada on their ready response to the calling out of the militia in anticipation of a breach with the United States. There was much, therefore, to set against the influence of French propaganda. The British Government, moreover, for its part, had been true to the promise of the Quebec Act. The Act of 1791, while superseding its constitutional provisions, had reaffirmed its policy of national toleration ... Very justly, therefore, had Bishop Plessis praised his people for their readiness to sacrifice everything rather than lose the protection of a Government that had both granted them a liberal constitution and preserved to them their ancient law ... The French Canadians served willingly and fought bravely in the militia; and, if it was on the citizen-soldiers of Upper Canada together with the British regulars and the colonial regiments newly raised in the Maritime Provinces and Newfoundland that the brunt of the fighting fell, their heroism would have been of no avail if the French Canadians had not held the flank in Lower Canada. The *voltigeurs* at Chateauguay take rank in history beside the British at Queenstown Heights and Lundy's Lane.

Reginald Coupland, *The Quebec Act*, 121–22, 186–89, 191–200.

S.D. Clark argues that the act by no means secured the French Canadians' loyalty, that Sir Guy Carleton was profoundly disappointed in its results, and that many French Canadians were ready to join the lusty "frontier revolt" that was the American Revolution. Their loyalty to the British Crown has been one of the great myths of Canadian history, a myth that will not stand up in the light of the facts.

Almost from the beginning of British rule in the colony, there had grown up a strong movement of opposition to the government and by the time the rebel attack upon the province was launched in the autumn of 1775 this movement had come to command the support of a large section of not only the English-speaking inhabitants but the French-speaking inhabitants as well …

Carleton … with all the prejudices of the aristocrat … steadfastly adhered to his policy of restoring to the noblesse many of their ancient privileges and powers in the belief that the securing of their support assured the support of the habitants. Expressions of satisfaction with the Quebec Act were taken by Carleton as emanating from the habitants as well as from the seigneurs …

The policy which found expression in the Quebec Act was put to the test during the summer of 1775 when the government faced the necessity of relying upon the support of the Canadians for the defence of the colony. The results proved bitterly disappointing to the authorities. "It has been said," a resident of Montreal had predicted as early as October 9, 1774, in writing to a friend in New York, "that some *Canadian* regiments would be raised and sent against you; but depend on it none will go willingly, except their officers; and for the others, it will require a regiment of soldiers to a regiment of *Canadians,* to oblige them to go."

Unable to form regular units, and faced with the imminent invasion of the province, Carleton on June 9 issued a proclamation declaring martial law and calling out the militia; seigneurs and former officers in the French army were employed to arouse the Canadians and form them into militia companies. Immediately there developed a widespread movement of resistance on the part of the habitants which amounted almost to rebellion against the state …

… When M. La Corne attempted to enlist the residents of Terrebonne in his seigneury and was compelled in the end to threaten calling upon the army to back up his authority, a riotous mob assembled armed with guns and clubs …

With the outbreak of hostilities in the late summer of 1775 it soon became apparent that few of the Canadians were prepared to fight in defence of the colony while many were ready to join the invading forces …

… Carleton had much reason for disappointment in the conduct of the people upon whom he had relied for the defence of the colony. "Can I enough lament," he wrote the Secretary of State, November 20, "the blind perverseness of this People, who frustrate all His Paternal Intentions for their own Protection, Interest and Happiness, by an unprecedented defection without even pretending the least Cause of Complaint." …

… It had become clear that the Quebec Act had not achieved the purposes for which it was intended. The truth was that by the time of the passing of this Act the old authoritarian order, built up about ecclesiastical rule and a feudal system of land holding, had come near to breaking down in French Canada … The picture of the Canadian habitants as a simple, religious-minded folk, respectful of authority and intensely attached to their ancient traditions and way of life, in contrast to American frontiersmen with their highly individualistic outlook … scarcely accorded with the facts.

S.D. Clark, *Movements of Political Protest in Canada 1640–1840* (Toronto, 1959), ch. 5.

14 ❧ Both Sides of the Rebellions

Was the British Government at Fault?

So often represented by Canadian writers as a distant and tyrannical force, the British Whig government of the 1830s finds in Helen Taft Manning a champion. Mrs. Manning argues that the British ministers were willing to grant the demands of the Canadas, Upper and Lower, but could not do so because the colonists were incapable of agreeing on what they wanted. It was not the British government that was at fault in the rebellions but the Colonists of both Canadas.

According to the traditional view, the policy of the mother country ... remained fundamentally unchanged until it was shaken to its foundations by the Canadian rebellion, and was reconstructed largely as a result of the work and the influence of Lord Durham and his able band of assistants. It is the purpose of these articles to show that this view of imperial history takes too little account of the changes in the mother country after 1830 and that ... the Whig ministers of the period were moving about as rapidly as they could in the direction of colonial self-government.

Although the Whigs certainly had no coherent plan of procedure, they did have firmly held principles. They really believed in giving the colonists control over their own internal affairs, and had the colonial assemblies been able to agree as to the form of self-government they wanted, they would probably have got it between 1835 and 1837 ...

... Even before the grievances of the Canadians became political ammunition for the aggressive wing of the Opposition, Mackintosh had created consternation at the Colonial Office by rising in the House of Commons whenever the old Tory régime proposed legislation for the Canadas, in order to insist that nothing should be done without first ascertaining the views of the colonists themselves ... To such arguments the Whigs and independent Tories lent a sympathetic ear, for it had long been an accepted principle of the House of Commons that British communities should pay for their own governments as soon as they were able to do so, and should be allowed to legislate for themselves, as well as to tax themselves ...

The work of the Whig ministers during their first term of office may be described as exploratory and tentative, as far as the North American colonies were concerned, rather than decisive. It is easy to condemn them as faint-hearted reformers, subject to pressure from the die-hard reactionaries in colonial capitals ... [But] No one who has studied the pages of the *Patriot* and the *Courier,* published in Upper Canada in these years, can doubt that the conservatives saw in the activities of the Whigs and radicals in England the writing on the wall as far as their own control over the province was concerned.

Helen Taft Manning, "The Colonial Policy of the Whig Ministers, 1830–1837," *Canadian Historical Review* 33, no. 3 (September 1952): 203–4, 235–36.

Louis Joseph Papineau—Strong or Weak?

Louis Fréchette, the poet, wrote a eulogy of Papineau in his La Légende d'un Peuple, which represented the leader of Lower Canada's 1837 Rebellion as the strongest force among his people. According to Fréchette, Papineau fought long and well for French Canada against its oppressors, and he deserves all the praise that can be given to him by future generations.

Papineau

Quarante ans, transformant la tribune en créneau,
L'homme-type chez nous s'appela Papineau!
Quarante ans il tonna contre la tyrannie;
Quarante ans de son peuple il fut le bon génie,
L'inspirateur sublime et l'âpre défenseur;

Quarante ans, sans faiblir, au joug de l'oppresseur
Il opposa ce poids immense, sa parole;
Il fut tout à la fois l'égide et la boussole;
Fallait-il résister ou fallait-il férir,
Toujours au saint appel on le vit accourir;
Et toujours à l'affût, toujours sur le qui-vive,
Du Canada français il fut la force vive!

Louis Fréchette, *La légende d'un peuple* (Paris, 1887), 223.

Fernand Ouellet, an authority on Papineau, argues that he vacillated at many crucial points during the rebellions. He was torn between his liberal ideas and his nationalistic goals, and he possessed certain weaknesses, such as irresponsibility, which contributed heavily to the failure of the rebellions. In the end, he fled the scene. Could such a man be truly regarded as a hero of French Canada?

Papineau always justified his actions on the grounds of liberal and democratic principles. He refused to admit nationalism as the factor motivating or determining his political attitudes. An analysis of his thought confirms both the duality of his attitudes and the importance of his nationalism. Whenever his liberal conceptions were in conflict with his nationalist positions, Papineau used them as an instrument for rationalization.

The duality which characterized his behaviour enabled Papineau to rally to the fold of the republican and patriotic party the French-Canadian middle bourgeoisie, some English-speaking Liberals, the Irishmen, the farmers of American origin settled in the Townships, and the French-Canadian peasantry. However, his politics met with absolute opposition among the English capitalists, the English farmers, the clergy, and the descendants of the old seigneurial nobility. After 1830, the conflict opposing these two groups entered a more violent phase. Papineau became the object of a veritable myth. For his supporters, he was the symbol of patriotism, disinterestedness, strength, energy, and courage. They saw in him the regenerator of the nation and the only man capable of bringing about and ensuring the emancipation of the French Canadians. Papineau himself came to believe in the "Papineau myth" and dreamed of becoming the president of a French-Canadian republic. Despite his rare leadership qualities, before 1837 Papineau did not succeed in giving the republican party a solid structure because he was not capable of assuming totally his responsibilities as a leader. His authoritarian behaviour, his lack of confidence in his subordinates and a noticeable fear of being supplanted account, in a large measure, for the defections and deep rivalries which existed within the party. This explains the lack of flexibility which characterized his parliamentary opposition. His political action was leading toward revolution, yet he was unable to envisage it coldly. He was equally incapable of officially detaching himself from the movement he had helped to create. The weaknesses led him to engineer the rebellion in such a way as to let the responsibility fall on the shoulders of the government ... The weaknesses of the revolutionary organization did not arise out of a lack of premeditation, but out of the very direction which Papineau had given the movement.

When arrest warrants were issued and British troops intervened, the patriots were divided, ill-equipped, and supported by a deficient organization. Papineau's attitude contributed to the confusion. His conduct at St. Denis and St. Charles was that of an irresponsible leader, dominated by fear. After his flight to the United States, Papineau ceased to believe that French Canadians could find within themselves the energy necessary to attain independence. He created in his own mind an illusion; that of a possible American, French, or even Russian intervention in favour of the revolutionary cause. His trip to France was not a voluntary exile. It was in answer to the aggressive attitude of the refugees towards him.

Fernand Ouellet, *Papineau: textes choisis et présentés* (Quebec, 1959), 9–10 (English translation).

THE DECLARATION OF SAINT-OURS

The Patriots gathered at Saint-Ours on the Richelieu River on 7 May 1837, and issued the following statements, echoing ideas of the French Declaration of the Rights of Man in 1789 and the American Declaration of Independence in 1776. The Declaration was published and distributed throughout French Canada by the literary and revolutionary newspaper La Minerve and the political newspaper Vindicator.

V. The people of this country have long awaited justice from the colonial administration at first, and later from the metropolitan government, and always in vain; during thirty years fear has broken some of our chains, while an insatiable love of power has added heavier ones. The high opinion that we had of the justice and honour of the English people made us hope that the parliament which represented it would provide a remedy for our grievances. Disillusioned of this last hope, we have renounced forever the idea of seeking justice on the other side of the ocean, and we have recognized at last how much this country has been misled by the lying promises which made it fight against a people which offered it liberty and equal rights in behalf of a people who prepared to enslave it. Sad experience forces us to recognize that our true friends and natural allies were on the other side of the 45th parallel …

VII. Regarding ourselves as no longer bound except by force to the English government, we shall submit to it as to a government of force, expecting from God, our valid rights and circumstances a better fate, the favors of liberty and a juster [sic] government. Meanwhile, as our public funds which the home government dares to dispose of without any control are going to become in its hands a new means of pressure against us, we regard it as our duty ... to resist by all means now in our possession to a tyrannical power ... and we resolve:

VIII. That we shall abstain, insofar as it may be in our power, from consuming imported goods, particularly those on which the higher duties are paid, such as tea, tobacco, wine, rum, etc. By preference we shall consume products manufactured in our own country ...

IX. In order to render these resolutions more efficacious, this assembly is of the opinion that an association should be established in this country, with headquarters in Quebec or Montreal, whose purpose will be to bind its members to consume only products manufactured in this country, or imported without the payment of duties ...

X. In order to effect more efficaciously the regeneration of this country, all should rally around a single man, following the example of Ireland. God has marked this man, like O'Connell, to be the political chief and the regenerator of a people. He has given him for that purpose an unsurpassed force of thought and word, a hatred of oppression, a love of a country which no promise or threat of the powers-that-be can break down. This man, already singled out by the country, is L .J. Papineau ...

La Minerve (Montreal), 11 May 1837.

THE CALL TO REVOLUTION

The revolutionary newspaper, La Minerve, after publishing the call to arms in the Declaration of Saint-Ours, ran the following editorial advising French Canadians on the action they should take. ("Friend Jonathan" meant the United States.)

Friend Jonathan will supply us with the articles which we cannot make here. Therefore let us aid the smuggler; from now on he is a brave fellow whom each of us will encourage. Vigorous youths, determined and well organized, must be trained for this career. Smuggling must be done on a grand scale. No more circumspection or temporizing. Major remedies are needed for major evils. The sources of the revenue must be dried up. The vaults will empty; the thieves will find nothing more there. Then England will listen to reason. Never has a struggle been more just. We have withheld the subsidies; this weapon is now taken from us and we must seek others more efficacious.

La Minerve (Montreal), 16 May 1837.

THE PLEA NOT TO REVOLT

Bishop Lartigue urged his people to abstain from civil strife, from which no good could come. His position, representing the attitude of most of the bishops, was denounced by the Patriots. At Chambly, when the pastoral letter was being read, there were cries of "A bas le mandement" and "Vive Papineau."

For a long time, brethren, we have heard only of agitation, even of revolt, in a country always renowned up to now for its loyalty, its peaceful spirit, and its love for the religion of its fathers. Everywhere brothers are seen arrayed against brothers, friends against friends, and citizens against their fellow citizens; and from one end of this diocese to the other discord seems to have broken the bonds of charity which existed between the members of one body, the children of one Church ...

We speak here on our own initiative, without any external pressure, solely from motives of conscience. We shall not give you our opinion, as a citizen, on the purely political question as to which is right or wrong among the diverse branches of the sovereign power ... but the moral question, i.e., what are the duties of a Catholic toward the civil power established and constituted in each state, this moral question, I say, is within our domain and competence ...

Do not let yourselves be seduced if some one wishes to engage you in rebellion against the established government, under the pretext that you form part of the "Sovereign People" ...

Have you ever considered seriously the horrors of civil strife? Have you pictured brooks of blood flooding your streets and your countryside, and the innocent engulfed with the guilty in the same sequence of misfortune? Have you reflected on the fact that, nearly without exception, every popular revolution is a bloody business, as experience proves; and that the philosopher of Geneva, the author of the *Social Contract,* the demagogue of the sovereignty of the people, says somewhere that a revolution would be bought too dearly, if it cost a single drop of blood?

Bishop Lartigue, 24 October 1837, *Mandements des évêques de Montréal*, vol. 1 (Montreal, 1867), 14; translation in Robert Christie, *History of the Late Province of Lower Canada*, vol. 4 (Montreal, 1866), 415–19.

Similarly, Etienne Parent, a moderate who was regarded as a vendu by the Patriots, stood against the rebellion. He wrote a letter of warning that was published in the newspaper Le Canadien.

If we emerge from our present plight without being crushed, let it be an eternal lesson to those who have not been able to learn from history, where it is written on every page, of the folly of agitating a people, of questioning the fundamental principles of the established social order, unless the oppression is directly felt by the governed and there remain no alternatives other than hard and dishonorable slavery or armed resistance. The agitation which has been aroused in this country has resulted in placing part of the population in open opposition to the government. But who would now say that the present government, with all its faults, is not preferable by far to the state of affairs which exists today in the district of Montreal? Would not the worst government be better than the anarchy which now grips the upper part of the province, even if anarchy were to be succeeded by a state of liberty; but no, it will be followed here as elsewhere by military despotism. That is not all. After the sword of the soldier has cut off the thousand heads of anarchy, then will come the law, which will arm the government with repressive measures that will necessarily retard the progress of the liberal cause …

Le Canadien (Quebec City), 22 November 1837.
The government-controlled Quebec Mercury used mockery as a weapon against the rebels. The editors ridiculed the appearance of the Patriots in their homemade garments.

Mr. Rodier's dress excited the greatest attention, being unique, with the exception of a pair of Berlin gloves, viz., frock coat of granite-coloured *étoffe du pays;* inexpressibles and vest of the same material, striped blue and white; straw hat and beef shoes, with a pair of home-made socks, completed the *outré* attire. Mr. Rodier, it was remarked, had no shirt on, having doubtless been unable to smuggle or manufacture one.
Dr. O'Callaghan's "rig out" was second only to that of Mr. Rodier, being complete with the exception of hat, gloves, and shirt (He had a shirt!) and spectacles.

Qtd. in Alastair Sweeny, *George-Etienne Cartier: A Biography* (Toronto, 1976) 39.

WAS THE REBELLION OF 1837–1838
A CONFLICT BETWEEN FRENCH AND ENGLISH?

S.D. Clark argues that it was not. Papineau's party contained many Irish and American settlers, particularly in the Eastern Townships, who were not at all concerned with French-Canadian grievances. Their revolt was a democratic one. It was a revolt of the poor against the privileged, and it had very little to do with French rights or the Roman Catholic religion.

By 1835 the frontier farm population of the Eastern Townships was beginning to make its influence felt. The radicalism of this population was the radicalism of the American back country, a radicalism developing very much out of an unbounded faith in the elective principle …

Increasing identification with the reform cause of the Irish population in Montreal and of the American population in the Eastern Townships arrested any tendency there may have been for political alignments to form along the lines of ethnic division and gave emphasis to the essential frontier character of the Lower Canadian reform movement. Indeed, after about 1835, the Papineau party could no longer be thought of as a *parti Canadien*. Rather, in its appeal to a population that had no great voice in the management of economic and political affairs, it had become a party of the disenfranchised, of the unprivileged, and underprivileged. As events moved closer to rebellion, it is true, support of the reform cause fell off among certain elements of the population and the ethnic character of the reform movement became more pronounced. But among the refugees seeking shelter in the United States were T.S. Brown, Dr. Robert Nelson, and the *Vindicator* editor, E.B. O'Callaghan, and, with the growth during 1838 of the patriot liberation movement, the close affinity between reform forces in Lower Canada and reform forces in the wider American society received new emphasis … By the late summer of 1838 there could be little question of the very considerable involvement of the Lower Canadian population in a movement rooted in American experience and giving expression to a political and social philosophy distinctively American in character. The uprising of 1838, if not the rebellion of 1837, was clearly related to, and indeed was essentially an outgrowth of the larger American revolutionary movement.

S.D. Clark, *Movements of Political Protest in Canada 1640–1840* (Toronto, 1959), 329–30.

The young George Etienne Cartier who fought with Papineau in 1837 believed that he was fighting for a dream—the liberty of French Canada, lost at the Conquest. In his later years, after he had attained a high position in the government of Canada, he cast aside the dreams of his youth and settled down to the reality of co-existence with English Canada. An independent Quebec was not possible, but for a brief moment it had seemed within the grasp of the French Canadians. Un Souvenir de 1837," which had one message: it urged a revolution of the French against British rule.

Un Souvenir de 1837

AIR: - *Combien j'ai douce souvenance.*
Dans le brillant de la jeunesse
Où tout n'est qu'espoir, allégresse,
Je vis captif en proie à la tristesse,
Et tremblant je vois l'avenir
Venir.

De longtemps ma douce patrie
Pleurait sous les fers asservie;
Et, désireux de la voir affranchie,
Du combat j'attendais l'instant
Gaîment.

Mais advint l'heure d'espérance
Où j'entrevoyais délivrance;
Eh! mon pays, en surcroit de souffrance,
Mars contraria tes vaillants
Enfants.

Et moi, victime infortunée
De cette fatale journée,
Le léopard sous sa griffe irritée
Sans pitié me tient mains et pieds
Liés.

La reverrai-je cette amie
Naguère qui charmait ma vie,
Souvent en moi son image chérie
Fait soupirer dans sa douleur
Mon coeur.

Adieu! ma natale contrée,
Qu'à jamais je vois enchaînée,
Fasse le ciel qu'une autre destinée
T'accorde un fortuné retour
Un jour!

G. E. Cartier, qtd. in Pierre Boileau, "La Fortune laurentienne du 'Montagnard émigré de Chateaubriand,'"
L'auteur-Montreal, 31 decembre 1987.

Lord Durham's Report

*In his Report, Lord Durham made some observations about Lower Canada and the desired
supremacy of the English people in North America.*

I expected to find a contest between a government and a people: I found two nations
warring in the bosom of a single state: I found a struggle, not of principles, but of
races; and I perceived that it would be idle to attempt any amelioration of laws or

institutions until we could first succeed in terminating the deadly animosity that now separates the inhabitants of Lower Canada into the hostile divisions of French and English ... The national feud forces itself on the very senses, irresistibly and palpably, as the origin or the essence of every dispute which divides the community; we discover that dissensions, which appear to have another origin, are but forms of this constant and all-pervading quarrel; and that every contest is one of French and English in the outset, or becomes so ere it has run its course ...

Nor does there appear to be the slightest chance of putting an end to this animosity during the present generation. Passions inflamed during so long a period cannot speedily be calmed. The state of education which I have previously described as placing the peasantry entirely at the mercy of agitators, the total absence of any class of persons, or any organization of authority that could counteract this mischievous influence, and the serious decline in the district of Montreal of the influence of the clergy, concur in rendering it absolutely impossible for the Government to produce any better state of feeling among the French population. It is even impossible to impress on a people so circumstanced the salutary dread of the power of Great Britain, which the presence of a large military force in the Province might be expected to produce ... Their more discerning leaders feel that their chances of preserving their nationality would be greatly diminished by an incorporation with the United States ... Yet none even of these considerations weigh against their present all-absorbing hatred of the English; and I am persuaded that they would purchase vengeance and a momentary triumph, by the aid of any enemies, or submission to any yoke.

There are two modes by which a Government may deal with a conquered territory. The first course open to it is that of respecting the rights and nationality of the actual occupants ... and without attempting any change in the elements of the community, merely incorporating the Province under the general authority of the central Government. The second is that of treating the conquered territory as one open to the conquerors, of encouraging their influx, of regarding the conquered race as entirely subordinate, and of endeavouring as speedily and as rapidly as possible to assimilate the character and institutions of its new subjects to those of the great body of its empire.

But before deciding which of the two races is now to be placed in the ascendant, it is but prudent to inquire which of them must ultimately prevail; for it is not wise to establish today that which must, after a hard struggle, be reversed tomorrow ...

There can hardly be conceived a nationality more destitute of all that can invigorate and elevate a people, than that which is exhibited by the descendants of the French in Lower Canada, owing to their retaining their peculiar language and manners. They are a people with no history, and no literature. The literature of England is written in a language which is not theirs; and the only literature which their language renders familiar to them, is that of a nation from which they have been separated by eighty years of a foreign rule, and still more by those changes which the Revolution and its consequences have wrought in the whole political, moral and social state of France ... In these circumstances, I should be indeed surprised if the more reflecting part of the French Canadians entertained at present any hope of continuing to preserve their nationality. Much as they struggle against it, it is obvious that the process of assimilation to English habits is already commencing. The English language is gaining ground, as the language of the rich and of the employers naturally will ...

A considerable time must, of course, elapse before the change of language can spread over a whole people; and justice and policy alike require, that while the people continue to use the French language, their Government should take no such means to force the English language upon them ... But, I repeat that the alteration of the character of the Province ought to be immediately entered on, and firmly, though cautiously, followed up; that in any plan, which may be adopted for the future management of Lower Canada, the first object ought to be that of making it an English province; and that, with this end in view, the ascendancy should never again be placed in any hands but those of an English population ...

I entertain no doubts as to the national character which must be given to Lower Canada; it must be that of the British Empire; that of the majority of the population of British America; that of the great race which must, in the lapse of no long period of time, be predominant over the whole North American Continent. Without effecting the change so rapidly or so roughly as to shock the feelings and trample on the welfare of the existing generation, it must henceforth be the first and steady purpose of the British Government to establish an English population, with English laws and language, in this Province, and to trust its government to none but a decidedly English legislature ...

The influence of perfectly equal and popular institutions in effacing distinctions of race without disorder or oppression, and with little more than ordinary animosities of party in a free country, is memorably exemplified in the history of the state of Louisiana, the laws and population of which were French at the time of its cession to the American Union. And the eminent success of the policy adopted with regard to that State, points out to us the means by which a similar result can be effected in Lower Canada ... The representation of Louisiana in Congress is now entirely English ... and the French language and manners bid fair, in no long time, to follow their laws, and pass away like the Dutch peculiarities of New York.

It is only by the same means—by a popular government, in which an English majority shall permanently predominate—that Lower Canada, if a remedy for its disorders be not too long delayed, can be tranquilly ruled. On these grounds,

I believe that no permanent or efficient remedy can be devised ... except a fusion of the Government in that of one or more of the surrounding Provinces; and as I am of the opinion that the full establishment of responsible government can only be permanently secured by giving these Colonies an increased importance in the politics of the Empire, I find in union the only means of remedying at once and completely the two prominent causes of their present unsatisfactory condition.

C.P. Lucas, ed., *Lord Durham's Report*, vol. 1, *Introduction* (London, 1912), 127 et seq.

THE REACTION TO DURHAM'S REPORT

When a nobleman advocates democratic institutions, we give him full credit for the benevolence of his intentions, but we doubt his sanity.

Thomas Chandler Haliburton, *Bubbles of Canada* (London, 1839).

The cause of popular agitation and of occasional collisions between the Assembly and other branches of government in the North American colonies is easily discerned. It lies on the surface. It is the tendency of democracy to swallow up everything, its impatience of any check ... If it be thought desirable to remove every obstacle to the absolute sway of the multitude whether their inclinations be just or unjust and whether their views be sound or unsound, then undoubtedly the system recommended in these pages is admirably adapted to that object. But how it can be imagined that such a system will confer tranquillity on a country is rather inexplicable.

John Beverley Robinson, member of the Family Compact of Upper Canada, to Lord Normanby (Colonial Secretary), 23 February 1839 (Archives of Ontario: Draft in the Robinson Papers, 23, 24, no. 18).

When this Report gets thoroughly before the Upper Canada people, I expect it will have the effect of tranquillizing the public mind in a great degree and thus militate against the "physical force men" at Rochester.

Dr. O'Callaghan, leader of the Rebellion in Lower Canada, to Louis Perrault, 2 April 1839 (Library and Archives Canada: Perrault Papers).

No document has ever been promulgated in British America that has given such general satisfaction as this report ... Thousands of copies have been distributed in pamphlet form, and the demand, instead of abating is greater than ever.

Examiner (Toronto), 24 June 1839.

Death to the Family Compact and up with the Durham Constitution! To sustain the latter, the masses are moving from Nelson and its back townships and the neighbourhood of Guelph, from Galt, Preston and Waterloo, from the Jersey settlement, Dumfries, Paris, Brantford and Ancaster, from Barton, Saltfleet and Glanford ... In numbers they will be overwhelming, in conduct they will be without reproach.

Journal (Hamilton), 2 August 1839.

The firm of the Baring brothers, which had heavy investments in Upper Canadian securities and stood to lose by civil strife, supported the union of the provinces and the sharing of the bankruptcy of Upper Canada with Lower Canada. As a young poet, Pierre Chauveau ridiculed this aspect of the Union, recommended by the Report, as the "Bankers Constitution."

C'est le jour des banquiers, demain sera notre heure.
Aujourd'hui l'oppression, demain la liberté;
 Aujourd'hui l'on fustige un peuple entier qui pleure,
Demain l'on voit debout tout un peuple ameuté;
Aujourd'hui le forfait, et demain la vengeance,
Aujourd'hui c'est de l'or, et demain c'est du fer ...
C'est le jour des banquiers, vous dis-je! c'est leur gloire
Que les placards royaux affichent sur nos murs;
L'Union que l'on proclame est leur chant de victoire,
Et tout devait céder à des motifs si purs! ...

Pierre-Joseph-Olivier Chauveau (Library and Archives Canada)

An act of injustice and despotism, in that it is imposed upon us without our consent; in that it deprives Lower Canada of the legitimate number of its representatives; in that it deprives us of the use of our language in the proceedings of the legislature, against the spirit of the treaties and the word of the governor-general; in that it makes us pay, without our consent, a debt that we have not contracted; in that it permits the executive power to seize illegally under the name of a civil list, and without the vote of the representatives of the people, an enormous part of the revenues of the country.

Louis-Hippolyte LaFontaine

Seduced, distracted after a fashion by its details, we have for a long time lost sight of the object of that measure, which, however, is every day recalled to our recollection by that invasion of ideas and institutions, foreign to our ideas and institutions, which renders each day the most desirable, in the midst of the confusion of institutions, that perfect labyrinth of laws, of manners and of language, which imposes upon us a double nationality, so as to render the one necessary, the other useless, that is to say, to make us lose ours and adopt the other …

L'Avenir (*Rouge* journal)

Tell us, gentlemen of *L'Avenir,* you who weep so much over the ruins of the past, and over imaginary evils—tell us at what period of our history has the French-Canadian nationality been more brilliant, more honoured, more respected, or has it occupied a higher position than it holds today? … The Union was brought about with the object of ruining us! But the Union has saved us, and after powerful and well-directed efforts, after having won a position which permits us to avoid its inconveniences and evil consequences, after having obtained the political rights for which we have struggled for fifty years, now it is, that the devoted and generous gentlemen of *L'Avenir* raise their voices against it …

But tell us, ye young and fiery apostles of French-Canadian nationality, what do you mean by the principle of nationality applied to the management of public affairs? It is not after our party has recruited its ranks from men of all origins, when our friends, the liberals of Upper Canada and those of Lower Canada of foreign origin, have made prodigious efforts to carry the elections and that together we have gained the most signal victory—it is not now that your appeal to prejudices and passions will have the least echo in the country.

La Revue Canadienne (journal of Louis-Hippolyte LaFontaine)

The Union has completely failed in its purpose. It was enacted with the sole motive of reducing the French Canadians under English domination. And the contrary effect has resulted! Those that were to be crushed dominate! Those in favour of whom the Union was made are the serfs of the others! ... I warn the ministry of peril ... I warn it that the course it takes is likely to throw the people of Upper Canada into despair, and to make them feel that if they are to be governed by foreigners, it would be more advantageous to be governed by a neighbouring people of the same race than by those with whom it has nothing in common, neither blood, nor language, nor interests.

Sir Allan MacNab, leader of the Tory Party in Upper Canada

15 ❧ The Confederation Debate

What Did English Canada Think of the Confederation Scheme?

The opinion of leading politicians was quite favourable. John A. Macdonald supported the Confederation plan wholeheartedly, although his personal preference was for an even stronger legislative union, such as Britain possessed. He put aside this preference for the sake of including not only French Canada but the Maritime Provinces, too, which also opposed a British-style legislative union.

Now, as regards the comparative advantages of a Legislative and a Federal union, I have never hesitated to state my own opinions. I have again and again stated in the House, that, if practicable, I thought a Legislative union would be preferable ... But, on looking at the subject in the Conference, and discussing the matter as we did, most unreservedly, and with a desire to arrive at a satisfactory conclusion, we found that such a system was impracticable. In the first place, it would not meet the assent of the people of Lower Canada, because they felt that in their peculiar position—being in a minority, with a different language, nationality and religion from the majority—in case of a junction with the other provinces, their institutions and their laws might be assailed, and their ancestral associations, on which they prided themselves, attacked and prejudiced; it was found that any proposition which involved the absorption of the individuality of Lower Canada—if I may use the expression—would not be received with favour by her people ... Therefore, we were forced to the conclusion that we must either abandon the idea of Union altogether, or devise a system of union in which the separate provincial organizations would be in some degree preserved.

Hon. John Alexander Macdonald, Attorney General, Canada West, Monday, 6 February 1865, addressing the Legislative Assembly in the Third Session, 8th Provincial Parliament of Canada. In *Parliamentary Debates on the Subject of the Confederation of the British North American Provinces* (Quebec, 1865), 25–45.

George Brown, the leader of the Clear Grits, or Upper Canada Reformers, favoured Confederation as a means of freeing his province, Anglo-Saxon and Protestant, from the shackles of the Union of 1840. Under Confederation, Upper Canada could go its own prosperous way.

The second feature of this scheme as a remedial measure is, that it removes, to a large extent, the injustice of which Upper Canada has complained in financial matters. We in Upper Canada have complained that though we paid into the public treasury more than three-quarters of the whole revenue, we had less control over the system of taxation and the expenditure of the public moneys than the people of Lower Canada. Well, sir, the scheme in your hand remedies that. The absurd line of separation between the provinces is swept away for general matters; ... local governments are to have control over local affairs, and if our friends in Lower Canada choose to be extravagant, they will have to bear the burden of it themselves. No longer shall we have to complain that one section pays the cash while the other spends it; hereafter, they who pay will spend, and they who spend more than they ought will have to bear the brunt.

Hon. George Brown, President of the Council, Wednesday, 8 February 1865, addressing the Legislative Assembly in the Third Session, 8th Provincial Parliament of Canada. In *Parliamentary Debates on the Subject of the Confederation of the British North American Provinces* (Quebec, 1865), 92.

John Rose represented the interests of the Montreal business community, which was largely English speaking. Businessmen were strongly in favour of Confederation, seeing in it the best means of developing an east-west economy whose profits should accrue to themselves. They were confident that their rights as Protestants living in the province of Quebec would be respected.

Now we, the English Protestant minority of Lower Canada, cannot forget that whatever right of separate education we have was accorded to us in the most unrestricted way before the union of the provinces, when we were in a minority and entirely in the hands of the French population ... I believe we have always had our fair share of the public grants in so far as the French element could control them ... I believe that everything we desire will be as freely given by the Local Legislature as it was before the union of the Canadas.

I speak particularly of those who have great interests at stake in the community which I represent—the great and varied interests of commerce, trade, banking, manufactures and material progress generally, which are supposed to centre in the city of Montreal. These men—and there are none more competent in the province—have considered the scheme in a calm and business-like way, and have deliberately come to the conclusion that it is calculated to promote the best interests and greatly enhance the prosperity of this country.

Hon. John Rose, Wednesday, 22 February 1865, addressing the Legislative Assembly in the Third Session, 8th Provincial Parliament of Canada. In *Parliamentary Debates on the Subject of the Confederation of the British North American Provinces* (Quebec, 1865), 410.

Christopher Dunkin, an English-speaking member of Parliament from the Eastern Townships in Quebec, was one of the few outspoken critics of the Confederation scheme on the English-Canadian side. He predicted a heightening of French-English tensions as a result of the new union.

But the moment you tell Lower Canada that the large-sounding powers of your General Government are going to be handed over to a British-American majority, decidedly not of the race and faith of her majority, that moment you wake up the old jealousies and hostility in their strongest form. By the very provisions you talk of for the protection of the non-French and non-Catholic interests, you unfortunately countenance the idea that the French are going to be more unfair than I believe they wish to be. For that matter, what else can they well be? They will find themselves a minority in the General Legislature, and their power in the General Government will depend upon their power within their own province and over their provincial delegations in the Federal Parliament. They will thus be compelled to be practically aggressive, to secure and retain that power ... there will certainly be in this system the very strongest tendencies to make them practically aggressive upon the rights of the minority in language and faith, and at the same time to make the minority most suspicious and resentful of aggression. The same sort of alienation, as between the two faiths, will be going on in Upper Canada ... The prejudices of the two camps are once more stirred to the depths; and if this scheme goes into operation, they will separate more and more widely, and finally break out into open war ...

Hon. Christopher Dunkin, Monday, 27 February 1865, addressing the Legislative Assembly in the Third Session, 8th Provincial Parliament of Canada. In *Parliamentary Debates on the Subject of the Confederation of the British North American Provinces* (Quebec, 1865), 510.

What Did French Canada Think
of the Confederation Scheme?

Aside from Cartier and his supporters, opinion was sharply divided and largely unfavourable. Sir Etienne-Paschal Taché was one of those who stood with Cartier and threw his weight behind the new union.

Lower Canada had constantly refused the demand of Upper Canada for representation according to population, and for the good reason that, as the union between them was legislative, a preponderance to one of the sections would have placed the other at its mercy. It would not be so in a Federal Union, for all questions of a general nature would be reserved for the General Government, and those of a local character to the local governments, who would have the power to manage their domestic affairs as they deemed best ... It would be tantamount to a separation of the provinces, and Lower Canada would thereby preserve its autonomy together with all the institutions it held so dear, and over which they could exercise the watchfulness and surveillance necessary to preserve them unimpaired.

Hon. Sir Etienne-Pascal Taché, Premier, Friday, 3 February 1865, addressing the Legislative Council in the Third Session, 8th Provincial Parliament of Canada. In *Parliamentary Debates on the Subject of the Confederation of the British North American Provinces* (Quebec, 1865), 9.

Louis Auguste Olivier, the member for De Lanaudière, was one of many French Canadians who opposed Confederation. He believed the plan gave too much power to the federal government, which would proceed to crush the provinces.

My opinion is that as much power as possible should have been entrusted to the local governments, and as little as is consistent with the functions it will have to discharge to the Central Government, and my reason for entertaining this opinion is, that the Supreme Government, with its power of purse and its control of the armies, will always be more disposed to stretch its prerogatives and to trench upon the domain of the local governments than to narrow down and retain its authority. The scheme then, in my opinion, is defective in that it inverts this order ... As it is now, if the scheme goes into operation, the local governments will be in danger of being crushed by the General Government.

Hon. Louis Auguste Olivier, Monday, 13 February 1865, statement made to the Legislative Council. In *Parliamentary Debates on the Subject of the Confederation of the British North American Provinces* (Quebec, 1865), 173–74.

Joseph Xavier Perrault from the Richelieu Valley viewed Confederation quite simply as a plan to deprive the French Canadians of their treasured rights, which they had fought for against the encroaching English for long decades.

... [E]ven if the scheme of Confederation was expedient, I maintain that the object of it is hostile. I gave a historical sketch of the encroaching spirit of the English race on the two continents. I pointed out the incessant antagonism between it and the French race. Our past recalled to us the constant struggle which we had to keep up in order to resist the aggression and the exclusiveness of the English element in Canada. It was only through heroic resistance and a happy combination of circumstances that we succeeded in obtaining the political rights which are secured to us by the present Constitution. The scheme of Confederation has no other object than to deprive us of the most precious of those rights, by substituting for them a political organization which is eminently hostile to us.

Hon. Joseph Xavier Perrault, Friday, March 3, 1865, addressing the Legislative Council. In *Parliamentary Debates on the Subject of the Confederation of the British North American Provinces* (Quebec, 1865), 585–648.

Antoine Aimé Dorion considered that Confederation was merely a plan concocted in the smoke-filled red chambers of the railway companies to help the Grand Trunk out of its financial difficulties. Beyond that, it was the first step toward a legislative union in which the French Canadians would be swamped.

This project [the Intercolonial Railway] having failed, some other scheme had to be concocted for bringing aid and relief to the unfortunate Grand Trunk—and the Confederation of all the British North American Provinces naturally suggested itself to the Grand Trunk officials as the surest means of bringing with it the construction of the Intercolonial Railway. Such was the origin of this Confederation scheme. The Grand Trunk people are at the bottom of it ...

Honorable members of Lower Canada are made aware that the delegates all desired a Legislative union, but it could not be accomplished at once. This Confederation is the first necessary step towards it. The British Government is ready to grant a Federal union at once, and when that is accomplished the French element will be completely overwhelmed by the majority of British representatives. What then would prevent the Federal Government from passing a set of resolutions in a similar way to those we are called upon to pass, without submitting them to the people, calling upon the Imperial Government to set aside the Federal form of government and give a Legislative union instead of it?

Hon. Antoine Aimé Dorion, Thursday, 16 February 1865, addressing the Legislative Council. In *Parliamentary Debates on the Subject of the Confederation of the British North American Provinces* (Quebec, 1865), 251.

Henri Gustave Joly from Lotbinière made one of the strongest personal attacks on George Etienne Cartier, Attorney-General for Lower Canada. Cartier, he said, had betrayed the trust of his people and was about to sacrifice their future on the altar of his own personal ambition for office.

When his [Cartier's] scheme of Confederation became public, a feeling of uneasiness pervaded all minds; that instinct forewarned them of the danger which impended. He has hushed that feeling to a sleep of profound security. I shall compare him to a man who has gained the unbounded confidence of the public, who takes advantage of it to set up a Savings Bank, in which the rich man deposits his wealth and the day labourer the small amount which he has squeezed out of his wages, against a day of need—both without a voucher. When that man has gathered all into his strong box, he finds an opportunity to purchase, at the cost of all he holds in trust, the article on which he has long set his ambitious eye; and buys it, unhesitatingly, without a thought of the wretches who are doomed to ruin by his conduct. The deposit committed to the keeping of the Attorney General is the fortune of the French Canadians—their nationality. That fortune had not been made in a day; it was the accumulation of the toil and the savings of a whole people in a whole century. To prolong the ephemeral existence of his administration for a few months, the Attorney General has sacrificed, without a scruple, this precious trust, which the unbounded confidence of his fellow-countrymen had confided to his keeping.

Hon. Henri Gustave Joly, Monday, 20 February 1865, addressing the Legislative Council. In *Parliamentary Debates on the Subject of the Confederation of the British North American Provinces* (Quebec, 1865), 358.

16 ❧ Assessments of Louis Riel

Was the Riel Rebellion a Primitive Revolt?

George F.G. Stanley, author of The Birth of Western Canada, *thinks that it was.*

... I feel that the significance of those troubles which marked the early history of Western Canada is to be found rather in their connection with the general history of the frontier than with the ethnic relationships of Quebec and Ontario. Both the Manitoba insurrection and the Saskatchewan rebellion were the manifestation in Western Canada of the problem of the frontier, namely the clash between primitive and civilized peoples. In all parts of the world, in South Africa, New Zealand, and North America, the penetration of white settlement into territories inhabited by native peoples has led to friction and wars; Canadian expansion into the North-West led to a similar result. Here both the half-breed population and the Indian tribes rose in arms against Canadian intrusion and the imposition of an alien civilization ... The rebellion of 1885 was the last effort of the primitive peoples in Canada to withstand the inexorable advance of white civilization. With the suppression of the rebellion white dominance was assured. Henceforth the history of the Canadian West was to be that of the white man, not that of the red man or the bois brûlé.

George F.G. Stanley, The Birth of Western Canada (Toronto, 1960), vii–viii.

Or Was It a Sectional Revolt?

W.L. Morton argues that the Riel Rebellion was but the first in a long series of western protests against control by eastern Canada. The following comment from S.D. Clark describes his point of view.

Professor Morton's study focuses attention upon the strong spirit of revolt which has been so characteristic of the Western Canadian community. It is a spirit with roots deep in the past. The history of political unrest in western Canada reaches back to the Red River insurrection of 1870 and the Northwest rebellion of 1885 ... The fact that these early struggles against outside control (by the Hudson's Bay Company or the Canadian federal state) were carried on largely by half-breeds has tended to obscure their significance ... Too often the half-breeds have been pictured as a slothful, irresponsible race of people scarcely civilized, led in 1870 and 1885 by a madman and demagogue. To place Riel's name alongside those of J.W. Dafoe, H.W. Wood, J.S.

Woodsworth, and William Aberhart would be thought to disparage the memories of these great leaders of reform. Even those people who were later most active in keeping alive the spirit of western revolt knew or cared little about this early champion of western rights ... Yet these half-breed uprisings were as true an expression of the grievances, and aspirations, of the West as the agrarian uprisings after 1900. What the West revolted against in 1816, 1870, and 1885, as in 1921 and 1935, was being taken over or being dominated by an outside power. Until 1885 this revolt found support within a distinctive ethnic-religious system—the Métis nation, but, if the sense of cultural unity was later not so strong, and never again was there a resort to arms, the feeling of being "a separate people" nevertheless persisted ... Throughout, the dominant note in the social philosophy of western people has been an unbounded confidence in themselves, a belief that their region was one with a great potential future if the hand of the outside exploiter could only be removed.

S.D. Clark, Foreword, in W.L. Morton, *The Progressive Party in Canada* (Toronto, 1950), vii–ix.

Did the White Settlers Support Riel—or Oppose Him?

The evidence is contradictory. On 28 July 1884, W.H. Jackson, a white settler in Prince Albert, issued a manifesto calling on the people to support Riel.

To the Citizens of Prince Albert:

Gentlemen: We are starting a movement in this settlement with a view to attaining Provincial Legislature for the North West Territories and, if possible, the control of our own resources, that we may build our railroads and other works to serve our interests rather than those of the Eastern Provinces ... We state the various evils which are caused by the present system of legislation showing:

1. That they are caused by the facts that the Ottawa legislators are responsible to Eastern constituents, not to us, and are therefore impelled to legislate with a view to Eastern interests rather than our own; that they are not actually resident in the country and therefore not acquainted with the facts that would enable them to form a correct opinion as to what measures are suitable to North-West interests ...

2. That the legislation passed by such legislators has already produced great depression in agricultural, commercial, and mechanical circles, and will continue to increase that depression unless the system is revised ...

Louis Riel of Manitoba fame has united the half-breed element solidly in our favour. Hitherto it has been used largely as the tool of whatever party happened to be in power in the East, but Riel has warned them against the danger of being separated from the whites by party proposals. The general impression is that Riel has been painted in blacker colors than he deserves; that in regard to his public attitude it is better to accept his services as long as he works for us ... As long as both elements work on the square, doing justice to each other, there will be no clash, but a marked advance toward our end, i.e., justice in the North-West.

Two weeks later, the Prince Albert Times ran an editorial against Riel, as did the Saskatchewan Herald published at Battleford. The Herald's editors were harshly critical of Riel on 9 August and referred to him as "an alien demagogue."

Instead of sending a deputation to a foreign country to bring in an alien demagogue to set class against class, and to mar the harmony between the races under which the country was growing prosperous and happy, they should have sent a representative to Ottawa to lay before the Government a statement of their claims; and, as the complaints of her citizens have always been listened to in the past, so would they be now. But we cannot believe the Government will seriously entertain any claims or propositions put forward by or through Riel.

Saskatchewan Herald, 9 August 1884.

SHOULD MACDONALD BE CENSURED FOR INACTIVITY?

J.S. Willison, editor of the Toronto Globe and long-time political opponent of the Prime Minister, argued that Sir John's neglect of the West made revolt inevitable.

... Time and again the Métis renewed their petitions. Time and again the North-West Council passed resolutions in support of their demands. Time and again bishops and clergy pleaded for action at Ottawa, and urged the dangers of delay. Ministers and officers of the Government passed up and down the West and heard the bitter story of the Métis grievances, and—forgot ... Col. Geo. T. Denison, in his interesting reminiscences of soldiering in Canada, deals in blunt and straightforward fashion with the Government's responsibility for the subsequent outbreak. He declares that the rebellion was caused by "a remarkable instance of departmental inefficiency and stupidity." ... Mr. Charles Mair, one of the originators of the Canada First movement, had lived for some years at Prince Albert. He knew the temper of the half-breeds, and saw that rebellion was certain if their claims were not recognized. "For two years or more before the outbreak," Col. Denison proceeds, "he had come all the way from Prince Albert to Ottawa, about 2,000 miles ... to impress upon the Government the danger ... He begged of the Government to make some concessions and warned them that there would be bloodshed." ... But six months passed and nothing was done. In

April 1884, Mair came down once more and made a further appeal to the government ... Mr. Mair was then so thoroughly convinced that a rising was inevitable that he bought a house at Windsor, returned to Prince Albert, closed out his business, and in the month of September brought his family down to Ontario to await in safety the rebellion that he so clearly foresaw, and which a fatuous Administration would not lift a finger to avert ... Nothing that was charged against the Administration by the spokesmen of the Liberal party, and nothing that the official documents reveal, more utterly condemns the Ministers who had the peace of the country in their keeping, or goes further in mitigation and justification of the leaders of the insurrection. Mair was neither a politician nor an agitator, and Col. Denison is an unprejudiced witness.

J.S. Willison, *Sir Wilfrid Laurier and the Liberal Party: A Political History*, vol. 1 (London, 1903), 430, 434, 435.

OR SHOULD RIEL BE CENSURED FOR DUPLICITY?

D.G. Creighton, in John A. Macdonald: The Old Chieftain, *the second volume of his prize-winning biography, maintains that Riel was not to be trusted.*

It was at this point, when the government expected negotiations and was prepared to make real concessions, that a most disquieting piece of news arrived from the north-west. Ever since, on the eve of his departure for England, Macdonald had received the account of the interview which Forget and Bishop Grandin had had with Riel, he had been very uneasy about the *métis* leader's real intentions; and now these doubts and suspicions were horribly confirmed ... Father André, the local priest, and D.H. MacDowall, the member for Lorne in the North-West Council, had paid a visit to the half-breed leader in St. Laurent; and the amazing revelations of the four-hour interview which followed were now spread before Macdonald's astonished eyes ... Now, before MacDowall and André, he [Riel] was cynically, almost brutally, selfish. Quite early in the interview, he announced that he had come back to Canada to press his own personal claims as well as to advocate the interests of the half-breeds; and he left his listeners clearly to infer that he hoped, by renewing and increasing his strong influence with the *métis*, to bring effective pressure to bear on the government in his own behalf. "He then proceeded to state," MacDowall continued with his incredible narrative, "that if the government would consider his personal claims against them and pay him a certain amount in settlement of these claims, he would arrange to make his illiterate and unreasoning followers well satisfied with almost any settlement of their claims for land grants that the government might be willing to make, and also that he would leave the north-west never to return." ... Riel had then proceeded calmly to appraise his own political value, basing his estimates on the various efforts which, he claimed, had been made to bribe him to leave the country after the Red River Rebellion. As much as thirty-five thousand dollars had, he asserted, been offered him on one occasion by an emissary from Sir John Macdonald! ... To Macdonald it was a shattering revelation. It made the whole agitation seem a malevolent sham. It utterly destroyed his faith in Riel's good will. "I believe," he solemnly told the House later, "he came in for the purpose of attempting to extract money from the public purse ... " ... Could the Canadian government stoop to the dangerous devices which this self-confessed political blackmailer was openly inviting it to adopt? It could not.

Donald G. Creighton, *John A. Macdonald*, vol. 2, *The Old Chieftain* (Toronto, 1955), 412–14. It is recommended that the student read Chapter 12 of *The Old Chieftain* in full.

ENGLISH CANADA CONDEMNED RIEL

An Ontario lawyer named O'Brien gave vent to his feelings in a letter to Macdonald.

Ontario is not going much longer to be sat upon by those Frenchmen and the priesthood. Quiet people here are beginning to talk savagely. The Anglo-Saxons will turn some day and make them "go halves" or drive them into the sea. The latter would be the best place.

O'Brien to Macdonald, 21 August 1885 (Library and Archives Canada: Macdonald Papers, vol. 5).

An Ontario Conservative candidate surveyed his riding, found the feeling unanimous against Riel, and reported the same to the Prime Minister.

During my canvass I have found that the Riel matter has, before any other question, engaged the attention of the farmers, and many of the very strongest of our friends have not hesitated to declare that, if the Rebel is not hung, they will never again vote on the Conservative side. They are very much in earnest over this question and evidently quite determined to carry out their threat to desert the party in the event of a reprieve being granted by the Government ... as one old farmer told me, "Well, the election is coming on at a rather bad time, but I'm glad it is before the 18th of September for I can give John A. Macdonald one more vote, but God help him next time if he don't hang Riel."

Ward to Macdonald, 26 August 1885 (Library and Archives Canada: Macdonald Papers, vol. 5).

The Toronto Evening News declared that it would not shed a tear if French Canada left Confederation, except for joy.

Ontario is proud of being loyal to England. Quebec is proud of being loyal to sixteenth-century France. Ontario pays about three-fifths of Canada's taxes, fights all the battles of provincial rights, sends nine-tenths of the soldiers to fight the rebels, and gets sat on by Quebec for her pains. Quebec since the time of Intendant Bigot, has been extravagant, corrupt and venal, whenever she could with other people's money ... Quebec now gets the pie. Ontario gets the mush, and pays the piper for the Bleu carnival ...

If we in Canada are to be confronted with a solid French vote, we must have a solid English vote. If Quebec is always to pose as a beggar in the Dominion soup kitchen she must be disfranchised as a vagrant ... She is no use in Confederation. Her representatives are a weakness in Parliament, her cities would be nothing but for the English-speaking people, and today Montreal would be as dead as the city of Quebec but for the Anglo-Saxons, who are persecuted and kept down by the ignorant French ... We are sick of the French Canadians ... Quebec could go out of Confederation tomorrow and we would not shed a tear except for joy.

Evening News (Toronto), 20 April 1885.

Likewise, the Orange Sentinel, champion of Protestant interests, looked to the break-up of the nation.

The French are as much French now as before Wolfe vanquished Montcalm upon the Heights of Abraham. The dividing line is sharply drawn, and although upon many previous occasions differences of race and religion have been strongly apparent, never before was the demarcation as distinct as over the present Riel imbroglio. The signs of the times point to the fact that this artificial nationality cannot last much longer.

Qtd. in the *Star* (Montreal), 11 September 1885.

FRENCH CANADA IDOLIZED HIM

L'Electeur, a popular newspaper in Montreal, wrote:

L'histoire te consacrera une page glorieuse et ton nom sera gravé dans le coeur de tous les vrais canadiens-français … Tes fautes personnelles s'effacent devant la sainteté de la noble cause dont tu t'es fait le champion. Jeanne d'Arc! Napoléon! Chénier! Riel! C'est avec le plus profond respect que l'on prononce vos noms sacrés. Chénier a son monument, Riel, tu auras le tien.

L'Electeur (Montreal), 25 June 1885.

L'Etendard, normally known for its Conservative views, defended Riel to the hilt.

Il ne nous est pas permis d'oublier quel rôle la constitution, les lois d'équité, la voix du sang, nous assignent vis-à-vis les minorités des autres provinces, notamment celles qui sont nos coreligionnaires et nos soeurs d'origine … On les hait peut-être pour leur origine française, et leur foi catholique; il n'est pas même impossible qu'on les ait persécutés à cause de nous; deux raisons qui nous feraient un devoir d'honneur et de loyauté d'accepter une part de solidarité dans leur situation.

L'Etendard (Montreal), 1 April 1885.

La Vérité compared the campaign against Riel in English Canada to the actions of Russia in crushing the Polish nation.

Le fanatisme orangiste qui voudrait l'extermination des métis français dans le Nord-Ouest, et qui a dû travailler à fomenter ces troubles afin d'avoir une raison de sévir contre la race détestée [est intolérable] … C'est ainsi que la Russie procède en Pologne.

Qtd. in *L'Etendard* (Montreal), 4 April 1885.

Louis Fréchette enshrined the martyred Riel in verse as the eternal hero of his people.

Le Gibet de Riel

Donc tout est consommé. Dans notre fière époque,
Quand de tous les côtés s'ébranle et se disloque
L'enchevêtrement noir des préjugés boiteux;
Quand les anciennes lois les vieux codes honteux,
Devant l'éclat vainqueur des lumières modernes,
Eteignent un à un leurs fumeuses lanternes; …
Quand, secouant partout le joug originel

De l'antique union des erreurs et des haines,
Les peuples, l'oeil tourné vers les aubes prochaines,
Semblent se dire enfin, dans un commun accord,
Qu'il est un droit plus saint que celui du plus fort;
Oui, dans ce siècle où tout s'élève et s'émancipe,
Chez nous, au plus flagrant mépris de tout principe
De clémence, d'amour, de paix et d'équité,
A la face du monde et de la liberté,
Sur le classique sol de toute indépendance,
Pris de férocité, gonflés d'outrecuidance,
On a vu des guerriers et des hommes d'Etat,
Juges, bourreaux, unis dans un même attentat,
Au-dessous d'un gibet qu'un peuple entier renie,
Groupés pour savourer un râle d'agonie!

Et voyez ce qu'on fait quand on est baptisé,
Qu'on est bon orangiste, et bien civilisé!

Louis Fréchette, *La légende d'un peuple* (Paris, 1887).

WHO BRIDGED THE GAP?

Much hinged on the action of the French-Canadian ministers in Macdonald's cabinet. Had they resigned, perhaps the nation would have been irreparably split. As it was, they chose to ride out the storm and face the wrath of their own people. J.A. Chapleau was one of those who stayed. He wrote to his chieftain of his fateful decision.

I believe in the guilt of the prisoner. His mental delusions would be the only extenuating point against the full application of the law in his case.

In the state of doubt in which I am with regard to that point, I prefer giving the benefit of the doubt to the law than to the deluded criminal.

We may be called upon to suffer, my Quebec colleagues and myself, I more than others, at the hands of our people, owing to the intense feeling which exists in our Province. (It is a further reason with me not to abandon my colleagues, as it would look like desertion at the hour of danger.)

However, I prefer the risk of personal loss to the national danger imminent, with the perspective of a struggle in the field of race and religious prejudices. We will have to fight, and perhaps to fall. Well, I prefer, after all, to fight and to fall in the old ship and for the old flag.

I would prefer in this case, that the minute of last evening's Council would record my assent to the decision of the Council.

Chapleau to Macdonald, 12 November 1885 (Library and Archives Canada: Macdonald Papers, 1873–85, confidential).

Much hinged, too, on the attitudes of the rising young Liberal politician, Wilfrid Laurier. He set himself firmly against a French-Canadian party and within two years had become Leader of the largely English-Canadian Liberal Party. Canadian parties, Laurier insisted, had to include both English and French members.

It would be simply suicidal for the French Canadians to form a party by themselves. Why, so soon as the French Canadians, who are in the minority in this House and in the country, were to organize as a political party, they would compel the majority to organize as a political party, and the result must be disastrous to themselves. We have only one way of organizing parties. This country must be governed and can be governed only on questions of policy and administration.

U. Barthe, Wilfrid Laurier on the Platform (Quebec, 1890), 256.

THE IMPERIALISTS

Sir Robert Borden was gravely impressed with the arms race between Britain and Germany and the danger to Canada and the Empire if Britain should lose. He questioned Laurier sharply on his naval policy, rejected it as inadequate, and urged that Canada make an immediate emergency contribution of dreadnoughts to the British navy.

Borden: Suppose a Canadian ship meets a ship of similar armament and power belonging to an enemy, meets her on the high seas, what is she to do? I do not ask what she will do if attacked, but will she attack, will she fight?

Laurier: I do not know that she would fight. I do not know that she should fight either. She should not fight until the Government by which she is commissioned have determined whether she should go into the war. That is the position we take.

Borden: The proposals of the Government seem to me in one aspect to be absurd and unworkable, but in another aspect they are dangerous and revolutionary ... It is absolutely inconceivable that if Great Britain were engaged in a naval war and the Canadian naval force acted as if it belonged not to the Empire or to Canada but to some neutral country, such a condition would not lead or at least conduce to the early separation of this country from the British Empire. Germany has put forward the greatest naval budget in her history ... My right hon. friend [Laurier] may dismiss all this with a wave of the hand and an eloquent phrase and he may say there is no danger and no peril ... I do not say there will be war ... I trust, I hope, I pray there will not be war. But, without war, without the firing of a shot or the striking of a blow, without invasion, German naval supremacy would bring the empire to an end. It is idle to assure that there will be no war. The war has already begun, the war of construction, and victory will be as decisive there as in actual battle ... I cannot ... understand how any man receiving and accepting the advantages of British citizenship, the safeguarding of our coasts, the security of our shores, the benefits and advantages of the diplomatic and consular service throughout the world can reconcile it with our self-respect to have every dollar of the cost paid by the over-burdened tax-payers of the British Islands ... When the battle of Armageddon comes, when the empire is fighting for its existence, when our kinsmen of the other great dominions are in the forefront of the battle, shall we sit silent and inactive while we contemplate with smug satisfaction our increasing crops and products ...? No, a thousand times no ... In the face of such a situation immediate, vigorous, earnest action is necessary. We have no Dreadnought ready, we have no fleet unit at hand. But we have the resources and I trust the patriotism to provide a fleet unit or at least a Dreadnought without one moment's unnecessary delay. Or, and in my opinion this would be the better course, we can place the equivalent in cash at the disposal of the Admiralty to be used for naval defence under such conditions as we may prescribe. In taking this course we shall fulfil, not only in the letter but in the spirit as well, the resolution of March last, and what is infinitely more important we shall discharge a great patriotic duty to our country and to the whole empire.

House of Commons debate on the Naval Service Bill, January 1910.

THE NATIONALISTS

Henri Bourassa published a pamphlet, Why the Navy Act Should Be Repealed, that protested any aid to Great Britain. Canada's first duty was to her own defences and interests. Let the rest of the Empire look after itself, Bourassa said. He rejected Laurier's Naval Service Bill as giving too much to the Empire.

Let the Navy Act be repealed.
Let our militia be thoroughly reformed.
Let the defence of our harbours and shores be organized.

Above all, let our system of transportation, by land and by water, be completed without a minute's loss. While we are talking "Dreadnoughts" and *"Niobes,"* populations, drawn to Western Canada by alluring advertisements, are clamouring for the means of selling and shipping their wheat. If our politicians lose their time in endeavouring to displace Imperial statesmen and save the British fleet and the motherland in spite of the British people, they may suddenly awaken from their magnificent dreams of Imperialism, and be confronted with serious troubles occasioned in Canada by their neglect to secure Canada's economical safety and national unity.

Let Canada first be looked after ... It is ... *the part of the Empire* committed to our care by the Crown of England and Imperial Parliament. If in order to do other people's work, we neglect our own, neither the British nor the Australians will come and help us in setting our house in order.

Henri Bourassa, *Why the Navy Act Should Be Repealed* (Montreal, 1912), 46.

LAURIER WAS CAUGHT IN THE MIDDLE

Laurier's philosophy of moderate compromise, embodied in the Naval Service Bill of 1910, has been described by his biographer, O.D. Skelton. Skelton warmly approved Laurier's actions and recommended them to his successor in the Liberal Party, Mackenzie King.

On Laurier's Philosophy of Governing Canada

The conception of Canada's status which Sir Wilfrid developed in his later years of office was that of a nation within the Empire. He became convinced that it was possible to reconcile what was sanest and most practicable in the ideals of independence and of imperialism. Canada might attain virtual independence, secure control of her own destinies at home and abroad, and yet retain allegiance to a common sovereign ... He approached the question in his own distinctive fashion. He would not draw up any elaborate theory or programme; he could meet only one problem at a time, and only when occasion compelled. He disliked sudden changes. His mind lacked what some would term the constructive, some, the doctrinaire bent. He was a responsible politician, working out each day's task as it came. He was anxious, again, to find a policy which would unite and express the dominant currents of Canadian opinion ... The compromise of nationhood within the Empire appeared to afford this basis.

O.D. Skelton, *Life and Letters of Sir Wilfrid Laurier*, vol. 2, 1896–1919 (Toronto, 1965), 110.

On Laurier's Naval Service Bill

In January, 1910 ... Sir Wilfrid Laurier introduced a Naval Service Bill ... It provided for the establishment of a naval force consisting of a permanent corps, a reserve, and a volunteer force, on the same lines as the militia, except that the provision of the Militia Act rendering the whole male population from seventeen to sixty years liable to service was not included; service was to be wholly voluntary. A naval college would be established, and a naval board set up to advise the Department of Marine. The force was to be under the control of the Canadian government, but the governor-general in council might in emergency place any or all of it at the disposal of His Majesty, subject to the immediate summoning of parliament if not in session ... In introducing the bill and again in the second reading, Sir Wilfrid defended the government's policy as a timely and moderate measure, a middle ground on which reasonable men could unite, and yet not a neutral and colourless compromise but a logical development of Canada's course since half a century.

O.D. Skelton, *Life and Letters of Sir Wilfrid Laurier*, vol. 2, 1896–1919 (Toronto, 1921), 325–26.

18 ❦ The Conscription Dilemma

How Many Men Did French Canada Contribute?

E.H. Armstrong argues that French-Canadian contributions lagged in World War I, but the statistics have to be read carefully.

To summarize French Canada's war effort, although she supplied two-fifths, or 40 percent of the total population of Canada, the estimated 32,000–35,000 French-Canadian members of the Canadian Expeditionary Forces constituted roughly only 5 percent of the 600,000 soldiers furnished by the Dominion as a whole. But in considering this percentage, it must not be forgotten that approximately 228,751, or roughly 33 1/3 percent, of the C.E.F. were British-born; while the English-speaking Canadian-born population, which constituted about 60 percent of the total, contributed less than 50 percent of Canadian soldiers.° In estimating the number of French Canadians in the Army it must also be remembered that not all French Canadians came from the province of Quebec, for there was a total population of 225,451 of French stock in the other provinces† ... In fact, of the total of 14,100 French Canadians serving on April 30, 1917, almost 50 percent were from other provinces than Quebec.

° Canada, *House of Commons Debates*, 19 March 1919, 164.
† *Fifth Census of Canada*, II, 340.

E.H. Armstrong, *The Crisis of Quebec 1914–18* (1974), 250.

How Was the Conscription Bill Presented? and Received?

Arthur Meighen, one of the ablest debaters ever to hold the floor in the House of Commons, presented the bill to Parliament. In the very act of presentation, it had to be defended against French-Canadian opposition. Part of his speech on 21 June 1917 read thus:

The right and honourable thing must be done. The right and honourable thing will be done. The right and honourable thing is embodied in this Bill. But the important duty of members of Parliament is to see to it that we make plain to every reasonable man to the four corners of this Dominion, that we pass this Bill, and enforce it, only because it is the right thing to do—that we do so, far from any spirit of vindictiveness, or for any unworthy or insufficient reason, but because, in this crisis of the nation, it is the only right thing to do ... The war in which we are engaged must be pressed on to victory by the only means in which it can be pressed.

I regard the forwarding of troops to the front as a necessary, as an all-essential, as something we cannot shirk ... No one has seriously argued in this House ... that we can dispatch 350,000 men overseas, commissioned by us to stand between our country and destruction and leave them to be decimated and destroyed. The obligation of honour is upon us, it is the plainest obligation that ever was placed on a nation ...

... Who can contend, with justification, that the voluntary system has not been adequately tried in Canada, both as to vigour of effort and as to length of time? ... In the two months through which we have just passed, the voluntary system yielded us not one man for four of those who were casualties among our armies in France. Add the casualties in France and the wastage in England to the wastage in Canada, and it is as plain as any rule of arithmetic that further reliance on the voluntary system will in time—perhaps in a very short time—so reduce our forces that we shall have no substantial representation in the war ...

... Strenuous effort is being exerted to show that the intention of the Militia Act was to limit compulsion to defence within this country, or, at all events, within this continent. I listened with great interest to the argument of the member for Kamouraska [Mr. E. Lapointe] and I address these words in particular to my French-Canadian friends. The Militia Act provides that all males between 18 and 60 shall be liable to service, and that liability may be exercised for the purpose of securing the defence of Canada within or beyond Canada ...

... The speech of the hon. member is made for the purpose of distribution throughout the province of Quebec, and for the purpose of urging his compatriots in that province against the adoption of the Military Service Act ... No honourable member can point me to a statement made by any constituted legal authority in Canada, at any time since the first Militia Act was passed in 1868 up to the present hour, who ever said anything else than that under the Militia Act our troops can be sent overseas ...

... I want to say something else, and I do so with special earnestness ... This bill is not designed and is not framed to be unjust to the province of Quebec or to any other section of this country ... We of English-speaking Canada have the kindest feelings towards our French-Canadian compatriots ...This Bill in its results will work more lightly on the province of Quebec than on any other province in Canada. In what way will it work more lightly? In the first place, the province of Quebec is an agricultural province ... Consequently under the terms of the Bill the exemptions to agriculture will far outnumber the exemptions to other avocations of our people. Therefore, the exemption clauses, applied evenly and fairly all over this Dominion, as is the intent, will, for just and good and sound reasons, be of more value to the province of Quebec than to any other province of Canada.

Secondly, in the province of Quebec, the young men marry at an earlier age than in the English provinces … Under this Act, the first three classes to be called out embrace only unmarried men between the ages of 20 and 34 … the Act will apply to a smaller proportion in the province of Quebec than in any other province.

We are ready, on our part, to do much to avoid the danger of disunion … We have been ready to pay a great price, to make a big sacrifice, if, by that price or sacrifice, we could avoid even the possibility of disunion in Canada … The leader of the Government has said to the great leader of the French-Canadian race: "I will share with you the reins of power."

Canada, *House of Commons Debates*, vol. 3, 21 June 1917, 2529–37.

On the other side of the House, the opposite view had been given six months earlier. In January 1917, replying to the Speech from the Throne, J.A. Descarries spoke for voluntary enlistment only.

The imperious needs of the struggle have suggested to certain individuals and to certain newspapers the possibility of the Government establishing obligatory military service. Should I say that the right hon. Prime Minister and many of his colleagues have refused to consider the suggestion … I believe in any case … and I think I am voicing the opinion of the majority of the hon. members in stating that the constitution of the country forbids sending our soldiers to fight outside of Canada, without special legislation being enacted in the House and that no such legislation altering the very basis of our Constitution would be enacted without its first being submitted to the people of Canada …

… There can be no question of conscription, obligatory enlistment is not needed. The people of Canada have given noble proof of their loyalty. Freely, voluntarily, 400,000 men have already answered the call. If they are required, 100,000 more will follow of their own free will—and thus the Prime Minister will have given to the Empire and the allied nations a royal and magnificent contribution to restore the peace of the world, which, let us hope, Providence will soon grant to Europe.

Canada, *House of Commons Debates*, vol. 1, 22 January 1917, 1124.

Was Laurier Right in Saying "No" to Coalition and Conscription?

Roger Graham, a biographer of Arthur Meighen, argues that Laurier was wrong and did the nation a great disservice by refusing to join the coalition government that Sir Robert Borden created by recruiting members of the Liberals to join his Conservatives—after he introduced conscription.

Laurier had spoken much about disunion but if it threatened was not he himself to blame? Meighen thought he was and said so bluntly. "If there is one man between the shores of this country who is responsible for the shadow of disunion I say it is the leader of the Opposition. It is only two months ago since an offer was made to the right hon. gentleman which, if it had been accepted, would have cemented together all, or almost all, in this House and throughout Canada who stand behind this war ... It is the fault of the leader of the Opposition, and on his head the charge will rest so long as time endures that in this ... the most perilous struggle in which this or any other nation ever engaged, there was not such a union of those who want to win the war as would produce for the sons of Canada the greatest assistance in their struggle to the death in Flanders ..." This speech, entirely unrehearsed and unpremeditated and all the more remarkable for its fluency and order on that account, was an expression of Meighen's innermost convictions about the war and the situation it had created in Canada ... The basic premise in this case was that the war was being fought, not only for the defence of Canada, but for her very survival as a free, democratic state. Meighen, in company with countless others, was intensely, passionately convinced of that. With the greatest of issues at stake, therefore, Canadians must be prepared to make every necessary sacrifice; the obligations of duty and honour could admit of nothing less ...

... His words were spoken more in sorrow than in anger: sorrow that Laurier, for whose gifts of leadership he had immense admiration, had not thus far responded to what Meighen thought were the self-evident requirements of the time; sorrow that Laurier by his repeated predictions of disunity had helped to bring about that dreaded condition; sorrow, finally, that Sir Wilfrid feared to pit himself against the malignant propaganda of the Nationalists. Meighen in fact, had more confidence in Laurier's remaining power and influence in Quebec than Laurier had himself. He believed that in a trial of strength between the Liberal chieftain and the Nationalist agitators Laurier would carry the day. Such a test of strength did not take place and, whether for that reason or not, Nationalism in Quebec was temporarily triumphant.

Roger Graham, *Arthur Meighen*, vol. 1, *The Door of Opportunity* (Toronto, 1960), 142–44.

J.W. Dafoe, a western Liberal, believed passionately that Laurier was mistaken. He wrote of his experiences in trying to persuade him to join the coalition and save the party and the country.

The Canadian house of commons was the vantage point from which Sir Wilfrid carried on the operations by which he unhorsed Bourassa. Here we find the explanation of much that appears inexplicable in the political events of 1916 and 1917. Laurier was out to demonstrate that he was the true champion of Quebec's views and interests ...

... His position in Quebec was now secure and unchallenged—even Bourassa, recognizing the logic of the situation, commended Laurier's leadership to his followers. If he could hold his following in the English provinces substantially intact the result was beyond question. He set himself resolutely to the task. Thereafter the situation developed with all the inevitableness of a Greek tragedy to the final catastrophe ... One thing he would not do; he would not deviate by an inch from the course he had marked out. Repeated and unavailing efforts were made to find some formula by which a disruption of the party might be avoided ... Sc ores of men had the experience of the writer; going into Laurier's room on the third floor of the improvised parliamentary offices in the National History Museum, spending an hour or so in fruitless discussion and coming out with the feeling that there was no choice between unquestioning acceptance of Laurier's policy or breaking away from allegiance to him. Not that Laurier ever proposed this choice to his visitors. He had a theory—which not even he with all his lucidity could make intelligible—that a man could support both him and conscription at the same time ... Sir Wilfrid in these conversations ... never failed to stress conditions in Quebec as compelling the course he followed; the alternative was to throw Quebec to the extremists, with a resulting division that might be fatal. There was, too, the mournful and repeated assertion—which abounds in his letters—that these developments showed that it was a mistake for a member of the minority to be the leader of the party ... Sir Wilfrid misjudged, all through the piece, the temper and purpose of the Liberals who dissented from his policy ... He saw political ambition. He saw unworthy desires to forward personal and business ends. But he did not see what was plain to view—that the whole movement was derived from an intense conviction on the part of growing numbers of Liberals that united national action was necessary if Canada was to make the maximum contribution to the war ... There followed the general election and the Unionist sweep. Laurier returned to parliament with a following of 82 in a house of 235. Of these 62 came from Quebec; and 9 from the Maritime province. From the whole vast expanse from the Ottawa river to the Pacific Ocean ten lone Liberals were elected; of these only 2 represented the west ...

The policy of shaping national programmes to meet sectional predilections, relying upon party discipline and the cultivation of personal loyalties to serve as substitutes elsewhere had run its full course—and this was the harvest!

John W. Dafoe, *Laurier: A Study in Canadian Politics* (Toronto, 1963), 97–105.

Two letters from Laurier give reasons for his stand—one to N.W. Rowell and one to Sir Allen Aylesworth.

... By conscription, you may undoubtedly assist the cause (of the war), but you will injure it more than you will assist, because you are going to create a line of cleavage in the·population, the consequences of which I know too well, and for which I will not be responsible. You will tell me, why should I not agree to conscription? Here are my reasons ...

... It is not only the people of Quebec who are opposed to conscription, but my correspondence satisfies me that in every other province there is amongst the masses an undercurrent [indicating] that they will be sore and bitter if at the present moment a conscription law is forced upon them ... This is the general idea. Now as to my own self.

When I introduced the Naval Policy, with the full approval of the Conservative party, as you will remember, I was assailed, viciously assailed, by the Nationalists of Quebec, on the ground that this Canadian navy—Canadian in peace time, Imperial in war time—was nothing short of a national crime; that under no circumstances should we fight for England; that it was the first step to conscription. I had to face the issue, and faced it by stating that the navy, Canadian at all times, in wartime might be placed at the service of the Imperial authorities; that Canada was a free country, and might, if it so chose, fight for England ... that enlistment for the naval service would be voluntary, as enlistment for the land service. I fought the issue upon those lines, always protesting that I was opposed to conscription.

Now if I were to waver, to hesitate or to flinch, I would simply hand over the province of Quebec to the extremists. I would lose the respect of the people whom I thus addressed, and would deserve it. I would not only lose their respect, but my own self-respect also.

Laurier to N.W. Rowell, 3 June 1917, in O.D. Skelton, *Life and Letters of Sir Wilfrid Laurier,* vol. 2 (Toronto, 1965), 190–91.

... Has a case been made out for conscription? There is a shortage of labour in agriculture and industry, in fact in every field where brawn and muscles are needed, and in the face of this condition people are still yelling for more men being taken away from occupations in which they are so much needed. If we had been in office a survey would have been made at once as to how many men could be spared from their usual occupations, and, having obtained a reliable statistical record, we would have endeavoured, and I think would have succeeded, in having in the field by voluntary enlistment the number of men which we could afford to give, and to that policy we would have adhered, instead of changing and again changing, with confusion worse confounded as a consequence. Every man in a certain section is striving to make himself more popular than the other by shouting for a larger number of soldiers ... Public opinion seems to have been swayed in Ontario to a feverish heat without any serious appreciation of the real situation.

Laurier to Sir Allen Aylesworth, 15 May 1917, in O.D. Skelton, *Life and Letters of Sir Wilfrid Laurier,* vol. 2 (Toronto, 1965), 187–88.

Ramsay Cook takes a balanced view of the differences between Laurier and the conscriptionists: there was something to be said for each side.

... The source of the conflict between Dafoe and Laurier over conscription and union government ... stemmed from a fundamental difference over the nature of the Great War and the role Canada should play in it. From the very outbreak of the conflict, Dafoe had taken the view that it was Canada's war and that the country's interests and aspirations were wagered upon its outcome ... Since it was Canada's war, Dafoe placed no limitations on the extent of the country's participation. When voluntary recruiting failed to provide the men necessary for a maximum war effort, Dafoe immediately agreed that compulsory enlistment would have to be put into effect. Union government was the best available means of achieving this end.

Laurier viewed the war as Britain's war, and Canada's contribution to it as the assistance given by a colony to the mother country ... Again and again he emphasized that it was "the duty of Canada to assist the Motherland to the utmost of Canada's ability" ... But since Canada was fighting for Britain, it would not be called upon to make the same sacrifices as the principal participants. For Laurier, that sacrifice fell just short of conscription ...

The nationalism of Dafoe and the nationalism of Laurier were at fundamental variance at this precise point. Dafoe viewed Canada, even in 1914, as part of a wider world in which it had international interests and responsibilities. Laurier saw Canada isolated from the world and, as far as possible, concerned only with its own pressing problems. These conflicting assumptions brought the rupture of 1917.

Ramsay Cook, *The Politics of John W. Dafoe and the Free Press* (Toronto, 1963), 84–85.

WAS CONSCRIPTION A SUCCESS?

A. M. Willms argues that it was, and in doing so he takes on the school of Whig historians.

The papers of Sir Wilfrid Laurier trace like a fascinating novel the collapse of the strong Liberal party around its tragic, white-plumed hero. They blame the catastrophe on the political machinations of the Government, and contend that conscription was neither necessary nor successful, but that it caused a serious rift between Quebec and the rest of Canada. Thus the Laurier Papers tend to confirm the story of conscription as it has been accepted by Canadian historians. But there are other versions of the story in such collections as the Borden Papers, the Rowell Papers, and the Dafoe Papers. In fact the cumulative effect of new materials is to show that not only was conscription militarily necessary—that Canada's contribution to the fighting lagged behind that of her principal allies and sister Dominions until conscription was employed—but also that the success of conscription was not achieved at the cost of a national tragedy …

It would appear that by the spring of 1917 the Canadian Government had exhausted the potentialities of voluntary recruiting … The trend of enlistment showed a fairly steady downward curve from about 30,000 a month in January, 1916, to under 5,000 a month in April, 1917.

Measures had to be adopted to check this trend. Drastic solutions were suggested and tried … Distinguished French veterans were sent from France to help the campaign in Quebec; and the help of the Catholic clergy from France was offered and accepted. But enlistments dropped to 3,000 in August, 1917. This was not enough to keep even two divisions in the field. The obvious answer to this manpower problem was conscription. Almost every country was using it and using it effectively. Selective conscription they found to be more efficient and more just than voluntary recruiting …

Despite the variety of evidence, the intensity of feeling among English-speaking Canadians on conscription has been generally disregarded by historians. One reason for this is that the English-speaking provinces were not united on the desirability of conscription whereas Quebec showed a solid front against it. Another reason is that until the election campaign of 1917 leadership was lacking for the pro-conscription forces; but then it emerged in great strength.

Most historians also seem to have accepted the thesis that conscription was a failure, that it did not produce worthwhile results. But this is not true. The Military Service Act was passed to enlist men as required; the first requirement was repeatedly announced as being from 50,000 to 100,000 men ... Conscription produced that number. The figures from different sources vary from less than 80,000 to over 170,000 ... In any case, the monthly enlistment was raised from 4,500 in December, 1917, to over 19,000 in January, 1918, while the average enlistment for the first eight months of 1918, until the war had been virtually won, was over 18,000 a month, whereas the average monthly enlistment during 1917 had been less than 6,000 ... Plainly, the Military Service Act was not a failure, and it was not ineffective ...

A.M. Willms, "Conscription 1917: A Brief for the Defence," *Canadian Historical Review* 37, no. 4 (December 1956): 338–51.

OR WAS IT A FAILURE?

O.D. Skelton argues that the policy of conscription was a total failure and provoked further unrest between French and English Canadians.

... The Military Service Act did more to win the election than to win the war. It failed absolutely in the ostensible aim of providing greater reinforcements than the voluntary system. The government had had a free hand in framing the measure. No effort or expense was spared in its enforcement. A huge administrative staff was set up, each office with its full equipment of shining desks and elaborate files; forms and instructions and regulations rained from the Printing Bureau ...

Yet the legions promised did not appear. The first shock to the sanguine supporters of the act came when it was found that of the 404,000 of the first class, unmarried men from 20–34, who had registered by the end of 1917, 380,000 had claimed exemption; the next, with the announcement that there were 118,000 claims for exemption from Ontario as against 115,000 from Quebec (out of 125,000 and 117,000 registrants). Local tribunals, particularly in Quebec, were charged with being farcically lax; on the other hand, the military representatives appealed nearly every exemption in Quebec, but allowed 90,000 in Ontario to go unopposed … Sir Robert Borden had insisted in June that it was absolutely essential to have 70,000 men by December 31, 1917. By March 31, 1918, the number ordered to report for duty was only 31,000, of whom 5,000 defaulted, the net yield being less than 26,000 …

When the end came in November, 1918, some 83,000 men had been enrolled under the act, or had reported voluntarily after its enactment; of these, 7,000 were on compassionate leave and 15,000 on farm leave, so that the actual yield was 61,000 men, of whom few ever saw France. Of these, Ontario yielded more than Quebec. The slacker remained a slacker still …

… The act, even with the cancelling of exemptions, did not yield as many men a month as the voluntary system, and even if allowance were made for the cumulative exhaustion of the supply of men, and the greater proportion available for infantry duty, it was clear that the test of experience had gone against the measure. It yielded no margin of reinforcements to balance the stirring of passion and the cleavage of race and province it provoked …

O.D. Skelton, *Life and Letters of Sir Wilfrid Laurier,* vol. 2, 1896–1919 (Toronto, 1921), 545–49.

THE METHODS OF MACKENZIE KING—NOBLE OR IGNOBLE?

J.W. Pickersgill argues that King's methods, like his aims in the war, were influenced by the highest principles of patriotism.

Mackenzie King undoubtedly loved office and the prestige of office, and it gave him deep satisfaction that the grandson of William Lyon Mackenzie had fulfilled the destiny of his grandfather. But he was not content to enjoy office for its own sake. From the outbreak of the war to its close, he never permitted any other aim to obscure his supreme objective that Canada should make a maximum contribution to the winning of the war. He believed that, to do so, it was essential that the country should not be torn by internal division or strife, and this it was his constant effort to minimize when it could not be prevented altogether.

Mackenzie King genuinely believed and frequently said that the real secret of political leadership was more in what was prevented than in what was accomplished. Yet his objectives were by no means negative. He always knew the direction in which he wished events to move and the political goals he sought to achieve. He was acutely conscious that political progress was possible only if public support was forthcoming, and he believed that nothing was so likely to set back a good cause as premature action. For him, leadership consisted in having the right objectives, picking the right time to act, and acting decisively and swiftly when that time had come ... He led his country successfully through the war with fortitude, with patience, with skill, and at times with audacity, and, at its close, the people of Canada gave him another vote of confidence.

J.W. Pickersgill, *The Mackenzie King Record*, vol. 1, 1939–1944 (Toronto, 1960), 9–10.

Roger Graham says that King's methods were deceptive and his goals entirely selfish.

... King's definition of the national interest seems to have consisted largely of the conviction that it could only be promoted by a Liberal government headed by himself, if, in fact, he did not believe that he was ordained to govern Canada by some divine right of King which rendered all his opponents either actual or would-be usurpers. To him the essence of the party leader's task was to listen to the many varied voices of the people. He was a "broker of ideas," to use a term much beloved of political scientists, taking from the infinitely complex and endlessly changing pattern of public opinion those thoughts, fears or desires which were politically important or exploitable. The leader, therefore, must respond to opinion, catering to it instead of trying to direct it along certain paths, and by being as many things as possible to as many people as possible seek to attract the support of the majority.

This intricate process was carried on by a compound of procrastination, inconsistency, compromise, equivocation, expediency, and misrepresentation. It ruled out candour as a political virtue and supplanted it with the cult of ambiguity. It required the carefully contrived confusion of issues, the dulling of the sharp edge of disagreement so that men of diverse opinions could come together in the capacious political church built by Mackenzie King ...

... Its logical end product was the unity of a one-party state, a state dominated by one massive, omnibus party which had something to offer to everybody and was bound to no fixed positions except an unremitting war against evil in which everyone could join with a good conscience.

Roger Graham, *Arthur Meighen,* vol. 2, And Fortune Fled (Toronto, 1963), 483–84.

Bruce Hutchison, in The Incredible Canadian, *says that, noble or ignoble, King's methods were successful and that Canadians recognized them as such. According to Hutchison, King compares with his predecessor and ranks higher than many.*

Grudgingly, in its Arctic fashion, the nation concluded, only when he had gone, that it had lost its indispensable man ...

Weighing success against failure, one must conclude that for volume and variety our Canadian registry holds no equivalent to his handiwork. There have been only two Canadians who challenge his place as a statesman, but Macdonald and Laurier dealt with problems far simpler than world war and revolution in which King swam blindly, without a chart. They were greater men. He was the greater statesman.

How, history will ask, did such a man achieve something so much larger than himself? To answer that it will be necessary to follow his life in detail. His actual methods of government are clear enough at a glance. Once, in a revealing moment, he described them to a friend as they strolled on the bank of the Ottawa.

"If," said King, pointing to a distant church spire beyond a bend in the river, "I try to reach that point directly I shall drown. I must follow the curves of the bank and ultimately I shall get there, although at times I may seem to be going somewhere else."

In the ceaseless zigzags of his administration he was often and rightly accused of inconsistency, but he always knew where he was going, and, above all, he knew how fast he could go. A Prime Minister, as he told his friend that day, must be a sponge, patiently soaking up the diverse trickles of public feeling until the time comes to extrude a policy. Only then, when a majority opinion has clearly formed, can a policy hope to work in this diverse country.

There was the method—the distant objective, the curving course of circumstance, the patient waiting for the tide of fortune to rise and then its sudden taking at the flood.

His art was the calculation of the flood. The oddest legend about King is that he made few mistakes because his judgments were formed deliberately on facts. In his largest verdicts he disregarded facts altogether and resorted to pure instinct ...

The combination of genius and chance required time for its consummation. With his equipment King could not hope for quick success. He could not blast the solid substance of Canada as Macdonald and Laurier had blasted it or even make the small dents left by the Meighens and Bennetts before the current swept them down. The rock must be worn away by steady drip, invisibly over the years.

Bruce Hutchison, *The Incredible Canadian* (Toronto, 1952), 5–11.

The Real Heroes in Quebec—Volunteers or Draft-Dodgers?

It is accepted almost without question that the heroes in war are those who volunteer their services and fight at the front. André Laurendeau, who campaigned strenuously for a "no" vote on the conscription plebiscite, suggests that to many in Quebec the real hero of the war was the man who refused to enlist. After all, 71 percent of the population in the province voted "no" to conscription.

There were two unequal forces present: we yielded. Through his art, Prime Minister King partially succeeded in masking the constraint. But there was constraint.

During the war, many French-Canadian Quebecers felt they were living in an occupied country. The English were the occupying nation, the one that dictated conduct and prevented the national will from being effectively expressed; our politicians were the collaborationists. It was, compared with Hitler's Europe, a benign occupation; thanks to the moderation of King, the yoke remained supportable. We risked only our liberties, and even at that, the menace was rarely realized. But it is sufficient that it existed for life to be poisoned.

The impression of having submitted to an occupation indicates to what point a large number of French Canadians then escaped, in their hearts and souls, from the bonds of the Central State. The greater the physical constraint, the less the moral adhesion and loyalty. To be sure, we respected the French-Canadian volunteers, because they risked their lives; but when on the basis of the courage they manifested on the battle fields, we were asked to adhere to King's policies, we experienced a violent movement of recoil. Our hero would have been the conscript in revolt, the rebel …

After all, it was a question of sentiment, but one of them is self-respect. Moreover, the world is full of sentiments, and I wonder why the only one we should refuse to allow is the one we hold with respect to ourselves, and which is called the sentiment of human dignity.

André Laurendeau, *La crise de la conscription 1942* (Montreal, 1962), 156–67 (English translation).

THE RECORD IN THE HOUSE OF COMMONS—
KING ON THE PLEBISCITE

Prime Minister King made this statement to the House of Commons on 11 May 1942.

(Plebiscite on April 27; final returns not yet available, May 11)
Over 2,926,856 voted in the affirmative—64% in favour
Over 1,618,730 in the negative—36% against

The total number of votes cast on the plebiscite is an impressive demonstration of the importance which the electors of Canada attach to giving to the government a free hand at a time of war.

The question on which the people of Canada were asked to express an opinion was:

"Are you in favour of releasing the government from any obligation arising out of any past commitments restricting the methods of raising men for military service?" By their vote, the people have decisively expressed the view that the government should be released from any such obligation. In other words, there no longer remains any issue which the government or members of parliament, because of past promises or pledges, are restricted from considering, discussing and deciding on its merits, in the light of what is best for Canada and for Canada's war effort.

The question of the plebiscite was of equal concern to all citizens of Canada. The result is a national expression of view on a national issue. It should be so viewed in all its aspects. In all of the provinces, and for that matter, in every constituency, affirmative and negative votes were cast. The vote was taken in a democratic fashion. It will be recognized throughout the country that, in a democracy, the will of the majority should prevail.

The vote in the plebiscite shows that the people generally recognize that the war has taken a course which was altogether unforeseen; that conditions wholly unexpected may yet arise, and that, in consequence, there should be no restriction upon the freedom of the government apart from its constitutional responsibility to parliament.

In the plebiscite the electors were not called upon to vote for or against the government. The result, therefore, is not to be construed as a vote for any political party. In fact, the plebiscite was selected by the government precisely because it afforded the best known means of obtaining an expression of the views of the people on a specific question, regardless of political parties, or party considerations. As, in some quarters, an effort has been made since the plebiscite to interpret the result as a mandate for conscription for overseas service, it is necessary for me to repeat that, in the plebiscite, conscription was not the issue. The government did not ask the people to say whether or not conscription for overseas service should be adopted. That was not the issue before the people. With regard to the issue of conscription, the result can only rightly be construed as leaving to the government and to parliament entire freedom to deal with that question on its merits.

Canada, *House of Commons Debates,* vol. 3 (11 May 1942), 2282.

WORDS SPOKEN IN THE HEAT OF THE CRISIS, NOVEMBER 1944

November was the height of the crisis as far as the members of Parliament were concerned. The issue had to be faced at last—was conscription for overseas service absolutely necessary? The question was faced and fought over during the last great debate.

Petitions laid before the House from English-speaking ridings:

CANADIAN FORCES

PETITIONS WITH RESPECT TO APPLICATION OF N.R.M.A. ACT

Hon. H. A. BRUCE (Parkdale): I desire to present a petition to this House of Commons from my constituency of Parkdale: The undersigned citizens of the Dominion of Canada—

Mr. SPEAKER: Order. Did I understand the hon. gentleman to say that the petition was presented to him?

Mr. BRUCE: No, Mr. Speaker; this is a petition to parliament, signed by 139 men and women of my constituency.

Mr. SPEAKER: Is it addressed to the houses of parliament?

Mr. BRUCE: It is addressed to the houses of parliament. I think it is perfectly in order.

That whereas the Prime Minister of Canada has pledged on behalf of his government to the House of Commons that if "circumstances should arise which would render the use of compulsion imperative, such for example as the maintenance of the necessary reinforcements for Canada's army overseas," the compulsory provisions of Bill 80 would become effective by order in council;

And whereas such circumstances have arisen;

And whereas your humble petitioners are of the belief that a grave emergency—

Mr. SPEAKER: Order. The hon. member may read the prayer of the petition, but not the whole petition.

Mr. BRUCE: It is, therefore, the earnest prayer of your humble petitioners that this force shall be at once dispatched overseas to the aid of our men now fighting at the front; And it is their further prayer that, since speedy victory can be gained at least cost of life only by a steady and adequate flow of reinforcements, and without such reinforcements lives must be needlessly lost, the policy of total conscription of man-power for overseas service to ensure support to our fighting forces now, and until victory is won, be made effective forthwith as provided by Bill 80, and approved by the great majority of the people of Canada recording their vote in the plebiscite of 1942.

Mr. McGREGOR: I desire to lay on the table a petition of a similar nature.

Mr. NOSEWORTHY: I desire to lay on the table two petitions of a similar nature.

Canada, *House of Commons Debates,* vol. 6 (22 November 1944), 6594–6615.

General McNaughton was closely questioned by the members of the House of Commons. He finally revealed on 23 November that those men drafted for service in Canada who did not volunteer for overseas service might be sent, nevertheless.

Mr. NOSEWORTHY: Mr. Speaker, may I continue my questions at the point at which I was interrupted. Am I to understand from the general that the answer to my question is, as the hon. member for Prince (Mr. Ralston) indicated, that there is to be no further recombing of the general service men for any part of the 16,000 extra men required for reinforcements?

Mr. McNAUGHTON: The answer is that there is constantly going on the combing of the general service personnel in Canada, that men from the N.R.M.A. Units who convert to general service will be in those figures that are going forward, and that any deficit in those figures will be made up under authority of the order in council from the men suitably trained under the N.R.M.A. There are several streams going in. I expect that the great bulk of the 16,000 men will be N.R.M.A. men, but I cannot say that that is the only source, because there will be other sources coming in to make up the stream.

Mr. NOSEWORTHY: Can you indicate at all the number that you expect to get by recombing the general service and the number that you will have to take from the N.R.M.A.?

Mr. McNAUGHTON: The number from general service which will be included in these transhipments of 5,000, 5,000 and three lots of 2,000 is not large. There will be some, but not many.

Mr. NOSEWORTHY: You would not care to indicate the actual number?

Mr. McNAUGHTON: I was only able to announce the decision, and there is a lot of detailed planning and staff work to be done before we shall know who will be in what shipment and so on.

Mr. NOSEWORTHY: Do we understand that you expect to get part of the first 5,000 by volunteer enlistments from the N.R.M.A. and that the remainders will be called up under the authority of the order in council?

Mr. McNAUGHTON: That is right.

Canada, *House of Commons Debates*, vol. 6 (23 November 1944), 6547.

On the same day, Charles G. Power resigned. An English Canadian, he declared he could not accept from McNaughton a policy he had rejected from Ralston.

Canada
Minister of National Defence for Air
Ottawa
23rd November, 1944.

Rt. Honourable W. L. Mackenzie King,
Prime Minister of Canada,
Ottawa, Ont.

My Dear Prime Minister:
It is with the deepest regret that I ask you to accept my resignation as a member of your cabinet.

I am unable to accept the policy which the government has now adopted with respect to the National Resources Mobilization Act. I do not believe such a policy to be necessary at this time, nor will it save one single Canadian casualty.

I parted company with Colonel Ralston after the most mature consideration largely on the grounds that the number of troops which he reported as being required was comparatively so small, the means to remedy the situation without placing undue strain on the men at the front so readily available, and the end of the war so imminent that weighing everything in the balance we were not justified in provoking a national scission.

I cannot accept now from a new minister, General McNaughton, a recommendation which I reluctantly felt obliged to reject when made by an old comrade and tried associate, Layton Ralston.

May I add that the task which you confided to me in May 1940 of organizing the British Commonwealth joint air training plan has now been completed and the plan is being wound up. The Royal Canadian Air Force overseas has reached the peak of its expansion. I shall always treasure the years of association with you and my colleagues and I thank you and them for all the kindness and consideration they have shown.

Yours sincerely,
Charles G. Power.

Canada, *House of Commons Debates,* vol. 6 (23 November 1944), 6591.

The policy of the government was under attack from the Conservatives and from Quebec nationalists. Victor Quelch from Acadia denounced the government succinctly, as did Jean-François Pouliot from Temiscouata. Pouliot crossed the floor and deserted the government. Each spoke of the feeling in his constituency.

In addition to that, its policy has, from the very beginning, been one of flogging the willing horse. What has been the consequence of that policy? The result has been this, that in various parts of Canada we find families in which the whole of the manhood of those families has been wiped out; and then across the road you may have a family that has made no contribution.

Victor Quelch in Canada, *House of Commons Debates,* vol. 6 (29 November 1944), 6649–50.

... I have been brought up in the respect and love of Liberal principles and traditions, and when I was young I learned English in the speeches made by great Liberal leaders of Ontario ... Since the beginning of the war I have done my best for the soldiers of my constituency and for some others ... ! regret very much that it is now impossible for me to agree with the policies of the government, for several reasons which I shall give in due course ... But when I have to make a choice between my constituents and the present government I cannot hesitate. I stand by the people of my constituency and this is my last word. I regret very much to have to cross the floor of the house right now.

Jean-François Pouliot in Canada, House of Commons Debates, vol. 6 (23 November 1944), 6562.

After the apparent reversal of the government's policy on conscription, the anger of French Canadians knew no bounds.

We have done more than you English-speaking Canadians of British descent. You have only obeyed the call of the blood ... What we have done could only be done through reasoning, and judging the situation as a judge would do when deciding a case presented to him. Try to imagine Canada as part of a French Empire, with the descendants of British citizens in the minority ... Would you be enthusiastic in defending that Empire as would be the Canadians of French descent? ...

... Think of the concessions which the French Canadians and their representatives have been making to bring about and maintain unity in this great land of ours ... by Sir Wilfrid Laurier, by Ernest Lapointe ... and by myself ... Where are your concessions, you British Canadians, in favour of the French Canadians? What have you ever done to preserve unity between the two great races in Canada ... Unity has been maintained owing to concessions made by French Canadians in this House of Commons and elsewhere ...

P.J. Arthur Cardin in Canada, *House of Commons Debates,* vol. 6 (29 November 1944), 6567 –68.

In the first place, Mr. Speaker, I regret very much that we did not have from the very beginning of the war a full-balanced conscription but a one-sided conscription. I regret very much the action of the DND which has given emblems for service only to those who have volunteered, thereby indicating that all the others who were contributing to the war effort in other ways were slackers just because they had not enlisted in the army ... What I mean with regard to the disastrous effect of what has been said throughout Canada regarding conscription and national unity is this: The province of Quebec is not at all opposed to a well-balanced conscription where the services of every man who is working in essential industry is recognized as a help to the war effort ... When on the one hand conscription is described as a good thing, and on the other hand the province of Quebec is described as opposed to conscription, and when what is described as a good thing is not imposed in this country on account of the opposition of Quebec, that is a great mistake which results in the province of Quebec being misjudged throughout the world ...

Jean-François Pouliot in Canada, *House of Commons Debates,* vol. 6 (24 November 1944), 6567.

... Protests are being heard against conscription not only from Quebec but from all sections of the country. I am still opposed to conscription with as much strength as I deployed in opposing the increase in defence estimates ... I cannot find words sufficiently scathing to condemn this new reversal of policy by a government which, at the end of its term of office, imposes this evil and anti-national measure. Never has a government broken so many pledges. Never has it thus sowed doubt and suspicion. A self-respecting administration, if they have any regard for the people, do not resort to all possible roundabout means to abuse the good faith of those under their jurisdiction.

... Since Canada has started participating in the war, we have lost all our prerogatives. We have reverted to century-old colonialism. Our country, thanks to the acts and errors of the government, is now trailing for good in the wake of the Empire to the great satisfaction of our partisans of colonialism.

Liguori Lacombe in Canada, *House of Commons Debates*, vol. 6 (29 November 1944), 6653.

THE FINAL VOTE

After what seemed the longest November on record, the vote was finally taken on the resolution put forward by Mackenzie King, "That this House will aid the government in its policy of maintaining a vigorous war effort." The House, exhausted, recorded its opinions numerically, and the conscription debate passed into history. Bruce Hutchison has described it thus:

On December 7, the criticisms, the replies, and the whole anatomy of The Crisis had been piled on the record and the House was ready to vote. When the division bells rang at last, the Quebec anti-conscription motion was defeated by 168 votes to 43. Only the French-Canadian members had voted for it, but they had detached two-thirds of the Quebec bloc from the Government—for the moment only.

The Conservative motion demanding total conscription fell by 170 to 44. Only the Conservatives supported it.

King's main motion of confidence provided a chance for a last dispirited chewing over of the conscription issue, with Cardin leading the attack ... No one was interested in further talk since nothing was left to talk about. Without excitement the House passed King's confidence motion by 143 to 70. On this vote the Conservatives were joined by 32 French Canadians, each group opposing the Government for opposite reasons.

It was a brief junction. The French Canadians had no intention of dislodging King to establish a more conscriptionist government. Now that the essential issue had been settled, they were ready to keep him in office.

Bruce Hutchison, *The Incredible Canadian* (Toronto, 1952), 397–98.

WAS THE CONSCRIPTION CRISIS OF 1944 NECESSARY?

Mason Wade argues that it was not. The military and political crisis was created by the Opposition for political gain.

The military outcome of the conscription crisis was long shrouded by censorship ... In all, 12,908 N.R.M.A. (National Resources Mobilization Act) men were sent overseas, the balance of the 16,000 provided for under the order-in-council not being needed. Casualties during November, December, and January proved considerably fewer than anticipated by the October estimate, and reinforcements overseas in April were 75 percent over the estimates of the secret session. From February until the end of hostilities in Europe "there was no serious difficulty in keeping our battalions in the field up to strength, and no question of disbanding Canadian formations ever arose," according to the official history of the Canadian Army in World War II.

In other words, Canada had nearly split itself apart in anticipation of a situation which did not materialize. The reinforcement crisis of 1944 was in great measure an artificial one brought on by the unscrupulous efforts of a party long in opposition to win power at any cost. The stake was not military victory in Europe, which was already assured, or the defence of Canada's reputation and honour, which had already been upheld beyond imputation, but control of Canada in a postwar world full of dangers for the conservative-minded ...

The collapse of their effort to win power did not prevent the Conservatives from pressing their case against French Canada's military record by close questioning of Mr. Abbott after his statement on April 5. Mr. Diefenbaker cited the statistics given in the February-March issue of *Canada at War* to show that Quebec had the lowest rate of volunteering and of N.R.M.A. call-ups. George Stanley White, an Ontario member, brought out that the Quebec military districts had the largest number of deserters, 7,800 and 3,713, out of a total of 18,943 for all Canada. On the following day Diefenbaker pointed out that over 50 percent of the Quebec N.R.M.A. men warned for overseas service had deserted.

Mason Wade, *The French Canadians 1760–1945* (Toronto, 1955), 1074–76.

Granatstein and Hitsman argue that even censorship could not conceal the ineffectiveness of conscripting the N.R.M.A. men, and that the wisdom of hindsight showed that they were not really needed.

... In all units, English-speaking or French-speaking, there was a high degree of absenteeism, and there were recurring bouts of rioting, sit-down strikes, and a definite reluctance on the part of NRMA men to "go active" even though that had advantages for them. There was also one famous case of a soldier who threw his kitbags and rifle into the sea as he went on board ship for overseas. This incident, magnified by gossip, was turned into a campaign charge by the Conservatives that hundreds of NRMA soldiers had so acted. The one incident, allegedly by a soldier with psychiatric troubles, had major political repercussions, and the Conservatives created the picture of an NRMA army that was riddled with dissension. Unfortunately that was not too far off the mark, and what some officers referred to as "Atlantic fever" was fairly widespread.

Word of the troubles with the NRMA men was largely kept from the public by censorship. The Toronto *Globe and Mail,* however, was convinced that the censorship was motivated by political reasons, not, as the Chief Censor maintained, for military security. The *Globe* and the Montreal *Gazette*, both Conservative papers, were tempted to burst the censorship bonds, but beyond an editorial by the Toronto paper denying that the security reasons were valid, an editorial that must have puzzled readers, the papers did nothing. Once the convoys had arrived in Britain, however, there was no longer any reason for censorship, and in late January there was a spate of articles that revealed, among other things, that over 200 of the 482 absentees in Pacific Command were G.S. volunteers! Nonetheless the state of affairs was bad enough among the NRMA, as the Gazette demonstrated in an editorial of 22 January:

> ... It is now a matter of official admission that of the 15,600 Home Defence troops advised that they were to be sent overseas, 7,800 or precisely one half, were at one time overdue or absent without leave. To the present time only 1,500 of these have returned or have been returned by police action.

These reports led to widespread unfavourable publicity in the United States.

They led as well to extensive efforts to crack down on deserters, to advertisements warning people that harbouring absentees was a criminal offense, and to raids on public places by RCMP and military police. In Drummondville, Quebec on 24 February a 100-man raiding party was attacked by a mob, their vehicles overturned and smashed, while fighting lasted in the streets for three hours, and scores required hospital treatment. There was no room for doubt that many of the NRMA men did not want to go overseas; nor was there any doubt that in Quebec at least, civilians too did not want them to go.

Curiously, once the NRMA soldiers did get overseas, they served very well indeed. The Loyal Edmonton Regiment's War Diary, for example, noted on 30 April 1945 that the NRMA reinforcements were treated the same as G.S. men and "in the few small actions they have engaged in so far they have generally shown up as well as all new reinforcements do." Other accounts stressed that once the men had been in action no one any longer cared who was or was not a "Zombie."

In all, 12,908 NRMA men went overseas and 2,463 were posted to units of the First Canadian Army in North West Europe. Of these 69 were killed, 232 were wounded, and 13 became prisoners of war. More important, the estimates of need that had provoked the crisis in October 1944, those guesses on the future course of events, proved to be in error. Action on the Canadian fronts was less heavy than the General Staff had expected; the corps in Italy was transferred to North West Europe and was out of action as a result, with a consequent saving of casualties; and the Germans collapsed rather more rapidly in the end than many had feared. Even without the reinforcements provided by the NRMA men, there would have been 8,500 men in the reinforcement pool overseas on 27 April 1945.

The NRMA crisis, then, fizzled out like a damp squib. Its importance was more symbolic than real, but that was importance enough.

J.L. Granatstein and J.M. Hitsman, *Broken Promises: A History of Conscription in Canada* (Toronto, 1977), 233–34.

19 ❧ THOUGHTS ON THE QUIET REVOLUTION

WHAT WAS HAPPENING IN QUEBEC?

Most observers are convinced that a revolution was taking place. Thomas Sloan, one of the more astute and sympathetic of the English-speaking observers of Quebec in the 1960s, argued that there were most certainly revolutionary changes going on and that more could be expected.

… Today's Quebec is no longer a folklore society of colourfully dressed old farmers and woodsmen dancing around the wood stove to the tune of the fiddle … It is the province of the Place Ville Marie, Place des Arts, of huge hydro-electric developments, of the new steel project. It is the province of new roads, new bridges, new northern towns and new ideas. It is the province of economic planning and the General Investment Corporation. It is the province where film censorship has practically disappeared and where more books are published and bought than any other part of Canada … Changes are taking place so rapidly and in so many fields that it is hard to keep pace with them. But at least, we must re cognize the fact of change and take it into all our calculations …

The new Quebec is, psychologically at least, more akin to the New France of the early days than to the Quebec of the more recent past. With its sudden release of energies and acceptance of change and experiment, it has more in common with the colony that was the stage for the exploits of the *coureurs de bois* and the explorers than it has with the ingrown, tradition-bound Quebec of the nineteenth and early twentieth centuries, ruled by politicians who were timid outside and all too often brazenly corrupt inside the province …

For it is a revolution, this process being experienced in Quebec. There are perhaps other words that could be used to describe it. Renaissance might be one. But when we consider the tremendous scope and impact of what is going on in Quebec, when we think of the speed and depth of the evolution of thought and institutions, the word revolution is not too strong. It is not a violent affair, except in some of its extremities; neither is it entirely consistent in all its parts. And perhaps the adjective *quiet* has been overworked in describing it. It is a lusty, brawling, enthusiastic, and occasionally angry forward movement that often disagrees within itself …

Thomas Sloan, Quebec. *The Not-So-Quiet Revolution* (Toronto, 1965), Preface, viii–x.

Jean-Paul Desbiens described the revolution as a moral and religious crisis.

I am not prophesying the outcome of the revolution, I am only describing the present state of affairs. For it is quite possible that in the end Christianity will have been thrown overboard. But if that happens it will have been the fault of the Christians themselves and not the result of a conspiracy of the MLF [Mouvement de Libération de la Femme]. If there are any Christians around here, they had better wake up; they had better show a bit of imagination, respect the freedom of others as much as they do their own, and spend a little less time maintaining the present easy but sterile methods and a little more in finding the almost non-existent methods of a productive system of education.

... In the *Impertinences* I said: "Things have already deteriorated beyond recognition. The young people whom we teach in class are as far from Christianity as they can go without making a commotion. Their ideas, their feelings, above all their feelings about money, women, success, love, are as foreign to Christianity as is possible." That opinion was based partly on intuition and partly on experience derived from my contacts with young men who came from a geographically-isolated region and lived among people who, at that time, were still in common agreement about everything. I have since learned that my opinions were much more correct than I had believed them to be. I was much concerned about it for a while. But I have now got over it.

There is no doubt that we are experiencing a religious crisis. Crisis means judgement. We are in the process of judging things for ourselves and making decisions. It is no longer possible to be a Catholic in the same way as having blue eyes. Each one will have to decide for himself. A major part of the population will, and has already, begun to throw off Christianity. But in fact there isn't much to throw off. It's simply a caricature which is being rejected, and as a matter of fact it is crumbling by itself more than it is being rejected. We are discovering that we are naked, as soon as our institutional trappings are removed. Our atheists and our free-thinkers are as good as our believers.

Jean-Paul Desbiens (Brother Anonymous), *For Pity's Sake* (Montreal, 1965), 115–16.

What Were Politics Really Like under Duplessis?

Herbert Quinn made an intensive study of the Union Nationale Party in the years of Duplessis and concluded that the electoral methods used to return the party to power were just about as bad as the Liberals said they were.

... In many electoral districts youth organizations, social and athletic clubs, and parochial organizations received donations of anywhere from $200 to $2,000 from the party. Influential individuals in every community who could not be looked after by giving them a government job ... were sometimes given gifts of a hundred dollars or more to induce them to come out openly for the party. The smaller fry were given presents as varied as sacks of potatoes, nylon stockings, hams, bags of flour ... Owners of cars were offered up to $25 for their participation in one of the innumerable parades ... Following the good old Roman custom of providing circuses, as well as bread, the party organization offered free entertainment in many constituencies in the form of wrestling matches, night club shows, movies, band concerts, and bingo games ... These different forms of entertainment were often timed to coincide with an important mass meeting called by the Liberal party in that particular town ... The distribution of beer, whiskey, and other kinds of alcoholic beverages played an important role in "softening up" the electorate in the two or three weeks immediately preceding polling day ... Parties were organized at which everyone was welcome and could drink to his heart's content.

Herbert Quinn, *The Union Nationale* (Toronto, 1963), 144.

But rather than placing the blame on the Union Nationale, Quinn saw the cause of corruption to be the lack of a democratic philosophy in the province. From the days of the Conquest, French Canadians had seen in politics the means of defending their nationality and of securing tangible material gains. The finer points of democratic idealism they left to their Anglo-Saxon neighbours.

From the point of view of democratic theory, parliamentary government was accepted by the people of Quebec for the wrong reasons. It was welcomed in that province, not because of any conviction that all government should be responsible to the governed, but because French-Canadian leaders were quick to grasp the value of representative institutions as a means of defending the interests and cultural values of the group against the autocratic rule of the colonial governor. Later on ... they ... were a weapon ... against any government, autocratic or otherwise, which happened to be dominated by the English ... This attitude has had a rather curious result: government expenditures made in the ordinary course of administration for such things as public works or social services have usually been looked upon, not as a right of the citizen, but as a special favour or privilege granted by the government. The party in power has a particular advantage as its expenditure of government money, particularly at election times, enables it to pose as a benefactor whose generosity should be rewarded by voting it back into office ... The average Quebec voter is left unmoved by flagrant breaches of the spirit of fair play on the part of the majority party towards the opposition in the legislature ... He is unconcerned whenever proper budgetary procedures are not followed by the government.

[ReadingSource.Start] Herbert Quinn, *The Union Nationale* (Toronto, 1963), 17–19.

SEPARATIST NATIONALISM—INSPIRING OR RIDICULOUS?

In April 1963, the Front de Libération Québécois published a remarkable manifesto. The authors passionately stated their case for a revolt of French Canadians against their foreign oppressors. It was a call to arms—for the sake of French-Canadian nationalism.

A Message to the Nation

by the *Front de Libération Québécois:* Ever since the second world war, the various enslaved peoples of the world have been shattering their bonds to acquire the freedom which is theirs by right ...

Like so many others before us, the people of Quebec have reached the end of their patience with the arrogant domination of Anglo-Saxon colonialism ...

The workers' eyes are daily becoming more attuned to reality: Quebec is a colony!

We are a colonized people, politically, socially, and economically ... Ottawa's colonial government has full powers in the following fields: economic policy, foreign trade, defence, bank credit, immigration, the criminal courts, etc... .

The federal government undividedly stands behind the interests of the Anglo-Saxon imperialists who both constitutionally and in practice play an overwhelming part in ruling the country ... Whenever a conflict arises between Anglo-Saxon and Quebec interests, it is Quebec's interests that must yield ...

We provide the labour, they bank the profits.

Socially, too, Quebec is a colony. We represent 80 percent of the population, and yet the English language prevails in many fields. French is gradually relegated to the realm of folklore, while English becomes the people's working language. The Anglo-Saxons' contempt for our people is as high as ever. Expressions such as "Speak White!" "Stupid French Canadians," and others of the same ilk are common ... The colonizers see us as inferior beings, and have no compunction about letting us know that they do ...

Quebec's patriots are not fighting over a name, but over a situation. A revolution is not a parlour game, played for fun. Only a full-fledged revolution can build up the necessary power to achieve the vital changes that will be needed in an independent Quebec. A national revolution cannot, of its very nature, tolerate any compromise. There is only one way of overcoming colonialism: to be stronger than it is! QUEBEC PATRIOTS, TO ARMS! THE HOUR OF NATIONAL REVOLUTION HAS STRUCK! INDEPENDENCE OR DEATH!

Claude Savoie, *La Véritable Histoire du F.L.Q.* (Montreal, 1963) (English translation).

Pierre Elliott Trudeau condemned such passionate outbursts as the Message to the Nation. Excessive nationalism was a waste of time for French Canada, he maintained, and no French Canadian had ever been better off for the ravings of the nationalists.

The Sorry Story of French-Canadian Nationalism

Let me explain—
We have expended a great deal of time and energy proclaiming the rights due our nationality, invoking our celestial mission, trumpeting our virtues, bewailing our misfortunes, denouncing our enemies, and avowing our independence, and for all that not one of our workmen is the more skilled, nor a civil servant the more efficient, a financier the richer, a doctor the more advanced, a bishop the more learned, nor a single solitary politician the less ignorant ... There's probably not one French-Canadian intellectual who hasn't spent at least four hours a week over the last year discussing Separatism. That makes how many thousand times two hundred hours spent just flapping our arms? ... The Separatists of 1962 that I have met really are, in general, genuinely earnest and nice people; but, the few times I have had the opportunity of talking with them at any length, I have almost always been astounded by the totalitarian outlook of some, by the anti-Semitism of others, and, in all cases, by their complete ignorance of basic economics.

Now this is what I call *la nouvelle trahison des clercs:* this self-deluded passion of a large segment of our thinking population for throwing themselves headlong—intellectually and spiritually—into purely escapist pursuits.

Cité Libre, April 1962.

WHAT WAS THE ENGLISH-CANADIAN REACTION?

At Laval University in 1961, Douglas Fisher claimed to represent the point of view of the average English Canadian. He was replying to a statement by René Lévesque that English Canada needed French Canada more than French Canada needed English Canada.

... I am tempted to say, "That goes double!" ... If I could come down without too great seriousness upon this whole question of French Canada from an English-Canadian point of view, it might go like this. If I was speaking to my constituents or anybody from Sudbury westward, trying to explain what little I know about the French Canadians, their reaction would be: "Well, what has the French Canadian to offer us, that we should be so excited about bonne entente and learning the French language and so on?" And I wonder what they would say about French-Canadian culture? I suppose for us the greatest impact of French-Canadian culture has been made by Maurice Richard and Lili St-Cyr. We did have Gisèle, of course, but she became Gisèle McKenzie and went off to the United States. I wonder whether we are to be fascinated by your marvellous police tradition, the magnificence of your telegraphers, the ingenuity that I witnessed when I was looking into the operation of the Jacques-Cartier bridge in Montreal. I wonder if we are to be tremendously impressed with the Courtemanches, the Pouliots, the Sévignys and such people whom we encounter at Ottawa. I wonder if we are to be impressed with your tradition of literary censorship, or whether your educational system has a great deal to offer us in a society where technocracy is becoming so much more important. I cannot honestly say I believe that we need your resources. You have lots of iron ore here, but so have we and so has much of the rest of Canada. You have a lot of base metals, but so have we. You have lots of water power, but so has British Columbia; and we've got all kinds of natural gas, oil, and coal in the rest of the country.

Le Canada : Expérience ratée ou réussie? (The Canadian Experiment: Success or Failure?) (Quebec, 1962), 155–56. The speech was to the First Congress on Canadian Affairs organized by Laval students, 15–18 November 1961.

Perhaps, in fact, some English Canadians were just as exclusively nationalistic as their counterparts among the radical left in Quebec. Perhaps unhyphenated Canadianism, as advocated by John Diefenbaker, was a form of English-Canadian nationalism, as jealous of its own as the francophone variety.

One misunderstanding should be cleared up at once. What is English-Canadian nationalism? English Canadians often deny it exists, claiming that any nationalism there is simply the all-Canadian brand—unhyphenated Canadianism, as Mr. Diefenbaker has described it. The supporter of this theory often considers himself a sincere Canadian patriot and gets extremely upset at French-Canadian nationalism, which seems to him a divisive sentiment, an obstacle to national unity. In so far as national unity is defined in terms of unhyphenated Canadianism, this is perfectly true. From the viewpoint of a French Canadian, however, unhyphenated Canadianism is merely another way of saying nationalism of the majority, or English-Canadian nationalism.

As grand a concept as unhyphenated Canadianism may be, the very existence of the French Canadians has always depended upon that same, miserable little hyphen. That is why the French Canadian will not and cannot give it up. That is why unhyphenated Canadianism is impossible. What the English Canadian must realize is that, objectively, his abstract Canadian is in reality an English-Canadian nationalism gone slightly hypocritical. By magnanimously doing away with the hyphen he is in fact forgetting the minority and creating Canadianism in the image of himself and of the majority to which he belongs. It would probably be much better to recognize that there is such a thing as English-Canadian nationalism, call it by that name and see what we could do to integrate it with the form dominant in Quebec.

Thomas Sloan, Quebec: *The Not-So-Quiet Revolution* (Toronto, 1965), 107.

Thomas Sloan wondered if English-Canadian nationalism is not sometimes separatism in reverse. Were not some anglophones anxious to ignore Quebec and to proceed as if the French part of Canada did not even exist?

… When discussing French-Canadian separatism there comes a point at which an English-Canadian observer from outside Quebec must stop, rub his eyes in disbelief, and take a completely new look at Canada and Confederation. He suddenly realizes that he has heard most of the arguments before, only reversed. He recalls his own compatriots' assertions that Canada is an English-speaking country; he remembers magazine articles, letters-to-the-editor, speeches by politicians … maintaining that French is a foreign language and that there is room for only one basic culture and language in Canada. There may be grudging acceptance of the right of "the French" to retain their language in Quebec, but under no circumstances should we surrender the exclusive rights and privileges of English elsewhere. How many times have we heard complaints that "Quebec is running the country," that "what we need is national unity," and that "we're going to have to show them where to get off"? Quebec is a thorn in our flesh …

What is this but separatism in reverse? Just like the Quebec brand, it is a rejection of the historical reality of this country, and it changes nothing that the English-Canadian separatist happens to be speaking with the comfortable voice of the majority. An English-Canadian rejection of Canadian duality is in fact perfectly acceptable to a member of the *RIN (Reassemblement pour l'Indépendance Nationale)*, who sees it as a confirmation of his own view that there is no place for French Canadians in Canada. As so often happens, the two extremes come together …

If he is at all logical, the English Canadian who holds such views will have to admit the justice of the Quebec separatist point of view and accept the break-up of Confederation. He has no other choice.

Thomas Sloan, *Quebec: The Not-So-Quiet Revolution* (Toronto, 1965), 94–95.

WHAT WAS NATIONAL BARGAINING?

It was a no-holds-barred argument over specific cases. In November 1962, Donald Gordon, president of the Canadian National Railways, was challenged in Parliament in the Sessional Committee on Railways, Air Lines, and Shipping to explain why there were so few French Canadians in high executive positions with the railway. This was part of the dialogue:

Mr. Grégoire: I had another point I wanted to mention, and it is in connection with the first page of the report. I note we have one president, seventeen vice-presidents, and ten directors, and none of them is French Canadian.
Mr. Gordon: How do you know?
Mr. Grégoire: Then, which ones are?

Mr. Gordon: I want to find out from you who is French Canadian.

Mr. Grégoire: Could you name for me the ones who are?

Mr. Gordon: I do not know how to define a French Canadian. But I will say this: these are all Canadians, every one of them ... Let me say quite clearly that the promotion policy of the Canadian National Railways has always been based upon promotion by merit. The man who, by reason of experience, knowledge, judgement, education or for any other reason, is considered by the management to be the best person fitted for a job will receive the promotion, and we do not care whether he is black, white, red, or French ...

Mr. Chevrier: You cannot make me believe that in an organization such as the Canadian National Railways there are no men of the standing and level of those who are listed on the second page of the annual report who are French speaking who could fill these positions. I do not want to be unfair or unjust, but it seems to me a misnomer for an organization such as the CNR to say that there are no French-speaking Canadians of that calibre. I do not believe such a statement.

Mr. Gordon: Mr. Chevrier, let me say this. What you really are asking for is discrimination.

Mr. Chevrier: I am not asking for discrimination at all.

Mr. Gordon: Yes, you are ... As long as I am president of the CNR there is not going to be a promotion or an appointment made just because a man is a French Canadian. He has got to be a French Canadian plus other things, and he has to be as able as the other fellow who has a claim on the job ...

Mr. Rouleau: Would it not be possible to make a special effort to find a qualified French-speaking Canadian for the job?

Mr. Gordon: You are asking me to discriminate.

Mr. Rouleau: It is only fair.

Minutes of the Sessional Committee on Railways, Air Lines, and Shipping (November, 1962), 59–66.

WHAT WERE THE TERMS OF THE OFFICIAL LANGUAGES ACT?

The Royal Commission on Bilingualism and Biculturalism, appointed in 1963, recommended an Official Languages Act to ensure respect for the status of French and English. The following passages have been selected from the act:

The English and French languages are the official languages of Canada for all purposes of the Parliament and Government of Canada, and possess and enjoy equality of status and equal rights and privileges as to their use in all the institutions of the Parliament and Government of Canada.

DUTIES OF DEPARTMENTS, ETC. IN RELATION TO OFFICIAL LANGUAGES

9-1 Every department and agency of the Government of Canada … has the duty to ensure that within the National Capital Region, at the place of its head or central office in Canada if outside the National Capital Region, and at each of its principal offices in a federal bilingual district established under this Act, members of the public can obtain available services from and can communicate with it in both official languages …

10-1 Every department and agency of the Government of Canada … has the duty to ensure that, at any office, location or facility in Canada or elsewhere at which any services to the travelling public are provided or made available by it … such services can be provided or made available in both official languages.

11-1 Every judicial or quasi-judicial body established by or pursuant to any Act of the Parliament of Canada has, in any proceedings brought or taken before it, and every court in Canada has, in exercising in any proceedings in a criminal matter any criminal jurisdiction conferred upon it by or pursuant to an Act of the Parliament of Canada, the duty to ensure that any person giving evidence before it may be heard in the official language of his choice, and that in being so heard he will not be placed at a disadvantage by not being or being unable to be heard in the other official language.

BILINGUAL DISTRICTS

13-2 An area … may be established as a bilingual district or be included in whole or in part within a bilingual district if:
    (a) both of the official languages are spoken as a mother tongue by persons residing in the area; and
    (b) the number of persons who are in the linguistic minority in the area in respect of an official language spoken as a mother tongue is at least ten percent of the total number of persons residing in the area.

COMMISSIONER OF OFFICIAL LANGUAGES

19-1 There shall be a Commissioner of Official Languages for Canada, hereinafter in this Act called the Commissioner.

19-2 The Commissioner shall be appointed by Commission under the Great Seal after approval of the appointment by resolution of the Senate and House of Commons.

19-3 Subject to this section, the Commissioner holds office during good behaviour for a term of seven years, but may be removed by the Governor in Council at any time on address of the Senate and House of Commons ...

25 It is the duty of the Commissioner to take all actions and measures within his authority with a view to ensuring recognition of the status of each of the official languages and compliance with the spirit and intent of this Act in the administration of the affairs of the institutions of the Parliament and Government of Canada and, for that purpose, to conduct and carry out investigations either on his own initiative or pursuant to any complaint made to him and to report and make recommendations with respect thereto as provided in this Act.

40-4 In relation to the appointment and advancement in employment of personnel the duties of whose positions include duties relating to the provision of services by authorities to members of the public, it is the duty

    (a) of the Public Service Commission, in cases where it has the authority to make appointments, and

    (b) of the authority concerned, in all other cases, to ensure that, in the exercise and performance of the powers, duties and functions conferred or imposed upon it by law, due account is taken of the purposes and provisions of this Act, subject always to the maintenance of the principle of selection of personnel according to merit as required by the *Public Service Employment Act.*

The Official Languages Act, 1969.

What Did Canadians Complain About to Mr. Spicer?

In 1970–1971, the Official Language Commissioner's Office opened its Complaints Service. It received 181 complaints, of which 105 (58%) were considered admissible under the terms of the Official Languages Act. In its second year of operation, it opened 745 files, of which it was able to close 602 (80%) by the year's end. The majority of complainants were French (76% the first year and 79% the second year) and most complaints related to the language of service in the federal government. The following selected files illustrate typical complaints:

FILE 6

The complainant had been transferred to Canadian Forces Base Bagotville (Department of National Defence) the previous year. He objected to the posting of unilingual French signs in the squadron hanger, and to daily orders being published only in French. He also commented unfavourably on the general treatment of English-speaking residents of Quebec.

While no specific action was requested, the Commissioner was of the opinion that the questions raised in the letter were of interest and significance. He promised to visit CFB Bagotville during a forthcoming tour of military bases, at which time he would invite the complainant and his associates to set forth their problems in greater detail.

FILE 39

This complaint concerned the daily weather forecasts prepared by the Meteorological Service of the Ministry of Transport and published by the Canadian Armed Forces Weather Office at Uplands (Ottawa).

The complainant stated that the bulletins were issued only in English, even though they were posted in various buildings owned or occupied by the federal government.

Investigation revealed that bilingual forms were indeed available to the Meteorological Service, but that the Service did not make use of them. The Commissioner brought this fact to the attention of the Deputy Minister, who ordered that thereafter bilingual weather bulletins be provided to the entire National Capital Region.

FILE 66

The complainant and his family visited the fortress of Louisbourg. At the museum entrance the official assigned to receive visitors was unable to answer the complainant in French and allegedly treated him somewhat arrogantly.

The Commissioner, stressing the symbolic importance of the alleged failure to provide service in both languages and of the employee's alleged attitude, brought this incident to the attention of the Department of Indian Affairs and Northern Development. The Department replied that 50 percent of the guides employed at the Fortress were bilingual and that tours were organized every day with commentaries in both official languages. It was natural, the spokesman added, for a number of guides to be unilingual English-speaking, since they are recruited in the Louisbourg area, where English-speaking people are in the majority. However, all guides have been instructed to direct French-speaking visitors to the reception centre, where a French-speaking guide will be provided.

As a result of the Commissioner's action, the Department issued an official directive instructing regional directors to assign bilingual employees to national parks and historic sites so that visitors may use the official language of their choice at tourist reception centres and campsites, and in park activities ...

FILE 324

Four persons who had stayed in the Queen Elizabeth Hotel in Montreal reported that an English-language daily newspaper was left outside each room in the morning with a slip of paper on which the following words were written: "A French-language newspaper is available on request from the Bell Captain." The complainants objected to the fact that guests wishing to obtain a French-language newspaper were obliged to make a special request in order to receive a copy, while English-speaking guests received their newspaper automatically.

The Commissioner brought this question of the inequality of the two languages to the attention of CN authorities. The administration of CN Hotels did not accept the Commissioner's suggestion to extend the existing service to both linguistic groups in the language indicated by clients on their registration; it preferred simply to stop automatic distribution of the newspaper in question at hotel room doors. However, guests may still receive a free newspaper on request, a service which—despite the additional effort demanded of them—puts French-speaking and English-speaking visitors on an equal footing.

The Commissioner of Official Languages, *The First and Second Annual Reports, 1970–1971, 1971–1972* (Ottawa, 1973).

WHAT DID THE FLQ WANT?

In the eyes of the law, they were terrorists and assassins who made demands on society and brutal threats if these demands were not satisfied. Their communiqué spelled out exactly what they wanted. It was read by radio station CKAC in Montreal on October 6, 1970.

The representative of Great Britain in Quebec, M.J. Cross, is in the hands of the Front de libération du Québec.

Here are the conditions that the ruling authorities must fulfill in order to save the life of the representative of the ancient racist and colonialist British system.

1   They must see to it that the repressive police forces do not commit the monstrous error of attempting to jeopardize the success of the operation by conducting searches, investigations, raids, arrests by any other means.

2   The political manifesto which the Front de libération du Québec will address to the ruling authorities must appear in full on the front page of all the principal newspapers in Quebec. The ruling authorities, after consulting with the latter, must make public the list of Quebec newspapers agreeing to publish our manifesto. But it should be quite clear that all Quebec regions must be covered.

   Furthermore, this manifesto must be read in full and commented upon by the political prisoners before their departure during a programme, the length of which will have to be at least thirty minutes, to be televised live or pre-recorded between 8 and 11 PM on Radio-Canada and its affiliated stations in the province.

3   Liberation of political prisoners: Cyriaque Delisle, Edmond Guénette and François Schirm …

4   A plane must be made available to the patriotic political prisoners for their transport to either Cuba or Algeria, once an official agreement has been reached with one of these two countries.

   Furthermore, they must be allowed to be accompanied by their respective lawyers and by at least two political reporters of two French Quebec dailies.

5   During a meeting attended by the Lapalme boys and the Postmaster-General—or a representative—the latter must promise to reinstate them. The reinstatement promise must take into account the standards and conditions already secured by the revolutionary workers of Lapalme prior to the breaking off of negotiations. This meeting must be held within forty-eight hours after the release of this communiqué and must be open to newsmen.

6   A voluntary tax of $500,000 in gold bullion must be put aboard the plane made available to the political prisoners. When one recalls the spendings caused by the recent visit of the Queen of England, the millions of dollars lost by the Post Office Department because of the stubborn millionaire Kierans, the cost of maintaining Quebec within Confederation, etc.... . $500,000 is peanuts!

7   The NAME and the PICTURE of the informer who led police to the last FLQ cell must be made public and published. The Front de libération du Québec is in possession of information dealing with the acts and moves of this louse ... and is only awaiting "official" confirmation to act.

Through this move, the Front de libération du Québec wants to draw the attention of the world to the fate of French-speaking Québécois, a majority which is jeered at and crushed on its own territory by a faulty political system (Canadian federalism) and by an economy dominated by the interests of American high finance, the racist and imperialist "big bosses" ...

Front de libération du Québec, CKAC Montreal, October 1970. Reprinted in John Saywell, *Quebec 70: A Documentary Narrative* (Toronto, 1971), 35–38.

The government accepted the second demand, and on October 8 Radio-Canada broadcasted the FLQ Manifesto. This stated the wider cause for which they stood and injustices they were protesting.

The *Front de libération du Québec* is not a messiah, nor a modern-day Robin Hood. It is a group of Quebec workers who have decided to use every means to make sure that the people of Quebec take control of their destiny.

The *Front de libération du Québec* wants the total independence of all Québécois, united in a free society, purged forever of the clique of voracious sharks, the patronizing "big bosses" and their henchmen who have made Quebec their hunting preserve for "cheap labour" and unscrupulous exploitation.

The *Front de libération du Québec* is not a movement of aggression, but it is a response to the aggression organized by high finance and the puppet governments in Ottawa and Quebec (the Brinks "show," Bill 63, the electoral map, the so-called social progress tax, Power Corporation, "Doctors' Insurance," the Lapalme guys ...)

The *Front de libération du Québec* finances itself by "voluntary taxes" taken from the same enterprises that exploit the workers (banks, finance companies, etc.... .)

We believed once that perhaps it would be worth it to channel our energy and our impatience, as René Lévesque said so well, into the Parti Québécois, but the Liberal victory clearly demonstrated that that which we call democracy in Quebec is nothing but the democracy of the rich. The Liberal party's victory was nothing but the victory of the election riggers, Simard-Cotroni. As a result, the British parliamentary system is finished and the Front de libération du Québec will never allow itself to be fooled by the pseudo-elections that the Anglo-Saxon capitalists toss to the people of Quebec every four years ...

We have had our fill of jobs and prosperity while we always remain the cowering servants and boot-lickers of the big shots who live in Westmount, town of Mount Royal, Hampstead and Outremont, all the fortresses of high finance on St. James and Wall Streets, while we, the Québécois, have not used all our means, including arms and dynamite, to rid ourselves of these economic and political bosses who are prepared to use every sort of sordid tactic to better screw us.

We live in a society of terrorized slaves, terrorized by the big bosses like Steinberg, Clark, Bronfman, Smith, Neaple, Timmins, Geoffrion, J.L. Lévesque, Hershorn, Thompson, Nesbitt, Demarais, Kierans. Compared to Rémi Popol the lousy no-good, Drapeau the Dog, Bourassa the lackey of the Simards, and Trudeau the fairy are peanuts.

The number of those who realize the oppression of this terrorist society are growing and the day will come when all the Westmounts of Quebec will disappear from the map ...

Our struggle can only lead to victory. You cannot hold an awakening people in misery and contempt indefinitely. Long Live Free Quebec!

Long live our imprisoned political comrades. Long live the Quebec revolution!

Long live the Front de libération du Québec.

Front de libération du Québec, Radio-Canada, 8 October 1970. Reprinted in John Saywell, *Quebec 70: A Documentary Narrative* (Toronto, 1971), 46–51.

How Did the Government Answer the FLQ?

The federal government, responding to the Premier of Quebec and the Mayor of Montreal, imposed the War Measures Act *on October 15, 1970. The Prime Minister's Office issued a formal statement explaining the action taken.*

Whereas the War Measures Act provides that the issue of a proclamation under the authority of the governor-in-council shall be conclusive evidence that insurrection, real or apprehended, exists and has existed for any period of time therein stated and its continuance, until by the issue of a further proclamation it is declared that the insurrection no longer exists.

And whereas there is in contemporary Canadian society an element or group known as *Le Front de Libération du Québec* who advocate and resort to the use of force and the commission of criminal offences, including murder, threats of murder and kidnapping, as a means of or as an aid in accomplishing a governmental change within Canada and whose activities have given rise to a state of apprehended insurrection within the province of Quebec.

Therefore, His Excellency the Governor-General-in-Council, on the recommendation of the prime minister, is pleased to direct that a proclamation be issued proclaiming that apprehended insurrection exists and has existed as and from the fifteenth day of October, one thousand nine hundred and seventy.

Prime Minister's Office, 15 October 1970. Reprinted in John Saywell, Quebec 70: *A Documentary Narrative* (Toronto, 1971), 86.

The federal Minister of Justice, John Turner, explained to the House of Commons on October 16 the reasons that lay behind the imposition of the War Measures Act. *He was replying to the charge from New Democratic Party leader, T.C. Douglas, that Friday, October 16, would be looked upon "as a black Friday for civil liberties in Canada." Others, such as Créditiste Leader Réal Caouette, were saying the action against the separatists was long overdue.*

The government of Canada has to take the final responsibility, but when the Government of the Province of Quebec, and the mayor of the largest city in this country, on the information available to them and the information available to us through our own law enforcement agencies, are of the opinion that the state has been reached where we ought to, as sound and commonsense human beings, anticipate a danger to our society in the form of insurrection and are willing to use that type of vocabulary to the Prime Minister of Canada, then that is material which we cannot ignore.

I want to recite a list of events that have contributed to the rapid acceleration of this dangerous situation in Quebec. They are the kidnappings, which in themselves if they were isolated would be a purely criminal affair but, within the context of a wider conspiracy and being used for ransom against a legitimately constituted government, are something else. We have the continuous threats to life and property in the communications of the FLQ of a seditious, violent and inflammatory nature. They have been issued and members are aware of them.

We have also a series of bombings and violence, a rising increase of thefts of dynamite now available in some hidden caches in the province of Quebec. More disturbing, we have a type of erosion of the public will in the feeling among some sincere people that an exchange of prisoners for the victims of the kidnappings would somehow ease the situation.

… I might say, too, that the recent call for a public manifestation by men like Gagnon, Vallières and Chartrand established and escalated the whole coming together of an infiltration of FLQ doctrine in certain areas of society in Quebec—in the unions, among universities and in the media—and growing feeling among the people of Quebec, particularly the citizens of Montreal, that they are living under a reign of terror. You do not have to ask me; ask any member from Montreal and the people they represent just what they have been undergoing last week in the city of Montreal.

Some hon. Members: Hear, hear!

Canada, House of Commons Debates (16 October 1970). Reprinted in John Saywell, *Quebec 70: A Documentary Narrative* (Toronto, 1971), 91.

The Prime Minister had an argumentative interview with a CBC reporter, Tim Ralfe, on the steps of the Parliament buildings, in which he defended the government's action and used the famous expression "bleeding hearts."

Question: Sir, what is it with all these men with guns around here?
Trudeau: Haven't you noticed? … It doesn't worry me. I think it's natural that as people are being abducted that they be protected against such abductions. What would you do if a Quebec minister—another Quebec minister—were abducted or a federal minister?

Question: But isn't that one of the …

Trudeau: Is your position that you should give in to the seven demands of the FLQ and … ?

Question: No, not at all. My position is completely the opposite.

Trudeau: What is your position?

Question: My position is that you don't give in to any of them … The proposition that perhaps it would be wise to use less inflammatory terms than "bandits" when you talk about a bunch of people who have the lives of two men in their hands?

Trudeau: You don't think they're bandits?

Question: Well, regardless of what I think, I don't think I would be inclined to wave a red flag in their faces if they held two of my friends or colleagues with guns at their heads.

Trudeau: Well, first of all, I didn't call them bandits. I called the people who were in jail now bandits, who had been tried before the law and condemned to a prison term and I said that you people should stop calling them political prisoners. They're not political prisoners; they're outlaws. They're criminal prisoners, they're not political prisoners, and they're bandits. That's why they're in jail.

Question: But with your army troops you seem to be combating them as almost as though it is a war, and if it is a war, does anything that they say have validity?

Trudeau: Don't be silly. We're not combating them as if it's war, but we're using some of the army as peace agents in order that the police be more free to do their job as policemen and not spend their time guarding your friends against some form of kidnapping.

Question: You said earlier that you would protect them in this way but you have said before that this kind of violence, what you're fighting here, the kind of violence of the FLQ, can lead to a police state.

Trudeau: Sure. That's what you're complaining about, isn't it?

Question: Well yes, but surely that decision is yours, not the FLQ's.

Trudeau: Yes, but I've asked you what your own logic is. It's to let them abduct anybody and not give any protection to anyone—call off the police … Yes, well there are a lot of bleeding hearts around who just don't like to see people with helmets and guns. All I can say is, go on and bleed, but it is more important to keep law and order in the society than to be warned about weak-kneed people who don't like the looks of …

Question: At any cost? How far would [you] go with that? How far would you extend that?

Trudeau: Well, just watch me … So long as there is a power in here which is challenging the elected representative of the people, I think that power must be stopped and I think it's only, I repeat, weak-kneed bleeding hearts who are afraid to take these measures …

The Canadian Broadcasting Corporation, *CBC TV National News,* 13 October 1970. Reprinted in Norman Sheffe, ed., Canadian/Canadien (Toronto, 1971), 110–113.

What Rights Are Claimed by the Charter of the French Language?

The Charter of the French Language was passed by the National Assembly on August 26, 1977. It became the center of much controversy and there were questions about its constitutionality. While there was a lot of sympathy for strengthening the position of French in Quebec, there was also concern about the anglophone and immigrant loss of rights. The following represents a summary of the main provisions of the charter.

TITLE I—Status of the French language
CHAPTER I Makes French the official language.
CHAPTER II Provides "fundamental" personal language rights—to be communicated with in French by government bodies, unions and business firms; to speak French at meetings and at work; as consumers to be informed and served in French; to receive instruction in French.
CHAPTER III "French is the language of the legislature and the courts in Quebec." The legislature: French to be used, bills drafted in French, only the French text official, English version published... The courts: corporations must plead in French, unless all parties agree to plead in English; all documents to be in French, if demanded. Judgments to be in French or "accompanied with a duly authenticated French version,"—which is official.
CHAPTER IV The Civil Administration—defined as the government, its agencies, municipal and school bodies, health. Social services: French names only, documents to be in French, communication with governments or corporations, and internally, in French; contracts, signs and posters to be in French; health and social services to be available in French; language tests (provincially supervised) for employees appointed or promoted. Certain exceptions relating to safety, public health, English municipalities, schools and health services. Traffic signs—French only ...
CHAPTER VI Labour relations ... An employer is prohibited from making the obtaining of an employment or office dependent upon the knowledge of a language other than the official language, unless the nature of the duties requires the knowledge of that other language. The burden of proof that the knowledge of the other language is necessary is on the employer, at the demand of the person or the association of employees concerned or, as the case may be, the *Office de la langue française. The Office de la langue française* has the power to decide any dispute ...
CHAPTER VII Commerce and Business ... Labels, menus, wine lists, catalogues to be in French; no toys or games using non-French vocabulary unless French version is available "on no less favourable terms." Contracts, employment application forms,

order forms, invoices etc. to be in French (minor exceptions allowed). Signs, posters, and commercial advertising to be in French only; firms names in French only; ethnic groups, firms with four employees or less, hospitals and social services may use own language in names if French version also given.

CHAPTER VIII Language of instruction. Provides for education in French, except where this chapter allows otherwise; the main exceptions are children whose father or mother received elementary education in English in Quebec; or if parents domiciled in Quebec on August 26, 1977, outside Quebec; children who were in English school during the 1976–77 session, and their younger siblings. Verification of eligibility is required by the Minister of Education. Appeals are allowed. Children with serious learning disabilities exempted. No secondary school leaving certificate issued to student without "speaking and writing knowledge of French" required by the province. Special provisions for native peoples. (72–88) …

TITLE II—*Office de la langue française and francization (Office)* …
CHAPTER V Concerned with francization of business firms and public utilities. Firms with fifty employees or more must obtain a "francization certificate" from the Office, attesting that it is carrying out an Office-approved program, or has reached the desired level of performance. Purpose:

141. The francization programme is intended to generalize the use of French at all levels of the business firm. This implies:
   (a) the knowledge of the official language on the part of management, the members of the professional corporations and the other members of the staff;
   (b) an increase at all levels of the business firm, including the board of directors, in the number of persons having a good knowledge of the French language so as to generalize its use;
   (c) the use of French as the language of work and as the language of internal communication …

TITLE V—Offences and Penalties—
Main penalties are fines: first offence from $25 to $500 for an individual, double that for a company; second offence $50 to $1,000 for an individual, $500 to $5,000 for a company. Firms doing business without a francization certificate, fine of $100 to $2,000 for each day in default. Posters, billboards, signs offending against the act may be removed on court order "within eight days" …

Appendix Four, Summary of Main Elements of Quebec Bill 101, Charter of the French Language, in Douglas Fullerton, *The Dangerous Delusion* (Toronto, 1978), 229–33.

WHAT WAS THE CASE FOR SOVEREIGNTY-ASSOCIATION?

In the Quebec government's White Paper entitled Québec-Canada: A New Deal, published in November 1979, the Canadian federal experiment was written off as a failure. It was noted that there was an urgent need for action in view of Quebec's declining numbers and influence, and the details of sovereignty-association were laid out, together with an appeal for support.

An Urgent Need for Action

While the federal government continues to invade our jurisdictions, and impose policies that clash with our interests, the demographic weight of Quebecers and of Francophones outside Québec is constantly decreasing. Demographer Robert Maheux predicts that in 1991, 73% of citizens of French ethnic origin outside Québec will have ceased to use the French language. Another demographer, Jacques Henripin, predicts that by about the year 2000 between 92% and 95% of Francophones in Canada will be living in Québec. As for Quebecers, who made up around 36% of the Canadian population in 1851, in 1971 they accounted for only 28% and this proportion will drop to 23% by 2001 if the current trend is maintained, because of Québec's low rate of birth and immigration.

These demographic losses necessarily result in a marked decrease ... [in] the political role played by Quebecers in Canada. From 1867 to 1979, the number of Québec Members of Parliament in Ottawa increased by 10, from 65 to 75; the number of Members of Parliament from other provinces increased by 91, from 116 to 207. And the trend grows stronger; in the last election, there was one new seat in Québec, seventeen in the rest of Canada. It is foreseen that in 20 years, the rest of Canada will have 250 Members of Parliament and Québec only 75. While they were more than one-third of federal Members of Parliament in 1867, Quebecers will account for less than one quarter by the end of the century.

Under these circumstances, it would be an illusion to believe that, in future, Francophones can play a determining role in the Government of Canada. On the contrary, they will be more and more of a minority and English Canada will find it increasingly easy to govern without them. In that respect, far from being an anomaly, the Clark government is a sign of things to come ...

THE PROPOSAL

... We hasten to state that the changes described here will not occur overnight after the Referendum, but will be, can only be, the result of negotiations between Québec and Canada, negotiations that will be started as a result of a positive answer in the Referendum ...

A. SOVEREIGNTY

Through sovereignty, Québec would acquire, in addition to the political powers it already has, those now exercised by Ottawa, whether they were assigned to the federal government under the British North America Act of 1867 or whether it assumed them since that time, directly or indirectly ...

LAWS AND TAXES The only laws that will apply on Québec's territory will be those adopted by the National Assembly, and the only taxes that will be levied will be those decreed by Québec law. In this way, there will be an end to the overlapping of federal and Québec services, which has been so often denounced, thereby enabling Québec to control the totality of its fiscal resources.

Existing federal laws will continue to apply as Québec laws, as long as they are not amended, repealed or replaced by the National Assembly.

TERRITORY Québec has an inalienable right over its territory, recognized even in the present Constitution, which states that the territory of a province cannot be modified without the consent of that province. Moreoever, since the agreements were reached on James Bay, there no longer is any lien on any part of the Québec territory. In becoming sovereign, Québec, as is the rule in international law, will thus maintain its territorial integrity.

Moreover, it would be desirable for Québec to regain the advantages that would normally come to it from its geographical position, putting an end to the uncertainties that have surrounded the issue of jurisdiction over the Gulf of St. Lawrence, Labrador and the Arctic regions.

CITIZENSHIP The Québec government gives its solemn commitment that every Canadian who, at the time sovereignty is achieved, is a resident of Québec, or any person who was born there, will have an automatic right to Québec citizenship; the landed immigrant will be able to complete residency requirements and obtain citizenship. The Parliament of Canada will have to decide whether Canadians who become Québec citizens may maintain their Canadian citizenship as well. Québec, for its part, would have no objection ...

MINORITIES The government pledges that Québec's Anglophone minority will continue to enjoy the rights now accorded it by law, and that other communities in Québec will be given the means to develop their cultural resources.

The Amerindian and Inuit communities, if they so desire, will be in full possession on their territory of institutions that maintain the integrity of their societies and enable them to develop freely, according to their own culture and spirit. As for Francophone minorities in Canada, Québec intends to fulfill its moral responsibilities towards them, as it has started to do, for that matter, despite its limited means ...

EXTERNAL RELATIONS   Québec will continue to be bound by the treaties to which Canada is now a signatory. It may withdraw from them should the occasion arise according to the rules of international law. Consequently, Québec will respect the agreement on the St. Lawrence Seaway and will become a full partner in the International Joint Commission. As for alliances such as NATO and NORAD, Québec will respect its responsibilities and offer its contributions in accordance with its aims.

In order to fully play its role on the international scene and defend its interests, Québec will ask to be admitted to the United Nations and to its specialized agencies.

Finally, while developing its relations and its cooperation with Francophone countries, Québec will consider remaining a member of the British Commonwealth.

B. ASSOCIATION

... Québec has never wanted to live in isolation; from the start it has accepted interdependence. However, it wishes to ensure that it will be directly involved in determining the terms of this interdependence. To this end, the Québec government intends to offer to negotiate with the rest of Canada a treaty of community association, whose aim will be, notably, to maintain the present Canadian economic entity by ensuring continuity of exchange and by favouring, in the long run, a more rapid and better balanced development of each of the two partners.

This treaty will have an international status and will bind the parties in a manner and for a term to be determined. It will define the partners' areas of common activity and confirm the maintenance of an economic and monetary union between Québec and the rest of Canada ...

AREAS OF COMMON ACTION

(a)   *The Free Circulation of Goods*
In order to ensure the free circulation of goods, the present situation in Québec and Canada will be maintained, and each party will renounce any right to customs barriers at common borders. With regard to foreign countries, the partners will jointly establish the tariff protection they deem necessary ...

(b)   *Monetary Union*
The dollar will be maintained as the only currency having legal tender, and real or liquid assets as well as letters of credit will continue to be expressed in dollars. Circulation of capital will be free, but each party will be entitled

to proclaim an investment code or to adopt, if need be, particular regulations applicable to certain financial institutions.

(c)   *The Free Circulation of People*
In order to ensure the free circulation of people from one territory to the other, the two States will give up their right to impose a regular police control at their common border. It goes without saying that no passport will be required between Québec and Canada …

C. COMMUNITY INSTITUTIONS
… The Québec government favours the establishment of four Québec-Canada agencies:

- A community council
- A commission of experts
- A court of justice
- A monetary authority

Quebec, *Québec-Canada: A New Deal,* édition official du Québec (Québec, 1979), 28–30, 54–58, 61.

WHAT HAPPENS WHEN ONE UNIT SECEDES FROM A FEDERATION?

Ronald L. Watts looked at the possible consequences and cited the examples of federations elsewhere.

The actual secession of a unit from a federation has usually been followed by one of three possible consequences. One is simply the general acceptance of permanent separation, as occurred with partitioned India, the shattered West Indies Federation, and the separated territories of the former Federation of Rhodesia and Nyasaland. This solution avoids continued civil war, eliminates the central government as a centre of political controversy, and produces a number of more compact independent political units. But it involves a considerable price since it entails the loss of economic and diplomatic benefits associated with the larger political union. The economic difficulties experienced by the remnants of the federations in the West Indies and in Central Africa after their dissolution, and the contemporary international trend towards larger economic units suggests that political balkanization is a regressive step. In external relations, whether in terms of diplomatic influence or of security, smaller political units such as these have proved weak and vulnerable to pressure from larger and more powerful neighbours.

An alternative consequence of federal disintegration is the attempt to establish, as a substitute for the federation, an economic union or confederacy. This solution seeks to avoid the full effects of balkanization and has often appealed to supporters of regional autonomy, since it may obtain some of the benefits of economic association while retaining for the component units their political independence and a veto over all central political decisions. But such a solution is not as simple as at first sight it appears. In practice such systems have found it almost impossible to isolate economic and political matters from each other. Economic unions, therefore, have proved politically unstable and have rarely lasted for long in the contemporary world. The European Economic Community represents an economic confederacy, but after an extremely effective beginning its progress has been slow and it has experienced some internal stresses. In any case, its main supporters regard it not as a final solution but merely as a stage on the road to fuller political federalism. Other contemporary examples, such as the East African Common Services Organization and the Central American Common Market, have not proved politically stable arrangements. It is perhaps worth noting that in the United States and Switzerland a federal system was adopted directly as a result of the deficiencies and difficulties experienced in the looser confederacy which had preceded it.

A third pattern of consequences following the declaration of secession by a state has been the resort to military force to maintain the union. The price of this alternative—civil war—may be high indeed in human lives, disruption, and the legacy of bitterness. Much depends, however, on the length and intensity of the civil war and upon the character of the federal reconstruction which follows. In Switzerland, where the war itself was brief and where the political settlement subsequently imposed was generous to the vanquished, the federal reconstruction was remarkably successful. In the United States, on the other hand, the length and ferocity of the civil war and the northern dominance which followed it left a much stronger and more enduring legacy of bitterness.

Richard Simeon, ed., *Must Canada Fail?* (Montreal, 1977), 57–58.

What Could the Economic Collapse
Caused by Separation Be Like?

Douglas Fullerton served as advisor to Lévesque and Lesage and as chairman of the National Capital Commission. He wrote an open letter to Lévesque in 1967 to plead Canada's cause. He beseeched Lévesque to consider the adverse economic consequences that could occur.

Cher René,

We have been friends for many years, and there is no one in public life for whom I have more respect.

You entered politics as a knight on a white charger, and few knights were ever more badly needed or more warmly received. To me, your recent manifesto is an honest document written by a man deeply troubled about his people and their problems ...

And yet you force me, on your central argument, to "stand up and be counted." If emotionally I can accept the depth of feeling behind your plea for independence, every reasoning bone in my Scots-Canadian body tells me that the financial and economic consequences of Quebec separation would be catastrophic for the province in the short run—and I leave the long run to look after itself.

In other words, the case that Kierans, Bourassa and others are making is a strong one and I can only add my voice to theirs in urging you to draw back from a policy of potential disaster ...

DEBT

1. Debt problems:

For five years Quebec's borrowing has run over $500 million a year, the amount needed to cover social capital expenditure and deficit spending. Today Quebec provincial and municipal bonds cannot be sold in Canada outside Quebec; in fact a substantial selling of outstanding bonds has been avoided only because investors are reluctant to sell and show large losses. Record high interest rates, together with the large volume of Quebec borrowing, have pushed bond prices down as much as 20 percent ...

The deterioration in the market for Quebec bonds has been in part due to heavy borrowing, but an important factor has been investor fears about nationalism, and uncertainty about Quebec's future. What would be the consequences of Quebec independence? I suggest that the initial effect would certainly be heavy selling of Quebec bonds—at any price—and a complete breakdown in Quebec's credit ...

2. Tax revenue and federal subventions:

Kierans sees this loss in revenue at close to $500 million per year, from the surrender of federal equalization payments and the decline in other tax revenues. I cannot appraise the accuracy of the calculation, but I suspect that as a "have-not" province, Quebec has been doing much better out of Ottawa than either side will admit (even if the Atlantic provinces get more on a per capita basis). Declining tax revenues would mean either or both of two things—less spending and fewer jobs, or more taxes. This latter prospect is not appealing to outside investors or entrepreneurs; the former is not palatable to Quebecers.

INVESTMENT
3. Direct investment:
Capital hates uncertainty, and the conclusions of the study by *la Chambre de Commerce*, that there is a widening gap between the rate of new direct investment in plant facilities in Ontario and in Quebec, does not contradict such fragments of evidence as cross my path. The uncertainties not only relate to Quebec's political status, but to the potential impact on the fabric of the system of abrupt and painful split.

4. Geography:
Quebec has many assets—the people, Montreal, the river, primary resources, but for a modern industrial state it has some surprising deficiencies. Industry is increasingly market-oriented, and Ontario is much closer to the main centres of North American populations. In fact 90 percent of Quebec is a barren, cold black-fly ridden land, remote from population centres and unattractive to colonists. Modern industry increasingly needs trained people and here again Quebec is behind most of the other provinces. Montreal is well-located, particularly for shipping and entrepot trade, but how much of that has stemmed from an east-west oriented Canada? My point is that Quebec may well have been exploited by outside capital, but its geographical assets are not promising.

ASSOCIATION
5.
You suggest that separation might be followed by setting up of some kind of a new association between the former component of the old Canada (a divorce followed by a common law relationship?). It sounds like a possible, logical and mutually beneficial proposal, but I have some nagging doubts.

First is the psychological consequences on English Canada of the split. The "Lévesque wrench" would be harder on them than the "Chinese water torture." English Canadians would tend to see themselves, rightly or wrongly, as the guiltless partner in the divorce proceedings—and would blame Quebec for tearing the country asunder. I wonder how amenable they would be in these circumstances to your "common market" proposal?

I wonder also how English Canadians would react to the economic dislocations caused by the actual act of separation. Canada west (Ontario to B.C.) would gain fiscally, which might offset the short run losses in economic efficiency, redeployment of resources etc., caused by the split, but the Atlantic provinces would be in desperate straits.

I feel myself that English Canada has the will to survive, but that there would be a strong feeling of betrayal—(the woman walked out on me—I don't want to see her again!). In summary, I don't think that your calculations about the costs to Quebec if it separates should underestimate the impact of English-Canadian backlash. Some of it, in a mild form, is being felt today in industrial decisions.

FLIGHT

6. The exodus:

How great a flight of capital—and people—there would be from Quebec is difficult for me to guess ... I think that any serious outflow of people or money would reflect itself quickly in Montreal property values. I have no data on this but there are some signs that a decline is in fact beginning to occur ...

PAYMENTS

6. Balance of payments and money:

Almost all the previous points have some bearing on the balance of payments of an independent Quebec, on both current and capital accounts. The money flows would be strongly against you, at least in the short run, and initially trade would be disrupted.

In these circumstances, can one conceive of a monetary union with the rest of Canada, with one partner in a more serious deficit position than the other? I don't see how it could work, for a kind of Gresham's law would be at work—bad money replacing good. Without monetary union, the Quebec dollar would depreciate more than the (new) Canadian dollar. If you asked me to put a figure on it, I could see the Quebec dollar at .70 and the new Canadian dollar at .80—in terms of U.S. currency. A new equilibrium would eventually be reached at the lower rate, but the disruptive consequences in the intervening period would be severe.

Finally what kind of grass-root support for separatism is there in Quebec, particularly if the public at large were made aware that the price-tag might be high? What about the impact of their own personal "rising expectations," which are more financial than nationalistic? I think that to be entirely honest with the people you must now come forward and talk about economic matters—and possible costs ...

En amitié

Douglas H. Fullerton

Douglas H. Fullerton, *The Dangerous Delusion* (Toronto, 1978), Appendix Three, a letter appearing in English in the Toronto Star and in French in *Le Devoir* on October 6 & 7, 1967, 224–28.

Ten years later, Douglas Fullerton again challenged Lévesque on economic grounds.

A 15 percent income drop when Quebec's free at last?

Debate still goes on about whether Quebec benefits or not from Confederation, but even Premier Lévesque admits that during the past few years the province has gained considerably on balance.

A more relevant subject for discussion is the impact of the apprehended, or actual, separation of Quebec upon its present weak and deteriorating economy. This is the issue to which all Quebecers should be giving hard thought.

First, the main weaknesses showing up now in the Quebec economy:

Unemployment close to 11 percent, well above the Canadian average. Impact softened by a rising flow of federal transfer payments—unemployment benefits, DREE and other make-work grants.

Employment, low as it is, has been artificially shored up by state projects financed with heavy borrowing—for James Bay, Olympics, roads. Total debt of Quebec and Quebec Hydro now over $12 billion, up $5 billion in the three years 1974–1976. Annual interest cost over $1 billion. No income from James Bay power until at least 1980—and $13 billion more borrowing required to complete the project.

Even apart from the impact of lender fears about separatism, this rate of borrowing cannot be sustained—and has already had to be curtailed.

Quebec taxes highest of any province, despite $1.3 billion in federal equalization payments this year, which is a good measure of below-average tax-raising capacity.

Weak industrial structure—above-average proportion of jobs are in service industries such as government employment, and large manufacturing concentration in tariff-protected but low-wage and threatened textile, show and related industries ...

An intransigent and militant union movement with above-average lost time from strikes; the highest minimum wages in Canada; the abnormally aroused expectations of Quebec wage earners; the impact of language legislation and other péquiste proposals—all these limit the attractiveness of Quebec for business investment, and creation of new jobs. That is the Quebec economy today, hardly the best launching pad for independence. An economy, in fact, that is a good deal more vulnerable than it was five years ago. But consider the further damage that would be done by the fears of imminent independence.

Further disincentives to investment, rising unemployment.

Flight of capital, more by Quebecers than outsiders, further worsening the balance of payments, coupled with growing inability to borrow to close the rising gap.

Rising government deficits and new taxes to offset falling tax revenues.

And if, in spite of all this, the péquistes win their referendum vote, and Quebec separates?

The mind boggles at the alternative scenarios, which range from the minimum damage of growing loss of jobs, declining output, loss of federal subsidies, to an exchange crisis and controls, rationing of imports such as cars and gasoline, and threatened economic collapse—perhaps staved off by emergency help from rejected Canada?

Cost to Quebecers: At best an income reduction of 15 percent, at worst a crisis that would wipe out all personal savings in a currency collapse.

Is this a wager Quebecers would be prepared to accept for independence, a price they would pay? Not if their leaders give them a few hard facts instead of rosy-eyed dreams about the glories of being free at last.

Douglas Fullerton, "A 15 Percent Income Drop When Quebec's Free at Last?" *Ottawa Citizen*, 9 June 1977), Appendix 5 in Douglas H. Fullerton, *The Dangerous Delusion* (Toronto, 1978), 234–35.]

A Satire on Post-Referendum Quebec

William Weintraub's Quebec after separation was long on patriotism but short on progress. The hero of The Underdogs worked by day in the old Sun Life Building in downtown Montreal, now an indoor farm, and by night he attended meetings of the Anglo Liberation Army.

In the Republic of Quebec, the entire month of June had been set aside to celebrate the twentieth anniversary of the founding of the state and its separation from the rest of Canada. The President called for revelry every night, and issued a proclamation declaring that during the month's span of thirty days there would be twenty-one holidays.

At first, only modest festivities had been envisaged, in view of the country's bankrupt condition. But four months before the anniversary, the Soviet Union had come through with a large loan. At once the government decided to spend the money on the most lavish party ever held in the young republic. The Soviets had stipulated that the loan be used to repair crumbling factories and rickety railroads, but the leaders of Quebec considered these projects to be of much lower priority than the need to stimulate national pride.

The *Bureau de la fierté nationale* went to work on plans for the merrymaking. There would be parades, fireworks, and dancing in the streets. Visits would be paid by foreign heads of state.

Thousands of costumed actors would appear in colossal pageants, depicting such historic events as the Fourth Referendum (June 24), the Proclamation of Sovereignty (June 25) and the Battle of Point Fortune (June 26).

In Montreal, blue-and-white bunting would flutter from every building. Statues of the Founding Fathers would be unveiled on the Boulevard du 15 Novembre, the elegant thoroughfare formerly known as Sherbrooke Street. Nearby, on the campus of the Université Maurice Duplessis, formerly McGill University, President Chartrand himself would open the Temple de la Langue Française, a new and magnificent structure built to apotheosize the official language of the state.

In the huge amphitheatre of the temple, poets, bards, and belletrists from many countries would attend a conference extolling the glory and the grandeur of the French language, which now reigned unquestionably supreme throughout the republic. For although a great many English-speaking people still lived in Quebec, the English language had no more status there than Swahili, Esperanto or Pig Latin.

"... et les savants venant du Sénégal, Mali, Gabon et Haute Volta ..." As the commentator described the preparations for the Congress of the French Language, Paul Pritchard listened intently to the little transistor radio clipped to his belt. At the same time he walked slowly along the furrow, sowing his cauliflower seeds in the soft, black earth. "... mettant la dernière main au temple magnifique ..." What idiocy, thought Paul. What the country needed was a modern fertilizer plant, not this monstrous temple, which would cost millions and serve no practical purpose.

By now he had come to the end of the last cauliflower row. He wondered whether he should start planting the celery. But at that moment his little radio emitted a few notes of the national anthem and a woman began to read the 5:00 p.m. news. Paul welcomed the sound of her voice, for it meant that the day's work was done ...

At the landing the sign was still there—HORS DE SERVICE. A glum group of workers trooped down the wide staircase. Paul fell in with Chucky Dwyer, who worked in carrots and parsnips, on the floor above. Chucky was twenty-four—two years older than Paul.

"When do you suppose they'll have the elevators fixed?" Paul asked.

"They don't need fixing," Chucky said. "There's nothing wrong with them."

"What do you mean?"

"They've been turned off. To save electricity."

Paul found this hard to believe. After all, this was no shoestring operation, this was the mighty Sun Life Building, in the heart of downtown Montreal. This was the structure that once boasted of being the largest office building in the British Commonwealth. Now, transformed into a farm, it had become a showplace for the Quebec government. Surely they wouldn't be stupid enough to cripple the elevators on purpose.

It was only two years since a special presidential ordinance had decreed that the building be converted to agriculture, and the government was immensely proud of the quality of the loam it had deposited on the marble floors, of the ceiling-based irrigation system it had installed, and of the powerful lights it had brought in to provide synthetic sunshine, day and night. It was a major enterprise—twenty-six storeys, each with more than an acre of first-class farm-floor …

They walked up the street toward the large building that housed part of the Ministry of Culture. There had been an explosion here, a big one that had blown in part of the building's façade. Near the hole a message had been painted, in huge red letters—FREE THE ANGLOS. The Anglo Liberation Army had struck again, during the night.

"I heard about it this morning, at work," Chucky said.

"That must have taken a lot of dynamite," Paul said.

They wanted to look more closely into the hole, but the area was roped off and policemen were hastening people along, so that no crowd could form. Meanwhile workmen were putting up their ladders to sandblast, paint over, or somehow obliterate the A.L.A.'s slogan. The words were not only seditious, they were in a language other than French, which was strictly prohibited.

"Free the Anglos," Chucky said. "What idiots! What a hopeless cause."

"I don't know, Chucky," Paul said. "Maybe it isn't so hopeless."

"Are you kidding?"

The aims of the Anglo Liberation Army were certainly visionary and perhaps quixotic. They called for total separation from Quebec and the creation of an independent Angloland. This would take in the western half of the Island of Montreal, traditional home of the urban Anglos, and part of the Eastern Townships, traditional home of the rural Anglos. The old Autoroute that linked the two areas would become a demilitarized corridor.

The name Angloland was provisional; one faction in the A.L.A. wanted to call it New Canada. But whatever its name, its advocates argued that it would be a perfectly viable country. Its area would be much bigger than Singapore or Mauritius or Malta or several other sovereign states. In fact, its size would be equal to the combined area of six European countries: Luxembourg, Liechtenstein, Vatican City, San Marino, Monaco, and Andorra. And its population would be twice as big as the combined population of those six sovereign states. Unlike Quebec, Angloland would enjoy good relations with the United States, and this would lead to trade and prosperity; this would be a country where Anglos could work in their own language, develop their own culture, and walk with their heads held high.

William Weintraub, *The Underdogs* (Toronto, 1979), 9–11, 68–69.]

Canada without Quebec—A Positive View

John Harbron argued that a brand-new start with a brand-new capital, Edmonton City, would be the best thing for Canada.

… Ottawa will be a forlorn city, stripped of its credibility as the federal capital, separated by only a river from the enthusiastic new republic on the other shore …

… Its formulas for holding the country together will have failed. Its bureaucracy will be discredited. Its ranks will be reduced by the departure of many of its Francophone members to work for the new Quebec state. Canada will need a new capital, a symbol of the new directions we will take after Quebec's departure.

A dynamic western Canada, which has chafed under the presecessionist division of power in favor of the east (Ontario and Quebec), will demand parity in the post-Quebec Canadian nation. I visualize Alberta and not Ontario as the new seat of the federal government.

I propose that Edmonton be considered for the new federal capital. Edmonton is a Brasilia of the north, a city symbolically located between the southern industrial sector and the Arctic frontier. It is already the jumping-off point for the Arctic, and would be the logical site for the new Canadian equivalent to the Soviet GLAVSEVMORPUT, if such an agency should be established. It was originally laid out as a large frontier community, and already has the administrative machinery of a provincial capital.

Edmonton is also close to Calgary, which is the heart of Alberta and an important centre for resource-based industries such as oil, gas, petrochemicals and food-processing. Calgary and Edmonton already display the kind of cooperation between industry and government which has fallen apart in eastern Canada. As a result Alberta under Premier Peter Lougheed is becoming an industrialized province, a "Ruhr of the West."

My belief is that a federal bureaucracy centered in Edmonton, next door to the dynamic business and investment climate of Calgary, would be forced to cast off the caution, conventional wisdom and laziness which have permeated the public service in Ottawa. The kinds of new relationships between multinationals and governments which are already emerging in other countries around the world could be more quickly developed in the West than in the present atmosphere of Ottawa …

The gloomy prognoses that Quebec on her own can only stumble, and that what is left of Canada can only disintegrate, are not in my view justified.

If the historical determinism propounded by Professor Bolton is to be our fate, with French America as an independent republic at last, then the challenges we face will largely be the ones we have ignored or not understood until recently.

We will need to assert our primacy as a hemispheric state, and define a national strategy and a national ideology for the future. And if we don't start doing these things before Quebec separates, Canada may require the kind of harsh direction we have not experienced since World War II to ensure our survival.

Yet restructuring Canada without Quebec will require more than this: it will require a rebirth of our self-esteem and an end to the demeaning and self-seeking attitude which has been the mark of our decline as a nation in the late 1970s. Separation must see the end of Canada as a "crybaby" nation.

Canada will be neither poor nor totally bereft when Quebec goes. We have creativity, a sense of purpose and some basic drives.

Let's not forget our times of greatness: the feat of Confederation, linking the infant nation by rail, great sacrifice in the two world wars, our economic and military role as a middle-sized world power in the 1940s and '50s, the spontaneous burst of patriotism during our Centennial year.

The Canadian identity will have to be for a time a more nationalistic one as we make efforts to keep intact what is left of Confederation.

It is also important that Canada relate to Quebec without rancor, even though many English Canadians will probably never understand why separation happened. We will have to negotiate with a republican government on a catalog of thorny crises. A radical restructuring of tariffs, negotiations on the operation of the St. Lawrence Seaway, acquiring a passage across Quebec to link Canada and the Maritime region, negotiations for disassembling the crown corporations—all will receive top priority.

And these will have to be conducted by a federal government which is trying to reorganize itself and other institutions at the same time.

When we formed Confederation in 1867, we rejected the Manifest Destiny that sought to plant the U.S. flag from the Isthmus of Panama to the North Pole. Now we will have to reject it again at a time when our intimate industrial, technological and financial associations with the U.S. will make independent survival more difficult than in 1776, 1812, or 1867.

Canada without Quebec will need both determination and magnanimity—to survive against American pressures for union, to assure peaceful coexistence with the new Quebec nation, and to rebuild a strong national presence in the world community.

John D. Harbron, *Canada without Quebec* (Toronto, 1977), 133, 150–51, 154–56. [ReadingSource.End]

Quebec within Canada: A Positive View

Mason Wade, general editor of the first and second editions of Search for a Nation, grew up in New Hampshire among Franco-Americans and acquired a lifelong interest in French Canada and its special problems in the larger Canada. In the preface and in the conclusion to his book The French-Canadian Outlook he states his sympathetic and positive approach to Canada's recurring crises.

This book is an attempt to show in brief, why the French Canadians think and act in ways differing from those of English-speaking North Americans. It is the story of the struggle of a minority group to maintain its cultural identity in the face of all manner of conscious and unconscious pressure to conform to the civilization of other ethnic groups and another culture. It is also in some measure an account of what the French Canadians call the "French fact in North America," for only by tracing out the cultural history of French Canada from its beginnings can the present position of Quebec be understood. The unifying thread of that history is the spirit known as "nationalism," which in this instance is actually a provincialism complicated by ethnic and religious factors. Therefore particular attention will be devoted to the extremists of a generally peaceful people who have a remarkable devotion to the golden mean as a principle of life. The attitudes of minority groups can often be explained only in psychological terms, and French-Canadian attitudes are a good example. Sir Wilfrid Laurier, perhaps the greatest French Canadian, once put this fact into words when he said, "Quebec does not have opinions, but only sentiments." So this short history will also be in some measure a psychological study.

There are certain advantages in writing the history of a country of which one is not a native. This is perhaps particularly true when writing of Canada, a country divided into two main cultural groups, between whom there is a serious lack of communication and understanding, and whose differences have long blinded the two groups to the intricate interweaving of the histories of Canada and the United States. Because of ancient difficulties and a tradition of diplomatic relations between English and French Canadians, an American, who has much in common with both, often finds that either sort of Canadian will unburden himself more fully to the stranger than he would to his fellow countrymen of the other ethnic origin ...

Today the great "Quebec problem" is to broaden the base of that mutual understanding (which began to appear after the Second World War), on a realistic rather than a diplomatic basis, and with mutual respect, for each group has something to give the other, and something to learn from the other. French and English will never be wholly one in Canada, but they can come to understand one another, and thus avert the recurrence of the crises here chronicled. The problem of Canadian union is merely a special case of the great world problem of our time, for mankind must learn to be equal without being identical, if it is to survive.

Mason Wade, *The French-Canadian Outlook* (Toronto, 1971), xiv–xv, 87.

21 ❧ Constitutional Debate, Defeat, and Compromise

"The Night of the Long Knives": Who Was Betrayed?

Bouchard said that Lévesque was "the best" of Quebec's negotiators. He could not be blamed for Quebec's isolation during the 1981 discussions about patriation that took place between Trudeau and the "Gang of Eight" premiers. The confusing story of who betrayed whom left Quebec out of the 1982 Constitution Act. The following commentary and press reports offer opinions.

The stage was set. On November 2, 1981. Most Premiers showed a certain amount of flexibility, except Lyon of Manitoba, Alberta's Lougheed and Lévesque of Quebec. Lévesque went so far as to exclude any possibility of negotiation on the Charter of Rights and boldly challenged Trudeau to consult the population on this score. This challenge would have significant consequences during the subsequent days.

On November 3, Davis of Ontario proposed a compromise: he would accept the amending formula concocted by the group of the eight, if a charter of rights was included in the Constitution. Trudeau, on the other hand, wanted to include linguistic rights for French-speaking Canadians in the Constitution. Surprisingly, his most stubborn opponent turned out to be Lévesque who was ready to sacrifice the rights of French speakers, except those living in Quebec. The other provincial leaders were left in a position where they had to choose between Trudeau and Lévesque.

The group of eight, which met every morning, had established that none of its members would modify their position without consulting the others. The solidarity of the eight fell apart on November 4, 1981 when René Lévesque eagerly accepted a Trudeau suggestion: if, in two years, there was no agreement on the Charter of Rights, the Charter would be voted on in a referendum. Lévesque, as we know, had been hoping for such a confrontation for a long time.

Later, René Lévesque, Claude Morin, Lucien Bouchard, Brian Mulroney and other politicians, as well as academics and journalists would say that Lévesque had been betrayed by his allies. But, the truth was captured in the newspapers. On November 5, the French daily *La Presse* reported the following:

> After two days of fruitless negotiations and an emergency cabinet meeting, on Tuesday evening, Mr. Trudeau finally made the following surprising overture at noon yesterday. As explained by Mr. Trudeau, at the conclusion of an extensive negotiation session in the morning, there was a "big story in the making." A Canada-Quebec alliance was developing. We shall try, during the next two years, to improve the Charter, said Trudeau. If there

is no agreement, we shall consult the population by asking the question: "Do you want a Charter, yes or no?" Commenting on the event, Lévesque then declared: "This provides us with a respectable and extraordinarily interesting way out of this whole imbroglio."

La Presse (Montreal), 5 November 1981, A10.

By suddenly aligning himself with Trudeau, Lévesque was not only breaking ranks with his colleagues in the group of eight, he was insulting them by not even bothering to inform them of his decision. And while the agreement between the eight premiers proclaimed the equality of the provinces, Lévesque quickly turned around and consented to a veto given only to Quebec and Ontario. As well, it seems inconceivable that he didn't know many of his colleagues in the group of eight were averse to a referendum. Who, then, had betrayed René Lévesque? Answer: Nobody. Lévesque himself violated the agreement he had signed on April 16, 1980.

Michel Vastel, then a columnist with Le Devoir, *wrote:*

The English-speaking provinces fought a pitched battle against Prime Minister Trudeau's referendum project. But at the end of the day, Mr. René Lévesque sided against his former allies in the group of eight ...

Le Devoir, 5 November 1981, 1.

In the November 6 issue of Le Devoir, Vastel explained further why the group of eight had reprimanded Lévesque's decision of November 4:

For the past two days, since Mr Lévesque's spectacular about-face in favour of the referendum project of Mr Trudeau, Quebec has been left with no allies. During the night of Wednesday to Thursday, while everybody thought negotiations were underway, a high-ranking Quebec public servant sat on the sidelines motionless, declaring disenchanted: "We have no more credibility after what happened at noon!"

Le Devoir (Montreal) 6 November 1981, 1.

When the other premiers, except Lévesque, finally found common ground, Richard Daignault of Le Soleil wrote:

What completely changed the situation?—It was the threat of a national referendum on the Charter of Rights. It was like holding a pistol to the temple of all the English-speaking provinces, because they did not want to hear of it. The provinces of Saskatchewan and Alberta had been quite open about it. And Bill Davis did not want a referendum in his province. Imagine how his Ontario Tories would have looked, campaigning in favour of a Trudeau project ....

Le Soleil, 6 November 1981, B1.

Roland Rainville added this commentary, claiming that Lévesque was not betrayed; he isolated himself:

Therefore, on November 4, the other provincial leaders had no other choice but to envisage a compromise with Trudeau. To camouflage René Lévesque's failure to Quebeckers in this instance, the journalists and the secessionist politicians successfully fabricated the concept of *"the night of the long knives,"* a scenario according to which, during the night of November 4 to November 5, 1981, Lévesque had been betrayed by his anglophone colleagues and Quebec left isolated.

The truth is that Lévesque himself, not Quebec, became isolated when he reneged on his agreement with the group of eight. Fortunately, this *"night of the long knives"* had nothing in common with the terrible Nazi slaughter of June 30, 1934, in Germany, which had resulted in thousands of deaths. Today, many Quebeckers, victims of the péquiste propaganda, ignore what really took place during this momentous conference which was held from November 2 to November 5, 1981.

Roland Rainville, "The Backstabbing That Never Was: The Myth of Lévesque's Betrayal" (see http://uni.ca, 20 July, 2007).

THE CHARTER OF RIGHTS AND FREEDOMS—NOTWITHSTANDING

The following excerpts make up a sample of individual rights and freedoms, together with the clause that enabled escape from them, added at the request of the provincial premiers. What was given could not be refused.

Whereas Canada is founded upon principles that recognize the supremacy of God and the rule of law:

1.   *The Canadian Charter of Rights and Freedoms* guarantees the rights and freedoms set out in it subject only to such reasonable limits prescribed by law as can be demonstrably justified in a free and democratic society.

Fundamental Freedoms
2.   Everyone has the following fundamental freedoms:
       (a) freedom of conscience and religion;
       (b) freedom of thought, belief, opinion and expression, including freedom of the press and other media of communication;
       (c) freedom of peaceful assembly; and
       (d) freedom of association.

Democratic Rights
3.   Every citizen of Canada has the right to vote in an election of members of the House of Commons or of a legislative assembly and to be qualified for membership therein ...

Mobility Rights

1. Every citizen of Canada has the right to enter, remain in and leave Canada.
2. Every citizen of Canada and every person who has the status of a permanent resident of Canada has the right
   - (a) to move to and take up residence in any province; and
   - (b) to pursue the gaining of a livelihood in any province ...

Legal Rights

7. Everyone has the right to life, liberty and security of the person and the right not to be deprived thereof except in accordance with the principles of fundamental justice.
8. Everyone has the right to be secure against unreasonable search or seizure.
9. Everyone has the right not to be arbitrarily detained or imprisoned.
10. Everyone has the right on arrest or detention
    - (a) to be informed promptly of the reasons therefor;
    - (b) to retain and instruct counsel without delay and to be informed of that right; and
    - (c) to have the validity of the detention determined by way of *habeas corpus* and to be released if the detention is not lawful ...

Equality Rights

15. (1) Every individual is equal before and under the law and has the right to the equal protection and equal benefit of the law without discrimination and, in particular, without discrimination based on race, national or ethnic origin, colour, religion, sex, age or mental or physical disability.

    (2) Subsection (1) does not preclude any law, program or activity that has as its object the amelioration of conditions of disadvantaged individuals or groups including those that are disadvantaged because of race, national or ethnic origin, colour, religion, sex, age or mental or physical disability.

Official Languages of Canada

16. (1) English and French are the official languages of Canada and have equality of status and equal rights and privileges as to their use in all institutions of the Parliament and government of Canada.

    (2) English and French are the official languages of New Brunswick and have equality of status and equal rights and privileges as to their use in all institutions of the legislature and government of New Brunswick.

    (3) Nothing in the Charter limits the authority of Parliament or a legislature to advance the equality of status or use of English and French.

17.   (1) Everyone has the right to use English or French in any debates and other proceedings of Parliament.

(2) Everyone has the right to use English or French in any debates and other proceedings of the legislature of New Brunswick …

Minority Language Educational Rights

23.   (1) Citizens of Canada

(a) whose first language learned and still understood is that of the English or French linguistic minority population of the province in which they reside, or

(b) who have received their primary school instruction in Canada in English or French and reside in a province where the language in which they received that instruction is the language of the English or French linguistic minority population of the province, have the right to have their children receive primary and secondary school instruction in that language in that province …

General

25.   The guarantee in this Charter of certain rights and freedoms shall not be construed so as to abrogate or derogate from any aboriginal, treaty or other rights or freedoms that pertain to the aboriginal peoples of Canada including

(a) any rights or freedoms that have been recognized by the Royal Proclamation of October 7, 1763; and

(b) any rights or freedoms that may be acquired by the aboriginal peoples of Canada by way of land claims settlement.

26.   The guarantee in this Charter of certain rights and freedoms shall not be construed as denying the existence of any other rights or freedoms that exist in Canada.

27.   This Charter shall be interpreted in a manner consistent with the preservation and enhancement of the multi-cultural heritage of Canadians.

28.   Notwithstanding anything in this Charter, the rights and freedoms referred to in it are guaranteed equally to male and female persons.

29.   Nothing in this Charter abrogates or derogates from any rights or privileges guaranteed by or under the Constitution of Canada in respect of denominational, separate or dissentient schools.

30.   A reference in this Charter to a province or to the legislative assembly or legislature of a province shall be deemed to include a reference to the Yukon Territory and the Northwest Territories, or to the appropriate legislative authority thereof, as the case may be.

31.   Nothing in this Charter extends the legislative powers of any body or authority.

Application of Charter

33. (1) Parliament or the legislature of a province may expressly declare in an Act of Parliament or of the legislature, as the case may be, that the Act or a provision thereof shall operate notwithstanding a provision included in section 2 or sections 7 to 15 of this Charter ...

Justice Canada, 1983

SECTION 33: THE NOTWITHSTANDING CLAUSE— AN ESCAPE CLAUSE FOR PROVINCIAL GOVERNMENTS

Section 33 is a Charter escape clause. It allows a government to make some laws as if the Charter doesn't exist. It can't be used to override voting, mobility or minority language education rights.

The Charter is a two edged sword. It means that governments can't just pass laws that trample on human rights, but it also limits the power of democratically elected officials to carry out the popular will.

Up to the year 2000, only two Provinces had invoked the "notwithstanding clause": Quebec and Saskatchewan. (Quebec has never signed the repatriated Constitution.) When the Charter came into force in 1982, all Quebec statutes were repealed and then immediately re-enacted with the Section 33 override (notwithstanding) clause added. As well, all new Quebec statutes are enacted with an override clause. That practice will eventually end. Then, in 1988, Quebec will use the notwithstanding clause to protect its language law requiring French-only signs, which the Supreme Court of Canada will rule violates the Charter.

Saskatchewan will use the clause to protect a back-to-work law introduced during a labour dispute. Ironically, the Supreme Court of Canada will rule that the law doesn't violate the Charter, so the notwithstanding clause wasn't even needed.

From *Human Rights in Canada: A Historical Perspective* (see www.chrc-ccdp.ca/en/index.asp).

Constitutional Amendment Proclamation, 1983

... And Whereas, following that conference, the Senate, the House of Commons and the legislative assemblies of at least two-thirds of the provinces that have, in the aggregate, according to the latest general census, at least fifty percent of the population of all the provinces, have, by resolution, authorized an amendment to the Constitution of Canada to be made by proclamation issued by the Governor General under the Great Seal of Canada; ...

Government of Canada, 1983]

The 1987 Constitutional Accord (the Meech Lake Accord): "Distinct Society and Unanimous Consent"

The Meech Lake Accord attempted to please everyone. It contained clauses to meet Quebec's demands, starting with recognizing it as a "distinct society" and continuing to amendment items that would give any province veto power—another way of saying that amendments to the Constitution required the "unanimous consent" of the provinces. This clearly constituted a step toward devolution of federal powers to the provinces. The provinces gained, and the federal government lost. Ironically, the Meech Lake Accord failed to get unanimous consent, and none of the following proposals became law.

The 1987 Constitutional Accord

WHEREAS first ministers, assembled in Ottawa, have arrived at a unanimous accord on constitutional amendments that would bring about the full and active participation of Quebec in Canada's constitutional evolution, would recognize the principle of equality of all provinces, would provide new arrangements to foster greater harmony and cooperation between the Government of Canada and the governments of the provinces and would require that annual constitutional conferences composed of first ministers be convened not later than December 31, 1988; ...

2.   The Government of Canada will, as soon as possible, conclude an agreement with the Government of Quebec that would ...

(b) guarantee that Quebec will receive a number of immigrants, including refugees, within the annual total established by the federal government for all of Canada proportionate to its share of the population of Canada, with the right to exceed that figure by 5 percent for demographic reasons ...

CONSTITUTIONAL AMENDMENT, 1987

1.   The *Constitution Act, 1867* is amended by adding thereto, immediately after section 1 thereof, the following section:

2.   (1) The Constitution of Canada shall be interpreted in a manner consistent with

    (a) the recognition that the existence of French-speaking Canadians, centered in Quebec but also present elsewhere in Canada, and English-speaking Canadians, concentrated outside Quebec but also present in Quebec, constitutes a fundamental characteristic of Canada; and

    (b) the recognition that Quebec constitutes within Canada a distinct society.

(2) The role of the Parliament of Canada and the provincial legislatures to preserve the fundamental characteristic of Canada referred to in paragraph (1) (a) is affirmed

(3) The role of the legislature and Government of Quebec to preserve and promote the distinct identity of Quebec referred to in paragraph (1)(b) is affirmed.

4.   An amendment to the Constitution of Canada in relation to the following matters may be made proclamation issued by the Governor General under the Great Seal of Canada only where authorized by resolutions of the Senate and House of Commons and of the legislative assembly of each province:

    (a) the office of the Queen, the Governor General and the Lieutenant Governor of a province;

    (b) the powers of the Senate and the method of selecting Senators;

    (c) the number of members by which a province is entitled to be represented in the Senate and the residence qualifications of Senators;

    (d) the right of a province to a number of members in the House of Commons not less than the number of Senators by which the province was entitled to be represented on April 17, 1982;

    (e) the principle of proportionate representation of the provinces in the House of Commons prescribed by the Constitution of Canada;

    (f) subject to section 43, the use of the English or French language;

    (g) the Supreme Court of Canada;

    (h) the extension of existing provinces into the territories;

    (i) notwithstanding any other law or practice, the establishment of new provinces; and

    (j) an amendment to this part.

THE SPICER COMMISSION: PROBLEMS
WITH THE PEOPLE'S SOLUTION, 1991

The travelling Citizens' Forum on Canada's Future (the Spicer Commission) was formed to consult the people on reform of the Constitution. It was called the "People's Forum" and represented pure democracy, direct democracy, free speech, the open door, populism. Comments by two commissioners indicate the problems that can occur when the people really do have their say.

Comment by Commissioner Richard Cashin

The people who spoke to us expressed opinion[s] on many matters. We have no way of knowing how their opinions on one matter were related to their opinions on other matters, or what priority particular issues may have had in their thinking. Nor do we have any way of knowing how representative the opinions we hear [sic] may be of the opinions of all Canadians. This is because the process of participation was self-selective.

My second concern has to do with the continuing emphasis which was given to American-style concepts of direct democracy.

These are not new ideas—they have been around since the time of the Progressive movement in the United States and Canada. Some of these notions were adopted in the United States but they were rejected in Canada. They were rejected because they do not fit well with our parliamentary system.

Consider, for example, the effect on our system of responsible government if a small but well-organized single issue group were able to use the recall to force by-elections in several ridings at the same time. Or, think what mischief a small group could do if it had the power to initiate a referendum on bilingualism or on equalization payments. Moreover, as the American experience shows, the referendum is a process that favours the wealthy and single issue groups.

Many of the proposed suggestions which reflected this agenda have been altered. But my concern remains. It is that we not allow the exercise through which we have gone to be used to legitimize notions of governance so at variance with the principles of British parliamentary democracy.

My third basic concern relates to the fact that, because of the multiplicity of issues that were raised and because of the breadth of our mandate, we might lose sight of the importance of focusing on the central issue, which is national unity.

I say this because, in the light of what we heard, it is by no means certain that Canada will stay together. If it does stay together, it could be a country that is dramatically, irrevocably and substantially altered.

The basic question is how does the rest of Canada accommodate Quebec and how does Quebec reconcile itself with the rest of Canada. How can this be done? From what we have heard, there are two ways to do it: either Quebec is recognized as a distinct society with certain arrangements (constitutional or otherwise) that are different, or federal power is devolved to all provinces.

Thus there is a real dilemma for those who believe in the need for a strong federal government and who, for this reason, are reluctant to recognize Quebec as a distinct society with different arrangements (constitutional or otherwise) …

We heard about many different issues and many different views about those issues, but before we can deal with them we have first to establish what the political community is—is it to be a political community with Quebec or without Quebec?

The resolution of that question will shape the kind of society we will be in the future. Its resolution will determine the respect we give to diversity, to minority rights, to collective rights and to differing regional interests …

Comment by Commissioner Robert Normand

I cannot subscribe to the content of the Forum's report without expressing the following reservations.

Firstly, let me say that I find deplorable the fact that the Forum was unable to get Canadians to express their thoughts regarding the future of the country in a broader perspective and that it basically limited itself to gathering only the superficial views of those Canadians who addressed it, in a fashion similar to that of open-line radio shows. In this context, citizens had a tendency to limit themselves to stating first impressions, often based upon erroneous information that was not corrected, and adopted radical positions without first evaluating their possible consequences. The information thus gathered is not devoid of interest, but it will have to be put into perspective in all cases where it is to be used as the basis for developing political solutions.

Several commissioners however, myself included, had asked, as early as January 1991, that the dialogue be "deepened," but the desire to put on a show for the media took precedence over the substance. Further, no commissioners' meeting was held between March 3 and May 7, in other words during a two month period (out of an eight-month mandate), despite my requests. This deliberate hiatus did nothing to improve matters!

I also deplore that the relationship between Quebec and the rest of Canada, in the context of an in-depth political restructuring, was trivialized, especially during the first few months. I would further like to underline that in most cases, the majority of participants at the Forum's group discussions I attended, tired after more than an hour's discussion on their own concerns and on native issues, were no longer up to speaking out as dispassionately on their vision of Quebec and were often tempted to apply to

Quebec the outlines of solutions they had just previously sketched for native issues.

The positive suggestions made by citizens (Part II of the report) and by the commissioners (Part III) are either too convoluted in form or too timid in content to be adequate for resolving the problems at hand; on the contrary, they might well contribute to maintaining the divisions that now exist in the country, as they bring out the lack of urgency English Canada attaches to the need to accommodate Quebec rapidly and responsibly. In this regard, the Forum's contribution is far from meeting my expectations. It is also unfortunate that the Forum did not devote more attention to the situation of the some 800,000 francophones living outside Quebec. Only a few observations in Part II are devoted to them. Furthermore, while the need for some form of bilingualism in Canada is underlined, what is being requested is a revision of the federal policy in this area, which revision could probably serve to water it down. Views were expressed against Quebec's Bill 178 that is considered as limiting the rights of anglophones, without at the same time paying enough attention to language laws applicable to francophones living outside Quebec. Here again, the report underlines the "political lyricism" of Canadians regarding the some 500,000 natives whose situation troubles them, and rightly so, but fails to deal with the appalling rate of assimilation of some francophone communities outside Quebec.

Though I found the Forum experience worthwhile in certain aspects, it was an unpleasant exercise for me in others …

A minister has been appointed to deal specifically with constitutional issues. Given the bitter confusion concerning the country's constitutional future, as brought to light in the report, and the Forum's inability to put forward satisfactory solutions, let me say: "Good luck to you, Mr. Clark."

The report of the Citizens' Forum on Canada's Future (The Spicer Commission report), 1991.

THE CHARLOTTETOWN ACCORD, 1992: "NO" AGAIN

The proposals in the Concensus Report on the Constitution *(the Charlottetown Accord) were based on many meetings called "Citizens' Forums," 3,000 submissions, and testimony from 700 individuals. There were also six televised national conferences between January and March of 1991. Where there was dissent concerning a proposal, this was recorded in the minutes; where there was consensus, the proposal was included in the following summary of* The Consensus Report on the Constitution, Charlottetown, August 28, 1992.

I: UNITY AND DIVERSITY

A: PEOPLE AND COMMUNITIES

1. *Canada Clause*

   A new clause should be included as section 2 of the Constitution Act, 1867 that would express fundamental Canadian values. The Canada Clause would guide the courts in their future interpretation of the entire Constitution, including the Canadian Charter of Rights and Freedoms ...

2.   (c)   Quebec constitutes within Canada a distinct society, which includes a French-speaking majority, a unique culture and a civil law tradition; ...

       (h)   Canadians confirm the principle of the equality of the provinces at the same time as recognizing their diverse characteristics.

       (i)   The role of the legislature and government of Quebec to preserve and promote the distinct society of Quebec is affirmed.

3. *Linguistic Communities in New Brunswick*

   A separate constitutional amendment requiring only the consent of Parliament and the legislature of New Brunswick should be added to the Canadian Charter of Rights and Freedoms. The amendment would entrench the equality of status of the English and French linguistic communities in New Brunswick, including the right to distinct educational institutions and such distinct cultural institutions as are necessary for the preservation and promotion of these communities. The amendment would also affirm the role of the legislature and government of New Brunswick to preserve and promote this equality of status ...

B: CANADA'S SOCIAL AND ECONOMIC UNION

4. *The Social and Economic Union*

   A new provision should be added to the constitution describing the commitment of the governments, Parliament and the legislatures within the federation to the principle of the preservation and development of Canada's social and economic union. The new provision, entitled the Social and Economic Union, should be drafted to set out a series of policy objectives underlying the social and the economic union, respectively. The provision should not be justiciable.

   The policy objectives set out in the provision on the social union should include, but not be limited to:

   - providing throughout Canada a health care system that is comprehensive, universal, portable, publicly administered and accessible;

- providing adequate social services and benefits to ensure that all individuals resident in Canada have reasonable access to housing, food and other basic necessities;
- providing high quality primary and secondary education to all individuals resident in Canada and ensuring reasonable access to post secondary education;
- protecting the rights of workers to organize and bargain collectively; and,
- protecting, preserving and sustaining the integrity of the environment for present and future generations.

A mechanism for monitoring the Social and Economic Union should be determined by a First Minister's Conference.

II: INSTITUTIONS

A: THE SENATE

7. *An Elected Senate*
The Constitution should be amended to provide that Senators are elected, either by the population of the provinces and territories of Canada or by the members of their provincial or territorial legislative assemblies.
Federal legislation should govern Senate elections, subject to the constitutional provision above and constitutional provisions requiring that elections take place at the same time as elections to the House of Commons and provisions respecting eligibility and mandate of senators. Federal legislation would be sufficiently flexible to allow provinces and territories to provide for gender equality in the composition of the Senate.
Matters should be expedited in order that Senate elections be held as soon as possible, and, if feasible, at the same time as the next federal general election for the House of Commons.

8. *An Equal Senate*
The Senate should initially total 62 Senators and should be composed of six Senators from each province and one Senator from each territory ...

10. *Relationship to the House of Commons*
The Senate should not be a confidence chamber. In other words, the defeat of government sponsored legislation by the Senate would not require the government's resignation.

11. *Categories of Legislation*
There should be four categories of legislation:

1) Revenue and expenditure bills ("supply bills");
2) Legislation materially affecting French language and French culture;
3) Bills involving fundamental tax policy changes directly related to natural resources;
4) Ordinary legislation (any bill not falling into one of the first three categories).

12. *Approval of Legislation*

The Constitution should oblige the Senate to dispose of any bills approved by the House of Commons, within thirty sitting days of the House of Commons, with the exception of revenue and expenditure bills.

Revenue and expenditure bills would be subject to a 30 calendar-day suspensive veto. If a bill is defeated or amended by the Senate within this period, it could be repassed by a majority vote in the House of Commons on a resolution.

Bills that materially affect French language culture would require approval by a majority of Senators voting and by a majority of the Francophone Senators voting. The House of Commons would not be able to override the defeat of a bill in this category by the Senate.

14. *Double Majority*

The originator of a bill should not be responsible for designating whether it materially affects French language or French culture. Each designation should be subject to appeal to the Speaker of the Senate under rules to be established by the Senate. These rules should be designed to provide adequate protection to Francophones.

On entering the Senate, Senators should be required to declare whether they are Francophones for the purpose of the double majority voting rule. Any process for challenging these declarations should be left to the rules of the Senate.

C. HOUSE OF COMMONS

21. Composition of the House of Commons

The composition of the House of Commons should be adjusted to better reflect the principle of representation by population. The adjustment should include an initial increase in the House of Commons to 337 seats, to be made at the time Senate reform comes into effect. Ontario and Quebec would each be assigned eighteen additional seats, British Columbia four additional seats, and Alberta two additional seats, with boundaries to be developed using the 1991 census.

An additional special Canada-wide redistribution of seats should be conducted following the 1996 census, aimed at assuring that, in the first subsequent general election, no province will have fewer than 95% of the House of Commons seats it would receive under strict representation-by-population. Consequently, British Columbia and Ontario would each be assigned 3 additional seats and Alberta 2 additional seats. As a result of this special adjustment, no province or territory will lose seats, nor will a province or territory which has achieved full representation-by-population have a smaller share of House of Commons seats than its share of the total population in the 1996 census.

The redistribution based on the 1996 and all future redistributions should be governed by the following constitutional provisions:

> (a)   a guarantee that Quebec would be assigned no fewer than 25 percent of the seats in the House of Commons; ...

29. *Culture*

Provinces should have exclusive jurisdiction over cultural matters within the provinces. This should be recognized through an explicit constitutional amendment that also recognizes the continuing responsibility of the federal government in Canadian cultural matters. The federal government should retain responsibility for national cultural institutions. The Government of Canada commits to negotiate cultural agreements with provinces in recognition of their lead responsibility for cultural matters within the province and to ensure that the federal government and the province work in harmony. These changes should not alter the federal fiduciary responsibility for Aboriginal people. The non-derogation provisions for Aboriginal peoples set out in item 40 of this document will apply to culture.

V: THE AMENDING FORMULA

Note: All the following changes to the amending formula require the unanimous agreement of Parliament and the provincial legislatures.

57.   *Changes to National Institutions*

Amendments to provisions of the Constitution related to the senate should require unanimous agreement of Parliament and the provincial legislatures, once the current set of amendments affecting the House of Commons, including Quebec's guarantee of 25 percent of the seats in the House of Commons, and amendments which can now be made under Section 42 should also require unanimity.

Justice Canada, 1991

Two Old and Former Friends

September 8, 1992, found Mulroney in an expansive mood introducing the Charlottetown Accord in the House of Commons. He was confident in the support of opposition leaders, all ten provincial premiers, and the Chief of the Assembly of First Nations. But the next day he clashed with the man he had once vigorously promoted. Now they were enemies, thanks to constitutional discord.

RIGHT HON. BRIAN MULRONEY—Prime Minister (Charlevoix): Mr. Speaker, this Agreement is the result of the most far-ranging and thorough process of consultation and discussion ever held by a Canadian government, and perhaps by any government, in a modern industrialized world.

For the aboriginal people, it proposes a new partnership in a federation that was created in 1867 without their participation. This generation of Canadians are now called upon to redeem the promises of equality first made to the aboriginal peoples several hundred years ago by representatives of French and English kings and never fulfilled. We propose to fulfil those obligations in the year 1992.

In 1608, French was already spoken in Quebec City. In 1763, when Canada was ceded to England, the 90,000 French people living here openly feared for their future. Long, long before Confederation, the ancestors of this country called themselves "Canadian," a name that generation after generation of pioneers bore with pride. This Agreement, Mr. Speaker, enables a new generation of Quebecers to say "yes" to Canada with pride and confidence.

We are faced today with the imperative duty of closing the circle of this constitutional round and getting on with the important work of readying Canadians to meet the sweeping demands of global competition and profound societal change that we find everywhere. Our history begs us to proceed and the world around us reminds us that we must. It is time for us all to find it in our hearts and in our souls to say without hesitation or doubt that a yes to Canada, a yes to this agreement, a powerful yes to liberating future generations of Canadians, for decades and decades to come, to achieve, to grow, to prosper, to share and to care in a manner the world has come to know as the Canadian way.

Canada, *House of Commons Debates* (8 September 1992), 12726–30.

Less than twenty-four hours later, the Speaker recognized an Hon. Member sitting deep to his left.

LUCIEN BOUCHARD (Lac-St-Jean): Mr. Speaker, the prime minister has been extolling the so-called virtues of the Charlottetown Accord, rallying to his cause such allies as the Leader of the Official Opposition, his new friend, and dead sovereignists. I would like to give the prime minister an opportunity to confront a real live sovereignist. I ask him to accept the challenge of meeting me in public debate in Quebec, anywhere and at any time during the referendum campaign.

MR. MULRONEY: Mr. Speaker, I am a real live Canadian, and I brought one into this world. For months, the leader of the Bloc Québécois has been insisting on public consultations. Well, there is going to be a referendum in Quebec and on October 26, you will know the outcome and what Quebecers really think.

LUCIEN BOUCHARD: Mr. Speaker, I think who brought who into t he world is beside the point. I want the prime minister to say whether he will accept my challenge, yes or no.

AN HON. MEMBER: He is scared.

MR. MULRONEY: The last challenge I accepted was in 1988, when I went twice to the riding of Lac St. Jean, with my wife, to get my hon. friend elected! There will be not one but many debates in Canada and Quebec, because when the Bloc Québécois and the Parti Québécois were asking for a referendum, they said it had to be a referendum on sovereignty.

MR. BOUCHARD: So let's have one.

MR. MULRONEY: I think I can hear the Bloc murmuring in the background. I can assure you that there will be a watertight question and a decisive outcome. Considering the commitment made by the leader of the Bloc, I assume that if the vote is not in his favour, he will do as he said and resign the next day.

Canada, *House of Commons Debates* (9 September 1992), 12766.

Charlottetown Accord Referendum Results

National Referendum on the Charlottetown Accord (October 26, 1992)

Province	Voted Yes	% of Yes Votes	Voted No	% of No Votes
Newfoundland	133,193	62.9	77,881	36.5
P.E.I.	48,687	73.6	17,124	25.9
Nova Scotia	218,618	48.5	230,182	51.1
New Brunswick	234,010	61.3	145,096	38.0
Quebec	1,710,117	42.4	2,232,280	55.4
Ontario	2,410,119	49.8	2,397,665	49.6
Manitoba	198,230	37.8	322,971	61.6
Saskatchewan	203,361	44.5	252,459	55.2
Alberta	483,275	39.7	731,975	60.1
British Columbia	525,188	31.7	1,126,761	68.0
Yukon	5,354	43.4	6,922	56.1
N. W. T.	14,750	60.6	9,416	38.7
Total Canada	6,185,902	44.6	7,550,732	54.4

Source: *Canadian Annual Review*, 1992, 27.

Note: The referendum in Quebec was held on the same day as in the rest of Canada but followed the rules as set in the Quebec Referendum law.

IS QUEBEC A NATION?

Dr. Michael Hill, president of the League of the South in Tuscaloosa, Alabama, and professor of history (retired) at the University of Alabama, wrote in his message of September-October 1995 that Quebec would become a nation if it had the courage to stand up and fight as the Confederacy once had.

In early September Quebec premier Jacques Parizeau, leader of the Parti québécois, fought back tears as the provincial flag was unfurled and a poet recited the preamble to a prospective declaration of independence from anglophone Canada:

> We, the people of Quebec, declare it our own will to be in full possession of all the powers of a state; to levy all our taxes, to vote on all our laws, to sign all our treaties and to exercise the highest power of all, conceiving, and controlling, by ourselves, our fundamental law.

If this sounds like glorious fiction, reality rolls around on 30 October when Quebec could choose by referendum to go its own way. Support for the separatists, according to polls, has risen recently to 50 percent, but it's a sure bet that Canadian Prime Minister Jean Chrétien will call on his New World Order buddies from the G-7 countries to exert political and economic pressure on the new nation, should it come to be. Bill Clinton, citing NAFTA regulations, already has threatened to cut trade ties with an independent Quebec. Like the United States and other Western "democracies," Canada is firmly in the grip of a globalist oligarchy that, according to the late Christopher Lasch, "see themselves as world citizens" at war with nationalists and regionalists of every stripe.

Those who mold public opinion in Toronto and Ottawa have mounted a fear-mongering campaign designed to undermine support among Quebec's moderate nationalists. Even in Montreal itself a cabal of anti-secessionist scholars (undoubtedly beneficiaries of Canada's liberal welfare program for academics) warned in *La Presse*: "We should face the fact that the Canadian community is much more real than a lot of sovereigntists (separatists) actually believe. Many Quebecers do not feel sufficiently different from other Canadians to demand with both force and enthusiasm a country all of their own." Former provincial Premier Daniel Johnson, leader of the unionist party in Quebec, accused the Parti québécois of engaging in "confusion and obfuscation" to trick Quebecers into a "yes" vote. For his part, Chrétien simply refuses to acknowledge the possibility of a separatist victory in October.

But Monique Simard, a high-ranking organiser of the separatist campaign, brushed aside such criticism and declared: "For the first time, English-speaking Canada is realising the 'yes' side could win." Simard went on to say that "without sovereignty, we're doomed to be an eternal minority or to disappear." After years of wrangling over the issue of Quebec's sovereignty, many Canadians are growing tired of Francophone agitation. Some undoubtedly would like to see the province's seven million inhabitants secede tomorrow.

But like the Scots National Party in Scotland, the Parti québécois and its supporters have been snared in the web of the welfare state. Writing in the September issue of The Rothbard-Rockwell Report, paleo-conservative Paul Gottfried notes that Canadians, both Anglo- and Franco-phone, have come to "accept their [socialist] rulers ... and lack the emotional and moral resources to oppose ... [them] effectively." Thus, it all boils down to the question: Do Quebecers really have the guts to form their own independent nation, cutting all ties with the Ottawa regime, or are they simply attempting to blackmail Chrétien's government into making concessions?

In 1980 separatists voted for a watered-down version of independence based on something called "sovereignty association." Had the referendum passed, it would have allowed Quebec to exercise a degree of "home rule" while the province still maintained certain formal ties (e.g. use of the national postal services) to the Canadian state. It appears that fifteen years later the separatists are again backing off from an advocacy of complete independence. In June Parizeau hinted that the Parti québécois would be satisfied with something less than an independent Quebec. The possibility of a "soft" referendum in October likely stems from the Harvard-educated Parizeau's tenuous commitment to a truly radical, populist solution and to the influence of his moderate allies, the Bloc québécois, which hold several opposition seats in the Canadian House of Commons, and the nascent Parti Action Democratique. But the Parti québécois may benefit from Prime Minister Chrétien's hard-line stance on the issue of provincial "home rule." Chrétien, taking his cue from an increasingly vocal Anglophone majority, refuses to promise special treatment to Quebecers as an inducement to keep them in the Canadian union. This time around, then, we can only hope that the majority of Quebecers will see secession as the only means of protecting their culture from a hostile majority.

It is clear that French Canadians, like Anglo-Celtic American Southerners, could, if they were determined, establish a "nation" in the real sense of the word. Organic nationalism, intuitively grounded in common language, poetry, literature, folkways, and religious beliefs, is the opposite of state-based civic nationalism in which people are "educated" to be cogs in a rationalist, technocratic, imperial machine. As the global elites push the world's nation-states toward interdependence, devolutionary forces are beginning to pull toward local rule and the break-up of nation-states cum empires. Thus the nation-state is caught in the middle. While Establishment elites seek their

New World Order, we witness movements for autonomy or outright independence not only in Quebec but also in Canada's western provinces, Scotland, Wales, Brittany, Lombardy, Catalonia, the Balkans, and other "ethno-regions."

We of the Southern League hope that the Quebecers are indeed serious about complete independence from Canada. However, considering the vacillating tendencies of the Parti québécois over the past 15 years, it seems unlikely that it will go beyond its tepid "sovereignty association" demands. If, as expected, Parizeau and his followers forge to the brink and then pull away, it should not dishearten Southern nationalists. Rather, we ought to learn an important lesson from Canadian antics: faux populist movements manipulated from above by Establishmentarians are slender reeds upon which to lean. So long as the chimerical allurements of socialism and its attendant welfare-state mentality rule the passions of a people, they will lack the willingness to sacrifice the comfortable life for the rigors of independence. If there is to be a new Southern nation, then we must begin by preparing ourselves to endure the common sufferings, so familiar to our Confederate ancestors, that weld a people into a nation. Unfortunately, Quebecers, lacking our historical experience, have yet to exhibit these hard tendencies.

Michael Hill, "Quebec: A Nation," *The Southern Patriot* (September-October 1995).

QUEBEC: THE OFFICIAL OPPOSITION

In January 1994 Bouchard, Leader of the new Bloc Québécois whose 54 seats made him Leader of the Official Opposition, addressed the House of Commons in Ottawa. He explained why the party was there and what it intended to do.

Many in English Canada were surprised by the Bloc québécois's achievement on October 25. To tell the truth, I am not surprised by that: the channels of communication from Quebec to English Canada are significantly distorted as they cross the border, so that the Quebec reality is perceived in a very confused way on the other side. That is a first justification for the presence of Quebec sovereigntists in this House.

Institutions often lag behind reality. The previous House of Commons was no exception to this rule: the stinging rejection of the Charlottetown Accord by voters in Canada and Quebec is striking proof. Today, the main architects of that accord have all disappeared from the political scene.

The voters have set the record straight. For the first time in contemporary history, this House which is now beginning its work reflects the very essence of Canada, its binational nature and the very different visions of the future which flow from that. Truth is never a bad advisor. As General de Gaulle said, one may well long for the days of sailing ships, but the only valid policy one can have is based on realities ...

We only have ourselves to blame if overlapping federal and provincial activities prevent the creation of cohesive programs and generate an outrageous amount of waste in human and financial resources. That reveals a second reality as inescapable as the economic crisis. Such inefficiencies are at the very heart of our system. They constantly affect each other and reflect the vicious circle of Canadian federalism. At the core of the economic crisis is a political crisis.

But for the better part of English Canada, there is no political crisis. Or, if there is one, they choose to ignore it. They have sent to Ottawa a new government with the mandate to better manage the present system without changing anything in it.

On the other hand, Quebecers not only sent a completely new team to Ottawa, but they gave their elected representatives the mandate to get prepared to bring about a new order. The Bloc Québécois was given a double mission: to manage the economic crisis and to handle the political crisis. Does the distribution of elected members in this House not prove the very existence of this second crisis? ...

More than 30 years ago Quebec awakened to the world and decided to catch up. The Quiet Revolution transformed Quebec. It did not take long before the spirit of reform in Quebec collided with the spirit of Canadian federalism in Ottawa. Thirty years ago the horns were locked. Thirty years later we are still at it, as if frozen in a time warp. We should learn from the past, and this we should have learned: The political problem with Canada is Quebec, and the problem of Quebec is Canada.

...

Some are willing to deny the obvious in order not to upset the status quo. They speak of one Canadian nation, whereas Quebec and English Canada are two different nations. Even when nobody in Quebec was contemplating sovereignty, the Canada that steered Quebecers was not of the same cloth as the Canada that seized the minds and hearts of Maritimers, Ontarians or Westerners. Quebecers were in the vanguard of the struggle for more Canadian autonomy under the Red Ensign and eventually for the political independence of Canada. This tends to be forgotten in certain quarters where Quebec bashing is a popular pastime.

... If one accepts the obvious, one must surely accept the consequences. Every nation has the right to self-government, that is to decide its own policies and future. We have no quarrel with the concept of federalism when applied to uninational states. It is a different matter when it comes to multinational states, particularly to the Canadian brand of federalism.

Canadian federalism means that the government of Quebec is subordinate to the central government both in large and lesser matters. Within the federal regime, English Canada in fact has a veto on the future development of Quebec.

When the theme of national sovereignty is brought up in English Canada a nice paradox almost always emerges. I shall call it the paradox of English Canada. First, the tendency to consider passé the concept of national sovereignty, what with the European Community, GATT, NAFTA and so on. This is a patent misreading of the situation. Take a look at the western world. Ninety-five percent of its population live in nation states.

The fact is that Quebec is the only nation of more than seven million people in the western world not to have attained political sovereignty. I invite members of this House to reflect upon this. As a political structure Canada is the exception rather than the rule, an exception that is not working well, to understate the case ...

Quebec sovereigntists advocate a modern concept of political sovereignty, one which is exercised within the framework of major economic structures and which is respectful of minorities. Under no circumstances will the 630,000 francophones outside Quebec be sacrificed. Moreover, Quebec sovereigntists were not the ones who rejected the Free Trade Agreement with the United States and NAFTA. There is a difference between withdrawing into oneself and pulling out in order to perform better in the new global economy.

The close economic integration between Quebec and Canada forces us to take a careful look at what is happening in Europe. What lessons can we draw from the European model?

Some pundits like to believe the European Community will gradually transform itself into something resembling Canadian federalism, and use this as an argument against Quebec sovereignty. Thus they reveal their lack of familiarity with European developments. In fact the other way around appears much more likely. To solve the Canadian political crisis our present institutions should evolve along the lines of the European Community.

A few facts seem in order. The European Commission in Brussels has a budget that amounts to 1.2 percent of the global GNP of the community. It has no fiscal powers and—such a tragedy—cannot run a deficit. The federal government in Ottawa spends 22 percent of GNP and has the whole gamut of fiscal powers. As for deficits we all know what has happened. The commission in Brussels has no army, no police, and a small bureaucracy when compared to national governments. Community decisions are in fact executed by national bureaucracies. If we exclude trade matters, national sovereignty remains the basic ingredient of the community.

For instance the 12 members could modify the structure and the workings of the EC without the commission having any say in the decision. For these countries co-operation is the master word, not subordination.

This is a far cry from the Canadian brand of federalism. Who will pretend, for example, that only the provincial governments determine the future of Canada? Who will pretend that the federal government is but a benevolent arbitrator of inter-regional conflicts? For Quebec, the central government is the problem. For English Canada, it is part of the solution ...

Canada, *House of Commons Debates* (January 1994), 32–36.

FACTS OR FANTASIES IN "J'ACCUSE"?—PIERRE ELLIOTT TRUDEAU

The French writer Emile Zola wrote a famous pamphlet, "J'accuse," in which he attacked the evidence presented against Captain Alfred Dreyfus, a French Jew who was exiled to Devil's Island in a notorious espionage case. He dared to attack the government's official version, just as Trudeau used the "facts" to expose Bouchard's revisionist "hallucinations."

I accuse Lucien Bouchard of having betrayed the population of Quebec during last October's referendum campaign. By distorting the political history of his province and of his country, by spreading discord among its citizens with his demagogic rhetoric and by preaching contempt for those Canadians who did not share his views, Lucien Bouchard went beyond the limits of honest and democratic debate.

Truth must be restored in order to rehabilitate democracy in Quebec—this, I shall do by examining some of Mr. Bouchard's assertions between Oct. 14 and 27, 1995 ...

IV Language, education and the veto

Mr. Bouchard's assertion:

1. The Constitution Act of 1982 "reduced Quebec's powers in the fields of language and education ... René Lévesque refused it. Claude Ryan refused it. The National Assembly of Quebec refused it. (Oct. 25, 1995, 7 p.m., Radio-Canada television)

The facts:

1. In the areas of language and education, the Constitution Act of 1982 enshrined precisely the "traditional requests from Quebec." Here is what Claude Ryan had to say about it the day after Lucien Bouchard made the above comment: "The Constitution Act of 1982 that Mr. Trudeau passed is not as dreadful as

some like to pretend. It is a very reasonable law: it gave a Charter of Rights to all Canadians, Quebecers and others alike, and it reinforced the protection of linguistic rights for francophones throughout Canada." And elsewhere: "I heard Mr. Bouchard last night saying that [the Constitution of 1982] has stripped Quebec of important rights in language and education. In my humble opinion, it's not true. It's just not true."

While he disapproved of the "fact that the act had been enacted without Quebec's signature," Claude Ryan recognized that "objectively, the changes brought about by the act of 1982 were very good changes, except where the amending formula is concerned" (Oct. 26, 1995. Interview with Bernard Derome, Radio-Canada television and Château Frontenac, RDI.)

2.   I, myself, shared Mr. Ryan's reservations with regard to the amending formula. But it should be remembered that the formula used in the constitution of 1982 was based on the one proposed by Mr. Lévesque and the seven other provinces that formed the Gang of Eight. This formula gave no veto to Quebec while the one proposed by my government included a veto.

Thus, on Dec. 2, 1981, *Le Devoir* published my reply to a letter from Premier Lévesque dated Nov. 25, 1981, requesting a veto for Quebec. I said, in part: "Between 1971 and Nov. 5, 1981, every government I headed put forth an amending formula which would have given Quebec a veto. We only abandoned the principle after you had done so yourself" by signing the Accord of the Eight and after "you had once again proposed [this accord] during our sessions of Nov. 2, 3, 4 and 5."

3.   Furthermore, failing that veto, the accord of the Eight gave the provinces a right to opt out which was enshrined in section 38 (3) of the Constitution Act of 1982. This right allows each province to refuse any constitutional change that would diminish its "legislative jurisdiction" or its "rights and privileges."

Consequently, Mr. Bouchard is showing that he knows nothing about the 1982 constitution when he alleges that the Chrétien government—after a No vote—will want "to perpetuate the current situation which gives the federal apparatus and the English-speaking provinces ... the power to impose anything they want on Quebec." (Oct. 17, 1995, 7:25 p.m., Westin Hotel, Montreal.) Such stupid allegations—and they were legion-flow more from hallucinations than from the science of politics...

By calling upon fallacies and untruths to advance the cause of hateful demagoguery, Lucien Bouchard misled the electors during last October's referendum. By his actions, he tarnished Quebec's good reputation as a democratic society and he does not deserve the trust of the people of this province.

Pierre Elliott Trudeau, "Lucien Bouchard, Illusionist," *Montreal Gazette,* 3 February 1996.

The Prime Minister Addresses the Nation, October 25, 1995

Jean Chrétien has been accused of taking a no/non victory in the referendum for granted. The last week in the campaign showed polls in favour of sovereignty, and, as was his custom, he reacted (instead of acting first) with a powerful speech, on the eve of the vote.

For the first time in my mandate as Prime Minister, I have asked to speak directly to Canadians tonight.

I do so because we are in an exceptional situation.

Tonight, in particular, I want to speak to my fellow Quebecers. Because, at this moment, the future of our whole country is in their hands.

But I also want to speak to all Canadians. Because this issue concerns them—deeply. It is not only the future of Quebec that will be decided on Monday. It is the future of all of Canada. The decision that will be made is serious and irreversible. With deep, deep consequences.

What is at stake is our country. What is at stake is our heritage. To break up Canada or build Canada. To remain Canadian or no longer be Canadian. To stay or to leave. This is the issue of the referendum.

When my fellow Quebecers make their choice on Monday, they have the responsibility and the duty to understand the implications of that choice.

The fact is, that hidden behind a murky question is a very clear option. It is the separation of Quebec. A Quebec that would no longer be part of Canada. Where Quebecers would no longer enjoy the rights and privileges associated with Canadian citizenship. Where Quebecers would no longer share a Canadian passport or a Canadian dollar—no matter what the advocates of separatism may claim.

Where Quebecers would be made foreigners in their own country.

I know that many Quebecers, in all good faith, are thinking of voting YES in order to bring change to Canada. I am telling them that if they wish to remain Canadian, they are taking a very dangerous gamble. Anyone who really wants to remain a Canadian should think twice before taking such a dangerous risk. Listen to the leaders of the separatist side. They are very clear. The country they want is not a better Canada, it is a separate Quebec. Don't be fooled.

There are also those Quebecers who are thinking of voting YES to give Quebec a better bargaining position to negotiate an economic and political partnership with the rest of Canada. Again, don't be fooled. A YES vote means the destruction of the political and economic union we already enjoy. Nothing more.

Through the course of this campaign, I have listened to my fellow Quebecers, and I have heard them say how deeply attached they are to Canada. I have listened—and I understand—that they have been hurt and disappointed in the past. I have also heard the voices for change that are echoing throughout Quebec and across Canada. Our country is changing. And we all know it. I ask you to remember all that this government has done over the last two years to help create change—positive change.

The end of Canada would be nothing less than the end of a dream. The end of a country that has made us the envy of the world. Canada is not just any country. It is unique. It is the best country in the world ... As a proud Quebecer and a proud Canadian, I am convinced that a strong Quebec in a united Canada remains the best solution for all of us. I ask those Quebecers who have not yet made their decision to ask themselves these questions when they vote on Monday:

Do you really think that you and your family would have a better quality of life and a brighter future in a separate Quebec?

Do you really think that the French language and culture in North America would be better protected in a separate Quebec?

Do you really think you and your family will enjoy greater security in a separate Quebec?

Do you really want to turn your back on Canada? Does Canada deserve that?

Are you really ready to tell the world—the whole world—that people of different languages, different cultures and different backgrounds cannot live together in harmony?

Do you really think that ties of friendship and understanding ... ties of mutual trust and respect can be broken without harm or rancour?

Have you found one reason, one good reason, to destroy Canada?

Prime Minister Jean Chretien's Address to the Nation, October 1995 (see Privy Council website, www.pco-bcp.gc.ca).

The Federalist Case or the Sovereigntist Case?

Professor John Trent of the University of Ottawa had a friend who challenged him to come up with ten good reasons why Quebeckers should want to remain in Canada. The Liberal Party tended to talk only about the economy but Quebeckers did not live by bread alone. Half a day's thought found eleven arguments that stressed other values.

1. Canada is a peaceful land ... Wherever we look, when different ethnic groups live side by side, whether within one country or across borders, there seems to be violence and fighting along ethnic lines. Canada is the exception to the rule. We have learned to manage our tensions together. Let us not tempt fate.

2. ... English and French have learned to live together, not without haggling but without violence. We live in tension but the tensions have taught us a certain respect for each other. English and French do not hate each other. If you think about it, this is a rather remarkable achievement ...

3. Quebec has flourished in Canada and proven it doesn't have to leave to achieve its needs. It has passed Law 101 making French its official language. It has increased its percentage of Francophones to the highest level ever—despite the increasingly English-speaking world around us. Francophones have taken over the Quebec economy and have produced some of Canada's and the world's leading technologies, companies and financial institutions like Bombardier, Hydro-Québec, SNC-Lavalin, le Cirque du Soleil and Caisse Populaire Desjardins.

4. Together in Canada we are all stronger and have an influence on the world.

    No other small or medium-sized country has been elected to the UN Security Council six times. We sit with the great powers in the Group of Seven (now Eight and a Half with Europe and Russia, sort of). United, Canada has a uniquely central position in world diplomacy. Would Quebec achieve as much all alone?

5. The French language has made great strides in Canada in the past fifty years. Quebeckers often belittle this fact because it is not all they want. But Canada is the only country where the number of French-speaking people has managed to grow since the Second World War. French has greatly increased in the National Capital Region, in the federal public service and the military forces. New Brunswick has become officially bilingual and Ontario has Law 8 on Francophone services. Despite the problems of assimilation, Francophones are better organized in every province and more and more run their own education systems. Each year 300,000 young Anglophones are in the French immersion system. Now, that is a real sign of respect.

6. Three decades of quarrels haven't limited the number of Francophones running Canada. Francophones are Prime Minister, Chief of the Supreme Court, Chief of Staff of the military forces, head of the federal public service, Governor General, Chief Electoral Officer and Chairman of the National Capital Commission. Surely this is a sign of great influence.

7. Canada is our country. Quebeckers helped shape it and should fight to hold on to it. Our forefathers founded Canada and left their imprint on it. They discovered the whole continent. English and French built Canada together through compromise and hard work. Francophones fought for their place and their rights …

8. Young people must be part of a country that prepares them for the 21st century. They don't need the old language battles of Johnson and Galganov, Villeneuve and Rhéaume. They don't need the English paranoia. And they don't need to feed the fantasies of 19th century nationalists who want to satisfy their own glory with their own little state. They do need to be prepared to live and compete in the global village. Independence is an illusion. Everything is international, from money to drugs, terrorism and pollution. Because French Canadians refused to be assimilated, Canada was forced to build the world's first bilingual, multicultural state. Many call it the world's first 21st century country.

9. Our capital, Ottawa, has monuments to peace, human rights and Sir Galahad. Other capitals have monuments to war …

10. Leaving Canada will lead to great economic uncertainty, instability and probably loss. Quebec could leave if it really wanted to. But it is just not wise …

11. What would happen if Canada were just to disappear? Crazy? Ask these questions. If Quebec were to separate, would Canada persist with a big hole in its middle? Would the West and the East stick around? Or would they try to join the United States? Come to think of it, wouldn't all the rest of Canada join the United States where they would speak the same language and have a higher standard of living? Then where would be the PQ's much vaunted partnership? Quebec would really be independent, a nice little island of six or seven million, trying to do business with a continent of nearly 300, 000, 000 angry Anglos. An instant recipe for success?

John Trent, speech given at University of Ottawa, October 10, 1998.

INTELLECTUALS FOR SOVEREIGNTY

Intellectuals for the Sovereignty of Quebec (IPSO) answered the question, "What does Quebec want? In an extensive paper, they outlined different facets of the case for sovereignty, from history, to economics, to politics and constitutional law, and finally to moral justifications. They appealed to intellectuals to monitor events closely should Quebec secede, lest the Canadian government display its customary intransigence.

Quebec's Moral Justifications

5.   Quebec's Moral Justifications

5.1   Canada refuses to consider itself a multinational state

     Quebecers have always tried to come to an agreement with their partners in the Canadian federation, in the form of a pact between peoples. They believe that one can belong to the Quebec people and also be part of a multinational State; they also believe that Canada is a multinational entity supported by two founding peoples who were called, at the time of confederation, French Canadians and English Canadians. Now, they are more commonly referred to as Quebecers and Canadians. Native peoples existed well before and independently of the creation of Canada in 1867. They were not considered one of the founding peoples of Canada because they were wrongly excluded. Yet it must now be acknowledged that they are also part of Canada's wide-ranging diversity and that their aspirations for self-government are legitimate. Acadians are also a people within Canada. This is the reality of Canada which should no longer be denied.

     Although Quebecers are open to the idea of belonging to a multinational sovereign state, they are still confronted with Canada's long-standing refusal to recognize the existence of the Quebec people. This refusal has existed since confederation in 1867, and is expressed constitutionally as well as politically and administratively. Canada refuses to acknowledge its multinational character in the constitution (except for the purely symbolic recognition of Native peoples which appeared for the first time in 1982). It refuses to grant Quebec full power over cultural (language, culture, communications) and economic (manpower training, unemployment insurance, regional development) matters. Within Quebec territory, these responsibilities should be under the control of the Quebec government. The federal government also refuses to limit its own spending power and continues to interfere, most notably by imposing so-called "national standards", in sectors which are under exclusive provincial control, such as education and health.

The Canadian government also refuses to explicitly recognize a genuine asymmetry in the sharing of powers which would reflect the fact that Quebec is one of the founding peoples of the country. Even though Quebec has its own Civil Code and language laws, and has just recently gained some control over immigration, on the whole the principle of equality among provinces takes precedence politically and constitutionally, which basically means that Quebec will never be able to attain special status within the Canadian federation as presently conceived …

Taken now collectively as a nation or a people, Quebec is not represented within the sovereign state of Canada. As stated above, Quebec never signed the Constitution which Canada tried to impose in 1982, and every Quebec government since then has refused to recognize the legitimacy of this constitutional order. Furthermore, constitutional documents make no mention of the Quebec people. Finally, the Canadian government did not even comply with the clause stipulating that they were to approve French translations of constitutional laws as quickly as possible. Delaying the implementation of a bilingual Constitution which reflects, albeit only partially, the wide-ranging diversity of its founding peoples, was one more way in which the federal government rendered the Canadian Constitution in valid within Quebec territory. Under these circumstances, how can one claim that Quebec is represented within Canada?

5.2   The Federal State has promoted unequal economic development

Quebec's desire for sovereignty also arises from the fact that the Canadian government has, through numerous policies implemented over the last thirty years, promoted the economic development of the Toronto region, at the expense of all the other regions of the country … Quebec is highly populated, closely located to the centre of the country's economic activity, and it has a wide variety of resources. Yet it is one of the poorest provinces and Montreal, its vital centre, is currently the poorest city in Canada … Through this inequality, for which it is largely responsible and which it has never tried to rectify, the Canadian government has violated the principle of equality between its founding peoples.

… Nonetheless, the appearance of a sovereignist movement in Quebec was first and foremost the result of unequal development, and not the cause of this inequality. Political uncertainty is the result of Canada's uncompromising attitude towards Quebec's political claims. The current federal government is maintaining political uncertainty, believing that this is how it can maintain the status quo. It states over and over again that the political climate is not conducive to investment and is adopting an increasingly hard line towards Quebec. It is therefore not surprising that investors choose to go elsewhere.

... A central government cannot favour one people at the expense of another. In this era of scarce public funds, federal transfer payments to the poorer provinces are continually put on the chopping block, while the economic effects of federal policies in favour of Ontario are permanent. We believe that this unequal economic development justifies Quebec's move toward sovereignty.

5.3   Quebec cannot choose its legal status within Canada

As discussed previously, Canada imposed fundamental constitutional changes on Quebec, despite an almost unanimous resolution against these changes by Quebec's National Assembly. Quebec is therefore governed by a Constitution which was imposed upon it and which it cannot amend, as the abortive attempts of Meech Lake and Charlottetown attest. The failure of the Meech Lake Accord clearly highlighted the inapplicable nature of the constitutional amending formula. For many issues, this formula requires the approval of every provincial legislatures [sic] within a three-year period. This makes it nearly impossible to reach an agreement on constitutional amendments. And the Charlottetown Accord was proposed to all Canadians mainly because it allowed the Canadian government to stave off another referendum on sovereignty in Quebec.

... Consequently, one can effectively argue that Quebec is no longer in a position to choose its own status within the Canadian Federation.

6.   Threats to Quebec's Democratic Framework

In reaction to Quebec's plans to hold a new referendum on sovereignty in the next few years, the Canadian government has been increasing its attempts to invalidate this endeavour. Canada has just taken the question of the legality of Quebec sovereignty to its Supreme Court, and it is clear that according to its Constitution, the court will declare that Quebec must obtain the consent of the other provinces and the federal government in order to attain sovereignty. Prime Minister Jean Chrétien has already stated that his government will contest the result of a referendum on sovereignty supported by the majority of the Quebec population. He claims that the federal government should formulate the referendum question, determine the percentage of the vote required in order to determine a sovereignist victory and even allow all Canadians to determine Quebec's destiny. The Canadian government has also openly supported the partitionist aims of certain groups, who claim that they will remain part of Canada in the event that Quebec separates. Quebec's referendum law is currently being contested, and this case will certainly be carried to the highest courts in Canada ...

Short of suggesting that Canada is willing to resort to force or duress during the debate on the future of Quebec, it is clear that all of these actions are calculated to heighten tension and intimidate people. They contribute nothing to the resolution of the problems within a framework of democratic discussion respecting each side's position. In participating in two referendums on the sovereignty of Quebec, the Canadian government has in fact already attested to their legitimacy.

Nonetheless, it seems that they acted in this way because they thought that they would be victorious on both occasions. Now that the political situation has changed and that Quebec sovereignty has become possible and even probable, the Canadian government is now attempting to change the rules of the game, and appears to be getting ready to resort to political authoritarianism. Quebec's democratic structure is being threatened by such attacks.

If the majority of Quebecers vote in favour of sovereignty during the next referendum, the will of the voters must be respected and the political emancipation procedure, which meets all required democratic guarantees, must be supported. The Canadian government will doubtless try to claim that secession is not covered in the Canadian constitution, and ask other members of the U.N. not to recognize the sovereignty of Quebec before it does so itself. This would simply be its roundabout way of imposing the will of the Canadian majority on the Quebec people, as it did in 1982. Criteria for the recognition of Quebec sovereignty must be based on democratic legitimacy, not constitutional law.

We appeal to your reflective and critical capacity as intellectuals and ask you to exercise caution in this matter. We feel that Quebec sovereignty is in keeping with an ideal shared by intellectuals around the world, and by people who favour a liberal polity. This ideal makes the aspirations of a people, rather than the power of the state, the focal point of democracy.

"What Does Quebec Want?" Intellectuals for the Sovereignty of Quebec (see www.rocler.qc.ca/turp/eng/Intellectuals/Intel.htm).

Quebec 1995: The Second Referendum

Referendum Question

"Do you agree that Quebec should become sovereign after having made a formal offer to Canada for a new economic and political partnership within the scope of the bill respecting the future of Quebec and of the agreement signed on June 12, 1995, Yes or No?" ...

Results

NO	50,58 %	2 362 648
YES	49,42 %	2 308 360
Valid ballots	98,18 %	4 671 008
Rejected ballots	1,82 %	86 501
Participation rate	93,52 %	4 757 509
Registered voters		5 087 009
"NO" majority	1,16 %	54 288

Source: Chief Electoral Officer, Quebec.

·&· BIBLIOGRAPHY FOR THE FIRST AND SECOND EDITIONS

This is a selective, not a comprehensive, bibliography on the subject of Canada's crises. By no means does it exhaust the material available, but the reader who wishes to pursue the general problem of French-English relations or any particular crisis will find that these books lead to a good basic understanding. Included are the major historical writings used in the preparation of the narrative and the sources and documents.

I COLLECTIONS OF DOCUMENTS AND REPORTS

Canada. Department of Militia and Defence. *Report upon the Rebellions in the Northwest Territories*. Ottawa, 1886.

Canada. *House of Commons Debates,* Ottawa, 1910, 1917, 1919, 1942, 1944, 1962, 1992, and 1994.

The Canada Studies Foundation. *One Land: Two Languages*. Ottawa, 1975.

The Commissioner of Official Languages, *Annual Reports 1971–1983*. Ottawa, 1971–1983.

Quebec. *Quebec-Canada: A New Deal* ("The White Paper"). Quebec, 1979.

Liberal Party of Quebec. *A New Canadian Federation* ("The Beige Paper"). Montreal, 1980.

The Royal Commission on Bilingualism and Biculturalism. *A Preliminary Report*. Ottawa, 1965.

Smiley, Donald V., ed. *The Rowell-Sirois Report*, Book I. Toronto, 1963.

The Task Force on Canadian Unity. *A Future Together: Observations and Recommendations*. Ottawa, 1979.

Waite, P. B., ed. *The Confederation Debates in the Province of Canada, 1965*. Carleton Library; Toronto, 1964.

II HISTORIES AND CONTEMPORARY STUDIES

Bell, David, and Lorne Teperman. *The Roots of Disunity*. Toronto, 1979.

Bergeron, Léandra. *The History of Quebec: A Patriot's Handbook*. Toronto, 1971.

Bernard, André. *What Does Quebec Want?* Toronto, 1978.

Butler, Rick. *Quebec: The People Speak*. Toronto, 1978.

Chaput, Marcel. *Why I Am a Separatist*. Montreal, 1962.

Clark, S.D. *Movements of Political Protest in Canada 1640–1840*. Toronto, 1959.

Cohen, Ronald I. *Quebec Votes*. Montreal, 1965.

Cook, Ramsay, ed. *French-Canadian Nationalism*. Toronto, 1969.

Coupland, Reginald. *The Quebec Act: A Study in Statesmanship*. Oxford, 1925.

Dawson, R. MacGregor. *The Conscription Crisis of 1944*. Toronto, 1961.

Denison, George T. *The Struggle for Imperial Unity*. London, 1907.

Desbarats, Peter. *The State of Quebec*. Toronto, 1965.

Dion, Léon. Quebec: *The Unfinished Revolution*. Montreal, 1976.

Driedger, Leo, ed. *The Canadian Ethnic Mosaic: A Quest for Identity*. Toronto, 1978.

Dumont, Fernand. *The Vigil of Quebec*. Toronto, 1974.

Dupont, Pierre. *How Lévesque Won*. Toronto, 1977.

Fullerton, Douglas. *The Dangerous Delusion*. Toronto, 1978.

Garneau, F.X. History of Canada, 3 vols. Montreal, 1860. [*Histoire du Canada, depuis sa découverte jusqu'à nos jours*, 4 vols., first published 1845–52.]

Geddes, Gary, ed. *Divided We Stand*. Toronto, 1977.

Granatstein, J.L. *Conscription in the Second World War 1939–1945*. Toronto, 1969.

Granatstein, J.L., and J.M. Hitsman. *Broken Promises: A History of Conscription in Canada*. Toronto, 1977.

Groulx, Lionel Adolphe. *Chemins de l'avenir.* Montreal, 1964.

———. *L'enseignement français au Canada.* Montreal, 1934–35.

———. *Histoire du Canada français depuis la découverte,* 4 vols. Montreal, 1950–52.

———. *Why We Are Divided.* Montreal, 1943.

Harbron, John D. *Canada without Quebec.* Toronto, 1977.

Harris, Richard C. *The Seigneurial System in Early Canada: A Geographical Study.* Quebec, 1966.

Harvey, Jean-Charles. *Pourquoi je suis antiséparatiste.* Montréal, 1962.

Howard, J.K. *Strange Empire.* New York, 1952.

Innis, H.A. *The Fur Trade in Canada.* Toronto, 1956.

Jacobs, Jane. *The Question of Separatism.* New York, 1980.

Kilrans, Eric W. *Challenge of Confidence.* Toronto, 1967.

Lamontagne, Maurice. *The Double Deal: A Response to the PQ White Paper.* Montreal, 1980.

Laurendeau, André. *La crise de la conscription, 1942.* Montreal, 1962.

Laxer, James, and Robert Laxer. *The Liberal Idea of Canada.* Toronto, 1977.

Lévesque, René. *An Option for Quebec.* Toronto, 1968.

———. *My Quebec.* Toronto, 1979. Translation of La Passion du Québec. Montreal, 1978.

Levin, Malcolm. *Crisis in Quebec.* Toronto, 1973.

McWhinney, E. *Quebec and the Constitution.* Toronto, 1979.

Mercer, John. *The Squeaking Wheel.* Montreal, 1965.

Milner, Henry. *Politics in the New Quebec.* Toronto, 1978.

Morf, Gustav. *Terror in Quebec: Case Studies of the FLQ .* Toronto, 1970.

Morin, Claude. *Quebec versus Canada: The Struggle for Self-Government 1960–72.* Toronto, 1976.

Morton, W.L. *The Canadian Identity.* Toronto, 1962.

Newman, Peter C. *Renegade in Power.* Toronto, 1963.

Nish, Cameron, ed. *Quebec in the Duplessis Era, 1935–1959: Dictatorship or Democracy?* Toronto, 1976.

Pelletier, Gérard. *The October Crisis.* Toronto, 1971.

Porter, John. *The Vertical Mosaic.* Toronto, 1965.

Postgate, Dale, and Kenneth McRoberts. *Quebec: Social Change and Political Crisis.* Toronto, 1976.

Quinn, Herbert. *The Union Nationale.* Toronto, 1979.

Rioux, Marcel. *Quebec in Question.* Toronto, 1978.

Rioux, Marcel, and Yves Martin, eds. *French-Canadian Society*, vol. 1. Toronto, 1964.

Saywell, John. *Quebec '70.* Toronto, 1971.

———. *The Rise of the Parti Québécois.* Toronto, 1977.

Scott, Frank, and Michael Oliver, eds. *Quebec States Her Case.* Toronto, 1964.

Sévigny, Pierre. *This Game of Politics.* Toronto, 1965.

Shaw, William F., and Lionel Albert. *Partition: The Price of Quebec's Independence.* Montreal, 1980.

Sheffe, Norman, ed. *Canadian/Canadien.* Toronto, 1971.

Simeon, Richard, ed. *Must Canada Fail?* Montreal, 1977.

Sloan, Thomas. *Quebec: The Not-So-Quiet Revolution.* Toronto, 1965.

Stanley, George F.G., *The Birth of Western Canada.* Toronto, 1960.

———. *The Story of Canada's Flag.* Toronto, 1965.

Stewart, James. *FLQ: 7 Years of Terrorism.* Montreal, 1970.

Trofimenkoff, Susan Man, ed. *Abbé Groulx: Variations on a Nationalist Theme.* Toronto, 1973.

————. *The Dream of Nation: A Social and Intellectual History of Quebec.* Toronto, 1982.

Trudeau, Pierre Elliott. *Federalism and the French Canadians.* Toronto, 1968.

Wade, Mason, ed. *Canadian Dualism/La dualité canadienne.* Toronto, 1960.

————. *The French-Canadian Outlook.* Toronto, 1964.

————. *The French Canadians,* 2 vols., rev. ed. Toronto, 1968.

Waite, P.B., *The Life and Times of Confederation.* Toronto, 1962.

III BIOGRAPHIES

Bishop, Morris. Champlain: *The Life of Fortitude.* Carleton Library; Toronto, 1963. [First published 1948.]

Black, Conrad. *Duplessis.* Toronto, 1977.

Borden, Henry, ed. *Robert Laird Borden: His Memoirs,* 2 vols. Toronto, 1938.

Bowsfield, Hartwell. *Louis Riel: The Rebel and the Hero.* Toronto, 1971.

————, ed. *Louis Riel: Rebel of the Western Frontier or Victim of Politics and Prejudice.* Toronto, 1969.

Boyd, John. *Sir George Etienne Cartier, Bart., His Life and Times; A Political History of Canada from 1814 until 1873.* Toronto, 1914.

Bradley, A.G. *Sir Guy Carleton.* Toronto, 1966. [Formerly *Lord Dorchester,* Makers of Canada Series, vol. 3 (1907).]

Cook, Ramsay. *The Politics of John W. Dafoe and the Free Press.* Toronto, 1963.

Creighton, Donald G. *John A. Macdonald. Vol. 1, The Young Politician.* Toronto, 1952; Vol. 2, *The Old Chieftain.* Toronto, 1955.

Dafoe, John W. *Laurier: A Study in Canadian Politics.* Carleton Library; Toronto, 1963. [First published 1922.]

De Celles, A.D. *Cartier.* Makers of Canada Series, vol. 5. Toronto, 1926. [First published 1904.]

————.*Papineau,* Makers of Canada Series, vol. 5. Toronto, 1926. [First published 1904.]

Desbarats, Peter. *René: A Canadian in Search of a Country.* Toronto, 1976.

Flanagan, Thomas, ed. *The Diaries of Louis Riel.* Edmonton, 1976.

Graham, Roger. *Arthur Meighen.* Vol. 1, *The Door of Opportunity;* Vol. 2, *And Fortune Fled;* Vol. 3, *No Surrender.* Toronto, 1960–65.

Hutchison, Bruce. *The Incredible Canadian.* Toronto, 1952.

Laporte, Pierre. *The True Face of Duplessis.* Montreal, 1960.

New, Chester. *Lord Durham's Mission to Canada.* Edited by H.W. McCready, Carleton Library; Toronto, 1963.

Osler, F.B. *Louis Riel: The Man Who Had to Hang.* Toronto, 1961.

Pearson, Lester B. *Mike: The Memoirs of the Rt. Hon. Lester B. Pearson,* vols. 1–3. Toronto, 1975.

Pickersgill, J.W. *The Mackenzie King Record,* vol. 1. Toronto, 1960.

Radwanski, George. *Trudeau.* Toronto, 1978.

Rosenstock, Janet, and Dennis Adair. *Riel* (novelization based on the CBC screenplay by Roy Moore, Markham, 1979).

Schull, Joseph. *Laurier.* Toronto, 1965.

Skelton, O.D. *Life and Letters of Sir Wilfrid Laurier,* 2 vols. Carleton Library; Toronto, 1965. [First published 1921.]

Stanley, George F.G. *Louis Riel.* Toronto, 1963.

Vallières, Pierre. *White Niggers of America: The Precocious Autobiography of a Quebec "Terrorist."* New York, 1971.

Willison, J.S. *Sir Wilfrid Laurier and the Liberal Party,* 2 vols. London, 1903.

IV LITERATURE

Crémazie, Octave. *Poésies*. Montreal, 1925.

Desbiens, Jean-Paul (Pierre-Jérôme, Frère). *The Impertinences of Brother Anonymous*. Montreal, 1962.

———. *Les Insolences du Frère Untel*. Montreal, 1960.

———. *For Pity's Sake*. Montreal, 1965.

———. *Sous le soleil de la pitié*. Montreal, 1965.

Fréchette, Louis. *La légende d'un peuple*. Montreal, 1941. [First published 1887.]

Garneau, *Saint-Denys*, Journal. Montreal, 1954.

———. *Journal*. Translated by John Glassco. Toronto, 1962.

———. *Poésies complètes*. Montreal, 1949.

Hémon, Louis. *Maria Chapdelaine*. Toronto, 1938. [First published in book form in 1915.]

Kirby, William. *Annals of Niagara*. Welland, 1896.

———. *The Golden Dog*. Toronto, 1904. [First published 1877.]

Weintraub, William. *The Underdogs*. Toronto, 1979.

V ARTICLES AND BOOKLETS

Bourassa, Henri. *Why the Navy Act Should Be Repealed*. Montreal, 1912.

Burt, A.L. *Guy Carleton, Lord Dorchester, 1724–1808*, rev. version. Canadian Historical Association Booklet no. 5. Ottawa, 1955.

Frégault, Guy. Canadian *Society in the French Regime*. Canadian Historical Association Booklet no. 3. Ottawa, 1954.

Manning, Helen T. "The Colonial Policy of the Whig Ministers, 1830–1837." *Canadian Historical Review* 33, no. 3 (September 1952).

Ouellet, Fernand. *Louis Joseph Papineau : Un être divisé.* Canadian Historical Association Booklet no. 11. Ottawa, 1960.

———. Papineau: *Textes choisis et présentés.* Quebec, 1958.

Scott, F.R., trans. *Saint-Denys Garneau and Anne Hébert.* Vancouver, 1962.

Scowan, Reed. *Reflections on the Future of the English Language in Quebec.* Montreal, 1979.

Wade, Mason. "An Age of Anxiety." *Report on Confederation* (vol. 2, no. 4, March 1979).

Willms, A.M. "Conscription 1917: A Brief for the Defence." *Canadian Historical Review* 37, no. 4 (December 1956).

❧ Bibliography for the Third Edition

Since publication of the previous edition of Search for a Nation, hundreds of books and articles have been published on the subject of French-English relations in Canada. The following bibliography of recent titles is therefore selective rather than comprehensive and is designed to provide the reader with studies that put the subject matter of the book, and the new chapters in particular, in historical context. The bibliographical entries for the previous edition appear before this bibliography, as they still have relevance for the earlier chapters and include the larger works from which sources and documents have been obtained.

Behiels, Michael, ed. *Quebec since 1800: Selected Readings.* Toronto, 2000.

Bernard, Jean-Paul. *The Rebellions of 1837 and 1838 in Lower Canada.* Ottawa, 1996.

Bosher, J.F. *The Gaullist Attack on Canada.* Montreal, 2000.

Bothwell, Robert. *Canada and Quebec.* Vancouver, 1998.

Cardinal, Mario. *Breaking Point: Quebec/Canada and the 1995 Referendum.* Toronto, 2003.

Dickinson, John. *A Short History of Quebec.* Montreal, 2002.

Gougeon, Gilles. *A History of Quebec Nationalism.* Toronto, 1994.

Greer, Allan. *The Patriots and the People: The Rebellions of 1837 in Rural Lower Canada.* Toronto, 1993.

Letourneau, Jocelyn. *History for the Future: Rewriting Memory and Identity in Quebec.* Montreal, 2004.

Resnick, Philip. *Toward a Canada-Quebec Union.* Montreal, 1991.

Romney, Paul. *Getting It Wrong: How Canadians Forgot the Past and Imperiled Confederation.* Toronto, 1999.

Rudin, Ronald. *Making History in 20th-Century Quebec.* Toronto, 1997.

Stevenson, Garth. *Community Besieged: The Anglophone Minority and the Politics of Quebec.* Montreal, 1999.

Tanguay, Brian. *Contemporary Quebec Politics and Society.* Peterborough, 1998.

Trent, John. *Quebec-Canada.* Ottawa, 1997.

Young, Robert. *Secession of Quebec and the Future of Canada.* Montreal, 1997.